Sebastian Speiser

Usage Policies for Decentralised Information Processing

Usage Policies for Decentralised Information Processing

by
Sebastian Speiser

 Scientific Publishing

Dissertation, Karlsruher Institut für Technologie (KIT)
Fakultät für Wirtschaftswissenschaften
Tag der mündlichen Prüfung: 20. Dezember 2012
Referenten: Prof. Dr. Rudi Studer, Prof. Dr. Hansjörg Fromm

Impressum

Karlsruher Institut für Technologie (KIT)
KIT Scientific Publishing
Straße am Forum 2
D-76131 Karlsruhe
www.ksp.kit.edu

KIT – Universität des Landes Baden-Württemberg und
nationales Forschungszentrum in der Helmholtz-Gemeinschaft

KIT Scientific Publishing 2013
Print on Demand

ISBN 978-3-86644-987-9

Zur Erlangung des akademischen Grades eines
Doktors der Wirtschaftswissenschaften (Dr. rer. pol.)
von der Fakultät für Wirtschaftswissenschaften
des Karlsruher Instituts für Technologie (KIT)
genehmigte Dissertation von
M. Sc. Sebastian Speiser.

Usage Policies for Decentralised Information Processing

Sebastian Speiser

Tag der mündlichen Prüfung: 20.12.2012
Referent: Prof. Dr. Rudi Studer
Korreferent: Prof. Dr. Hansjörg Fromm

Karlsruhe 2012

Abstract

Sharing information for re-use in new and innovative contexts increases the value of the information. Standardised access methods and semantic technologies facilitate the integration of information across different sources. However, not all information can be freely used for arbitrary purposes. Owners impose usage restrictions on their information, which can be based on a number of foundations including privacy laws, copyright law, company guidelines, or social conventions. In this work, we introduce technologies to formally express usage restrictions in a machine-interpretable way as so-called policies. Such policies enable systems that assist users in complying with usage restrictions.

Existing policy approaches support static processes that are under the central control of one entity. In practice, however, information is processed in more complex constellations, e.g., providers manage information on behalf of the owners (e.g., social networking, cloud-based storage); or information is processed by dynamically changing networks of providers (e.g., a service outsources billing to an external provider). The consequence is that there is no central view let alone control of the systems that process protected information. We, thus, need decentralised systems for managing and processing information. Also the policy language for formalising usage restrictions must adapt to such decentralised systems, where each information processor has only knowledge of his local actions but not of the overall process in which it participates.

In this thesis, we propose methods that enable the creation of decentralised systems that provide, consume and process distributed information in compliance with their usage restrictions. We derive the requirements for our work by studying use cases from different domains. We base our approach on contributions in three categories: (i) we define vocabulary and semantics of a policy language for expressing usage restrictions from a localised view that allows the evaluation of the compliance of isolated usages; (ii) as in the end we have humans as the actual information owners and consumers, we develop user-friendly methods to interact with the machine-interpretable formal policies; and (iii) we extend the Linked Data architecture to support policies, information services and query processing guaranteeing formally defined completeness notions.

We evaluate our approach in three ways: (i) realisation of the use case scenarios; (ii) conducting performance experiments; and (iii) validating that our policy language correctly models real world usage restrictions. The validation includes that we model the Creative Commons licenses in our language and show that we can automatically compute the correct compatibilities between the individual licenses.

Acknowledgements

First of all, I want to thank my advisor Rudi Studer for his support, guidance, and the great work environment that he has created. I am grateful that I could pursue my PhD in an environment that could only exist under his unique leadership style.

Special thanks to my co-advisor Hansjörg Fromm for giving both very detailed comments and high-level insights from practice.

I would like to thank all the members of AIFB, KSRI, and IME for providing inspiration, helpful criticism and many occasions for having a good time. In particular, thanks to Andreas Harth for sharing his knowledge and insights about the web, research, and among other things the importance of a haircut during a phase of hyperinflation. I also thank Steffen Lamparter, Sudhir Agarwal, and Markus Krötzsch for their guidance and many useful discussions.

I thank Natalie for her support and encouragement. Special thanks also to my family and my friends for their understanding, their reassurance, and the distraction.

Contents

Chapter 1

Introduction

More and more information is shared and re-used in new contexts, enabled by the ever in-creasing availability of computing and networking capacities. For example, organisations collect an increasing amount of data about their transactions and their environment and base their decisions on analysis of this data [The10, MCB$^+$11]. The smart grid vision includes that energy consumption data is not only used for billing purposes but also for energy pro-duction planning and energy demand control [Eur06]. Photos previously kept locally on the computer of the photographer are now shared with friends in social networks or with the public in photo communities [ME07].

Information re-use and sharing can be beneficial for all involved stakeholders: consumers can satisfy their information needs by accessing new services; service providers create value by managing, aggregating, combining, analysing, or simply presenting information; and information creators and owners increase the value of their information by enabling its use in different contexts.

However, additional uses also pose new risks. Using information in new contexts can have negative consequences, e.g., analysts releasing reports based on company confidential information can lose their jobs; people publishing their energy consumption data can reveal absence times which burglars can exploit; or the creator of a web site can be sued when consuming a photo without permission of the copyright holder.

Usage restrictions with the goal to prohibit the wrong uses of information are widely available, e.g., privacy laws, copyright law, company guidelines, or social conventions. The problem with those regulations, which apply to all information of a certain kind, is that they tend to be overly general and employ a prohibit all regime. For example, in copyright law, all rights to use protected information are by default reserved exclusively for the information creator. Users, however, publish information so that it can be used and re-used, though not for all purposes. Furthermore, usage restrictions are more fine granular than binary decisions, i.e., a usage is allowed or prohibited, and potentially different for each information artefact in question, e.g., one individual allows the use of his energy consumption data only to his energy producer for billing purposes, whereas another individual also allows use by an optimiser service for consulting; users share their scenic photos with the public under an open license, but their party photos only with their friends.

In practice, information is completely missing statements about allowed and restricted usages [Dod10], or such statements are frequently ignored as illustrated by the following example. Seneviratne et al. estimate that 70% – 90% of re-uses of Flickr images with

Creative Commons Attribution license actually violate the license terms [SKBL09]. The Creative Commons Attribution license terms are very generous, basically allowing every use and derivation as long as the original creator is attributed, making malicious intentions an improbable cause for the high number of violations. Rather we think that such violations can be explained by the fact that the effort for re-using information is low, while finding and evaluating its usage restrictions requires a high effort.

Standardised ways to link to usage restrictions from individual information artefacts support readily available and fine-granular restrictions [KSW03]. Furthermore, formalising the usage restrictions in a machine-understandable way enables automated tools that evaluate the restrictions, thus reducing the gap in efforts for re-using information and re-using it in a compliant way. We denote such formalised restrictions as usage policies. Usage policies can be partially enforced, e.g., we can disable unauthorised access to private information. After releasing protected information, we can in general not prevent all potential misuses, as even digital rights management (DRM) systems [Ian01] that restrict information usage to a closed software environment can be circumvented by malicious attackers [BEPW03, Doc04]. Still, policies can support tools, which make it easier to adhere to usage restrictions than to break them. Encouragement of compliant usage and accountability for non-compliant usage corresponds to the way that other legal and social norms are enforced [WABL⁺08].

A special challenge for policy-aware systems in the considered scenarios is their decentralised nature. Information is not released from the owner to one information processor, but rather we encounter more complex processes: providers manage information on behalf of the owners (e.g., social networking, cloud-based storage); dynamically changing networks of providers process information (e.g., an energy producer outsources billing to an external provider); unanticipated usages come up after information is released (e.g., a company wants to print a brochure using a photo published in a blog post).

The contribution of this thesis is to create an approach for information usage policies in decentralised systems. Due to the lack of a central view and central control of the information-using processes, we need (i) a decentralised architecture for sharing and retrieving information; and (ii) a formalism for expressing usage restrictions from a localised view that allows to evaluate the compliance of isolated usages. Finally, (iii) as in the end we have humans as the actual information owners and consumers, we need user-friendly methods to interact with the machine-interpretable formal policies.

The rest of this chapter is structured as follows. We present our hypotheses in Section 1.1. In Section 1.2 we give an overview of our approach. In Section 1.3 we list our contributions and give an outline of the thesis.

1.1 Hypotheses

The goal of this thesis is to develop technologies, which enable us to build decentralised systems that consume and process distributed information in compliance with their usage restrictions. We capture this goal as a hypothesis, which we substantiate in our work. The main hypothesis is given in the following.

Main Hypothesis: Decentralised systems can be built that support end users in the creation of services and applications using information in compliance to applicable usage restrictions.

We split our main hypothesis into three subhypotheses capturing the individual components of our work: the policy language, the policy interaction methods, and the architecture for decentralised information processing. We outline for each subhypothesis our approach that we develop in this work in order to verify it.

Subhypothesis 1: Information usage restrictions can be formalised in a way such that compliance of an information use can be checked without a complete view on the containing process.

Approach: Develop a vocabulary and logic formalism that can express restrictions on an information usage independent of the history of the used information and independent of the future use of produced information.

Without a complete view on the process in which an information artefact is used, it is not possible to base compliance decisions on the presence or absence of actions in the unknown history or future. Instead, we limit the context of a usage to the policies of the used artefacts (representing the relevant information about their history) and the policies of produced artefacts (representing the relevant information for their future).

Subhypothesis 2: Policy specifiers and information consumers can interact with a policy-aware system without being exposed to logic formalisms.

Approach: Design a method to compose policies from existing building blocks, which can be described in natural language, and develop an explanation facility that presents natural language justifications to users for the non-compliance of their intended information usages.

Policies expressed in formal logic are machine-interpretable and thus the task of checking compliance of an information usage can be automated. However, the actual origin of usage restrictions are still human beings just like the users creating services using policy-aware systems. Non-experts cannot create or understand formal logic. Thus, we develop interaction methods that allow users to deal with policy-aware systems without having to work directly with formal logic.

Subhypothesis 3: Decentralised systems can provide a uniform view with well-defined borders on information and policies distributed over a wide range of data sources.

Approach: Extend an existing architecture by means of attaching policies to information artefacts, integrating information services, and answering information needs under precisely-defined completeness notions.

We base our architecture on the Linked Data principles, which already provide a solution for managing decentralised and interlinked information. We extend the architecture to integrate information provided by dynamic services and develop notions of completeness for query answering, which establish clear boundaries of relevant data sources for given information needs.

1.2 Design Choices

Our approach includes the development of three components: (i) a policy language for formalising usage restrictions, (ii) methods for interacting with policies, and (iii) a decentralised architecture for policy-aware systems. When designing these components, we encounter a number of fundamental aspects, where we have to make design choices. In this section, we present several relevant aspects, discuss the available alternatives, and argue for the choices we make.

Usage Policies vs. Access Control Policies

Access control policies are declarative specifications in a formal language that unambiguously define who can access protected information or services. Different approaches to access control, such as discretionary access control or role-based access control [FK92], express explicitly or implicitly an access control matrix [Lam71]. In our scenarios, access control decisions are not sufficient as restrictions still apply to the use of information, even after the initial access was granted.

We thus design our policy language to be able to express usage restrictions, which encompass access restrictions as well as constraints on all following uses of protected information artefacts and their derivations. This thesis focuses on expressing usage restrictions. We regard enforcement of restrictions as complementary, which can be solved using technologies from usage control [PS02, PS04] or information accountability [WABL⁺08]. However, we introduce an information request model that can enforce the access control aspects of usage policies.

Data-centric vs. System-level Policies

System-level policies are general rules that restrict the processes in which a certain class of protected information artefacts is used as a whole, e.g., [ZPPPS04, LPB06, JCZ07, CT09]. Such policies can for example formalise a privacy law that applies to all customer data in the IT system of a company. System-level policies are not suitable in decentralised scenarios, as restrictions can differ for each individual artefact and there is no single entity overlooking or controlling all involved IT systems. We need the ability to assign a policy to each specific artefact. We ensure that the policy is accessible at usage time by making the policy sticky, i.e., always attached to the artefact [KSW03, RS10].

We propose the concept of data-centric policies, which are sticky and employ a localised view on single information uses. The advantages of data-centric policies include (i) that they can be applied in partially unknown processes, (ii) that intermediate artefacts of processing steps have explicit policies, and (iii) that policies can be shared across data processor boundaries. We enable the local view by allowing policies to restrict the policies that can be assigned to copies or derivations of the protected artefact. Together with the assumptions that used artefacts have correctly attached policies and that produced artefacts will be used in accordance with the assigned policies, the local view can be restricted to the current information usage without regarding any previous or future actions.

Content-based vs. Name-based Policy Restrictions

Data-centric policies are based on a local view of uses, which include restrictions on policies that can be assigned to derived information. One possibility to restrict the admissible policies is to list all choices by their names. Such name-based policy restrictions introduce incompatibilities in cases where a policy with compatible meaning but different name should be assigned to an artefact [Les05]. The lack of canonical names has to be expected in scenarios with heterogeneous actors.

In this thesis, we thus propose content-based policy restrictions, which specify the usages that an admissible policy should allow at least, respectively at most. Our logic formalism enables such content-based restrictions by introducing a special relation that represents the containment between policies. A policy is contained in another policy, if all usages allowed by the first policy are also allowed by the second policy. While policy management commonly uses policy containment, we integrate containment in a novel way into the language itself. Specifically, we enable the containment relation as part of policy conditions.

User Interaction in Natural Language vs. Formal Logic

We cannot expect that users interacting with policy-protected information are experts in formal logic or computer science. Information re-use and sharing is easily possible for lay people using for example blogging software, content management systems or mashup editors. Such users are both consumers and producers of information and will thus come in contact with policies particularly in two situations: (i) specifying a policy that formalises their intended usage restrictions, and (ii) learning from a policy engine that their intended use is non-compliant. Policies will not be widely used, if users have to directly read and write logic formulae.

Instead, we propose a simple structured model for policy specification. With the structured model, users can compose policies from existing building blocks comparable to the Creative Commons approach [AALY08].

For the situation of a non-compliant use, we propose a system to generate natural language explanations for the violation. We exploit the user-specified structure and labels of a policy to aggregate and structure the explanation as introduced by Kagal et al. [KHW08], which is in contrast to using heuristics and automatically generated text (e.g., [CR02, BOP06]). Our approach generates complete explanations, meaning that the explanations are the only way to reach compliance and meaning that fixing the issues contained in one explanation leads to compliance. Complete explanations are not always found in [KHW08].

Decentralised Information vs. Data Warehousing

Data warehouses are centralised databases that integrate information from a number of distributed and potentially heterogeneous sources via an extract-transform-load (ETL) process [DM88]. Creating such centralised databases is not suitable for our scenarios for the following reasons: (i) different entities use the same information in different contexts leading to the need for an own warehouse for every context or entity thus creating redundant copies of the information, which are hard to keep in sync; (ii) the centralised database needs a global data model, which is not a realistic requirement considering the wide range of information domains and providers; (iii) many information sources provide access only through restricted interfaces and thus cannot be loaded completely into a warehouse.

Instead, we base our approach on a decentralised architecture based on an interlinked data model. The Linked Data principles enable such an architecture by publishing information with a uniform representation format and access mechanism using web technologies [BL06]. The principles facilitate the exposure of a sizable amount of data; alone the Linking Open Data (LOD) project maintains a cloud of datasets containing approximately 30 billion statements in the form of RDF triples [BJC11]. However, some of the information sources that are most popular with users and applications are missing from the LOD cloud, e.g., Facebook, Twitter or Flickr. Web APIs of popular commercial sites are commonly provided as services instead of fully materialised and browsable datasets. Besides the obvious reluctance to give arbitrary access to one's data based on commercial considerations, there are other reasons to expose data via service-based interfaces, e.g., if data is constantly changing or is generated depending on inputs from a possibly infinite domain. In this thesis, we develop an approach to integrate service-accessible information with Linked Data, related to other current efforts under the label *Linked APIs*, e.g., [NK10, VSD+11, SH11].

Defined Boundaries vs. Closed Systems

In centralised and closed systems, an answer for an information need is reached by evaluating a query over the complete database. In decentralised and interlinked information systems always more and more data can be found by following links in already discovered data sources. Such a link following approach for answering queries is realised for Linked Data by a number of systems, e.g., [HBF09, LT10, HHK+10]. In contrast to a closed system, such query engines operate on the potentially infinite set of all data on the web and thus cannot adhere to the same completeness notion.

Instead of stopping source discovery at an arbitrary point, we develop precisely-defined completeness notions for Linked Data queries.

1.3 Contributions and Outline

In our work, we develop an approach for decentralised information processing in compliance with applicable usage restrictions. In Chapter 2, we present three concrete scenarios: (i) open licenses for copyright-protected information; (ii) information mashups for decision support;

and (iii) data privacy in the smart energy grid. Based on the scenarios, we identify twelve requirements for supporting information usage policies in decentralised systems. Finally, we describe the components of our approach and outline how they address the requirements. We introduce the foundations of our approach in Chapter 3 including basic definitions and formal notation.

In Chapter 4, we present our policy language and make the following contributions:

- We develop the syntax and semantics of a general policy language framework that supports meta-modelling in the form of policy containment as part of policy conditions. The framework is based on first-order logic with an extended greatest fixed point semantics. We define syntactic restrictions on policy definitions and background theories that ensure plausible inferences.

- Based on the framework, we develop a data-centric policy language with support for content-based policy restrictions. The language includes a vocabulary for modelling information uses. We instantiate the language for OWL and Datalog.

In Chapter 5, we develop the following methods for policy interaction:

- We present a structured policy model, which enables user-friendly tools for policy interaction. With the structured model, tools can provide interfaces to compose policies from re-usable building blocks that are described with natural language.

- We develop a component that exploits the structured model of a policy for explaining to a user why a planned usage is non-compliant.

- The non-compliance of an information use can be due to either a policy violation or an obligation that is not yet fulfilled. Certain obligations can be fulfilled automatically, e.g., the deletion of a stored artefact within a given time span. We present an approach to identify domain-specific obligations.

We introduce the following extensions to the Linked Data architecture in Chapter 6:

- We develop the Linked Data Services (LIDS) approach to integrate information services into the existing Linked Data architecture.

- We define three formal completeness notions for query processing over Linked Data. Especially the notion of query-reachable completeness is practical as it requires access only to a manageable set of data sources and provides all results available on the web under certain assumptions. We evaluate the appropriateness of the assumptions by analysing large amounts of existing Linked Data.

- We implement an engine that processes queries over Linked Data in accordance to our proposed completeness notions. Furthermore, the engine supports LIDS and rule-based reasoning.

Chapter 7 describes our implementation and applies it to evaluate the feasibility and performance of the presented concepts. The evaluation includes the following parts:

- We discuss how our presented methods can realise the scenarios.

- We validate the semantics of the policy language by modelling the Creative Commons licenses and ensuring that we infer the correct compatibilities between the individual licenses.

- We show a translation of P3P – the W3C standard for privacy policies – into our language.

- We develop a number of LIDS, which wrap existing services. The LIDS are used in a number of experiments.

- We perform experiments with the query engine using data from our scenarios, and existing benchmarks for querying Linked Data and queries with background knowledge.

Finally in Chapter 8, we summarise our work, conclude on the findings and present opportunities for future work. Existing work and its relation to this thesis is discussed within the technical chapters (see Sections 4.8, 5.6, and 6.4). We list at the beginning of each technical chapter our relevant previous publications on which the chapter is based.

Chapter 2

Scenarios and Requirements

In this chapter, we introduce three scenarios that are representative for decentralised systems that process distributed information with usage restrictions. The scenarios have diverse types of restrictions and are presented in Section 2.1. Based on the scenarios, we collect requirements for the decentralised information system architecture and the policy language in Section 2.2. In Section 2.3, we give an overview of the components of our approach and discuss how they address the requirements.

Parts of the scenarios and the derived requirements were presented in several publications: the Creative Commons licenses are a topic in [Spe12b, KS11b], information mashups are discussed in [SS10b, Spe11a, SS10a, SH11, SH10], and the Smart Energy Grid in [SH12, Spe12a, WSRH10, WJSH11]. The requirements analysis overlaps with the one presented in [SSD10].

2.1 Scenarios

This section introduces three scenarios, which we use to collect requirements for a policy-aware architecture for decentralised information systems. The scenarios cover a wide range of different systems with diverse information artefacts and diverse usage restrictions, including creative works protected by copyright, company-internal information protected by company rules, and personal information protected by privacy laws. Despite their differences, the scenarios show common characteristics that underly the identified requirements:

- Information is used in different contexts that cannot be anticipated when the information is created or collected, e.g., energy consumption data can be used for billing but also for analysing customer behaviour.

- There is a wide range of types of information with different usage restrictions, e.g., publicly available statistical information is integrated with company-internal confidential data.

- Restrictions can differ largely between information artefacts depending on their owner or subject even though they might belong to the same category, e.g., one person has different privacy requirements for his birthday than another person.

- There is no central storage for information, e.g., it would be infeasible to centrally store detailed energy consumption information about every energy consuming device in the world.

- There is no central entity controlling the processes performed on data artefacts, e.g., bloggers using copyright-protected information such as pictures or Wikipedia texts to create new information sources host their web pages at diverse providers and the web pages can again be used by different entities publishing it in ever more ways and places.

2.1.1 Open Licenses for Copyright-protected Information

Original works are protected by laws in most countries, giving the creator exclusive usage and exploitation rights. Such laws are commonly known under the notion of copyright. Original works can include creative works (e.g., photos, videos, text), databases (e.g., a database of royal families, their members and relations), and software. The copyright protection also applies to information artefacts representing such original works. By default only the creators of such a work are allowed to use it. Creators can license their content to others, giving them usage rights. Enabled by the Internet, today copyright-protected information is re-used in many different contexts, with the results often being published again on the Internet. Examples include (i) blog posts that embed photos from Flickr; (ii) videos on YouTube that are based on other videos, e.g., replacing the sound; (iii) texts quoting from Wikipedia articles. Open licenses share the common goal of enabling re-use as an alternative to the "forbidden by default" approach of traditional copyright. However, open licenses still impose some usage restrictions in contrast to putting a work in the public domain, i.e., allowing every usage to anybody for any purpose.

Creative Commons (CC) provides a popular family of open licenses for publishing creative works on the web. Each license specifies how the licensed work may be used by stating, e.g., in which cases it can be further distributed (shared) and if derivative works are allowed. The most permissive CC license is Creative Commons Attribution (CC BY), which allows all types of uses (sharing and derivation) provided that the original creator of the work is attributed. Various restrictions can be added to CC BY:

- NoDerivs (ND): the work can be used and redistributed, but it must remain unchanged.

- NonCommercial (NC): re-use is restricted to non-commercial purposes.

- ShareAlike (SA): derived works have to be licensed under the identical terms.

The CC ShareAlike restriction is particularly interesting, as it does not only restrict usages of the protected information, but also the policy of information artefacts generated by those usages. ShareAlike is formulated in legal code as follows:

> "You may Distribute or Publicly Perform an Adaptation only under: (i) the terms of this License; (ii) a later version of this License [...]; (iii) a Creative Commons

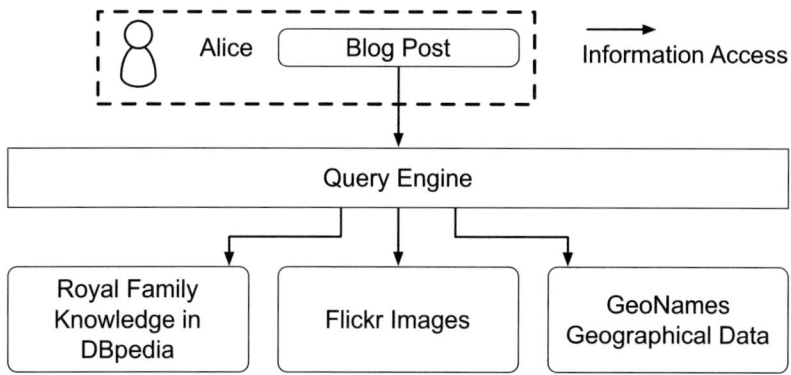

Figure 2.1: Scenario: Open Licenses for Copyright-protected Information

jurisdiction license [...] that contains the same License Elements as this License [...]"[1]

Thus derived artefacts can only be published under some version of the exact same CC license. Such a restriction has the effect that the CC licenses are propagated to all derivations of CC-licensed information, to all derivations of derivations, and so forth. This effect can be desired, e.g. for the GPL which thus ensures its "viral" distribution. However, the effect is not intended for Creative Commons, as noted by Lessig who originally created CC: rather, it would be desirable to allow the combination of licenses that share the same intentions but that have a different name, e.g. to specify that a derived information artefact must be published under a license that allows only non-commercial uses instead of providing a list of all (known) licenses to which this characterisation applies [Les05].

We consider the example of Alice who wants to write a blog post about the English royal family. For this, she wants a complete list of all descendants of Queen Elizabeth II and for each descendant a photo with information about where it was taken. Alice has access to a query engine, which implements a system that can answer declaratively specified information needs by accessing information sources and services. For Alice's need the engine accesses DBpedia, a database containing facts extracted from Wikipedia, to get the descendants; the Flickr API to search with the descendants' names for matching photos; and the GeoNames API to determine from the photos' geographical locations a name for the place. In Figure 2.1 we visualise the information accesses that Alice performs to create her blog post. Important for Alice is that she can freely use the retrieved information, i.e., the descendant list and the photos, without having to pay license fees. Her blog is maintained for non-commercial purposes and she is willing to give attribution to the creators of information. She uses a policy-aware blogging software and so expects that the attributions are automatically added to her post.

---

[1]Section 4(b) in http://creativecommons.org/licenses/by-nc-sa/3.0/legalcode, accessed July 20th 2012

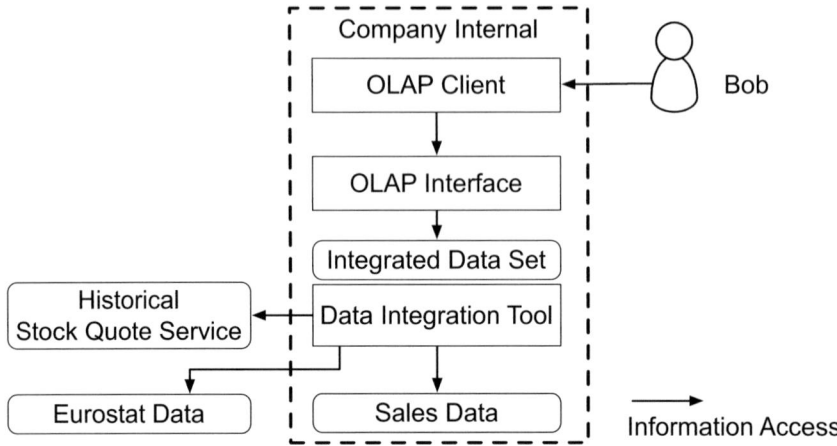

Figure 2.2: Scenario: Information Mashups

Furthermore, we are interested in answering the question about compatibility of Creative Commons licenses. We consider a license A compatible to a license B, if we can assign A to an information artefact that we derived from another information artefact with license B. For Creative Commons, the compatibilities are explicitly listed in a table[2]. We expect that we can automatically derive the compatibilities from a correct formalisation of the licenses.

2.1.2 Information Mashups for Decision Support

More and more decisions in companies become data-driven instead of being based on intuition. This is facilitated both by the increasing amount of available data and also by the growing abilities to integrate, process and analyse the data. A transformation is taking place in companies: previously the business side would explain their need for data to the IT department, which then would collect and integrate the data to provision it to the requestor. The trend goes in the opposite direction: IT makes data available with no knowledge about possible uses of the data; business people will browse the data and build new combined data sets for analysis based on the available data. Data is available from a wide range of different sources and can be combined without being confined to system or provider borders. Sources include company internal data sets, such as sales data or customer databases; external services, such as stock quote services or weather information; and open data sets, containing e.g. statistical or encyclopedic knowledge. Availability of the data and the ability to process it enable new applications on a technical level, but one also has to consider usage restrictions of the data. For example, sales data might only be accessible to managers of a company, who may use it for analysis but are not allowed to freely redistribute it to other employees or the public. Information services might restrict their provided data, e.g., a company obtaining a

---

[2]see Point 2.16 in http://wiki.creativecommons.org/FAQ, accessed 9th March 2012

license for a stock quote service might use the quotes in internal reports, but is not allowed to provide the quotes on their public homepage. Open datasets generally pose few restrictions on their usage, but some of them could have large impact on their suitability for certain applications: some open licenses do not allow commercial usage, or require that derived data is also made available under an open license.

In the following, we consider the example of Bob, a manager for the publicly listed company Acme. We visualise the information flow between the systems and information sources that Bob uses in Figure 2.2. Bob wants to create a dataset for analysing the company's performance in different geographical regions over time and the effect on the company's stock price. He uses a tool that integrates the different data sources and makes the data available for Online Analytical Processing (OLAP) software. The performance is derived by company-internal sales data, to which the managers of Acme have access, and are allowed to use it for analytical purposes, and share the results with other managers. The sales data contains location information, which can be linked to Eurostat data about geographic regions and their demographics, which is available under an open license allowing commercial and non-commercial redistribution under the requirement that Eurostat is acknowledged. Historical stock price data is available via a service for which the company purchased a license to use the data for company-internal purposes. Bob wants to make the integrated dataset available to all employees, but gets the hint from the policy-aware data integration tool, that this is not possible due to the usage restriction of the sales data, which only allow redistribution of the data to other managers.

2.1.3 Data Privacy in the Smart Energy Grid

The smart grid is the goal of current efforts to do a radical redesign of the current aged energy grid. Instead of centrally planning and producing energy in a top-down way, the aim is to create a network of distributed energy suppliers implementing a demand-driven production [Eur06]. The smart grid is a prominent example of a solution approach to problems occuring due to the increasing concentration of population in city areas. Like other smart city systems, the smart grid builds on information exchange between large numbers of heterogeneous entities. In order to make energy grids more efficient and reduce environmental impact, the smart grid requires up-to-date and fine-granular data about energy consumption and production. Besides its obvious uses for billing and statistical purposes, there are also various scenarios how energy consumption and related data can be both used for additional value-added services and misused to the disadvantage of individuals. Collected data includes not only consumption data, but for example also geographical locations of electric vehicles, information about clothes and used detergent for a run of the washing machine, or floor plans obtained through a vacuum cleaning robot. The goal is to establish an ecosystem of services creating value using information provided by smart appliances and at the same time protecting the privacy of individuals. Traditional means, i.e., organisational control for ensuring compliance with usage restrictions are not sufficient in the smart grid, due to the heterogeneity of available services and individuals' privacy requirements. A special challenge is the lack of a central control of the systems processing privacy-relevant information. Cou-

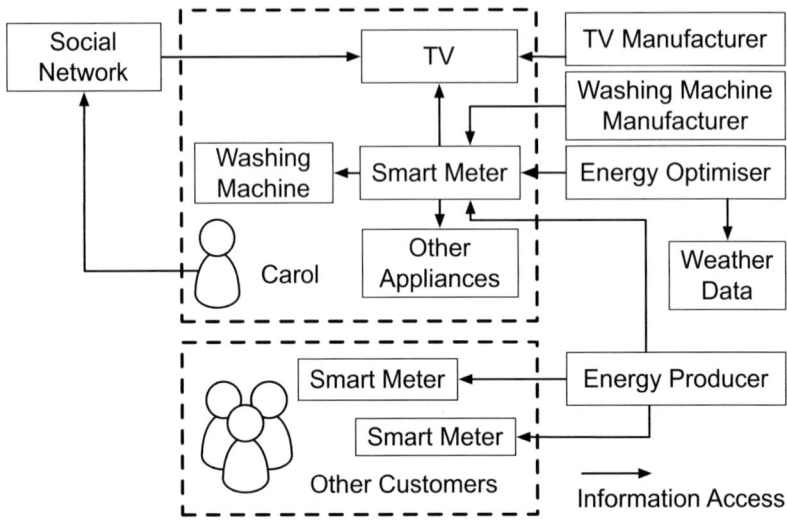

Figure 2.3: Scenario: Data Privacy in the Smart Energy Grid

pling smart grids with other smart city systems, such as smart factories, further intensifies the effects of a missing central control and the heterogeneity of information providers and processors.

In the following, we describe a concrete scenario about an individual participating in the smart grid. Figure 2.3 illustrates the information accesses in the example. Carol lives in an apartment equipped with a smart meter and smart appliances, which track in detail her consumption of electrical energy. She has to share consumption data with her energy producer for billing purposes, and also allow the producer to store the data for one year, in order to protect himself in case of a dispute about the bills. The energy producer needs a querying facility, where he can ask for all the consumption data from all of his customers. The producer does not want to miss any of the data as this would mean he cannot bill for energy that he has delivered. Consumption data is collected in a decentralised way at each customer's premise, so the provider has to decide which of the distributed information sources he needs to access. In order to guarantee that the energy producer has received all required sources, we need a notion of completeness, which specifies the relevant information sources. A further aspect is to restrict the sources that can specify certain data, e.g., a customer can only specify his own consumption, but not his neighbour's. Carol furthermore wants to share her consumption data with an energy optimiser service, which consults her about potential ways to save energy, respectively energy costs. The optimiser service uses the collected data from different customers and historical energy pricing information in order to improve its service. Carol allows such further usage only after her data was anonymised, in which case she also allows usage for statistical purposes and sharing of her data for the same purposes. Carol's washing machine does not only provide consumption data, but also information about the washing behavior, including selected washing programs, load of the machine, and used detergent. Carol gives the manufacturer of the washing machine access to this information for maintenance purposes, so that the manufacturer can monitor the relation between energy consumption and usage and can discover occurring problems in a timely fashion. The TV of Carol provides a functionality to post to a social network which movies Carol watched. Carol wants to share this information with her friends in the network, but does not want that her friends can share it further with third parties. The TV manufacturer has some basic support for privacy policies in previous devices based on the P3P standard for privacy on the web. Thus the manufacturer is interested in migrating its legacy P3P documents to the policy approach used in the smart grid.

2.2 Requirements Analysis

In this thesis we develop an approach for decentralised information systems, which integrate formalised usage restrictions of data artefacts as policies. Components of such a system that we develop or extend include: (i) a formalism and vocabulary for a usage policy language, (ii) methods to integrate dynamic information services into an existing decentralised information architecture, and (iii) completeness notions for query processing over the distributed information sources. The components are designed to be part of systems for supporting the proposed scenarios. Based on the scenarios, we identify a number of requirements that have to be fulfilled by the policy language and the information system. We list the derived requirements in Table 2.1 and discuss them in detail in the remainder of the section. In Section 2.3 we summarise and discuss how our work addresses the requirements.

Requirement R1: Web Compatibility
The presented scenarios show the need for interoperability between different, heterogeneous entities. To facilitate communication between the entities, it is important to be aligned to existing standards and best practices. The web architecture has proven to be very scalable both from a technical and social viewpoint. The used standards are generally open, i.e., no licensing of the standard itself or used patents is required, and supported by many implementations, including open source libraries. Thus, the adoption of new technologies based on the web architecture and related standards is of relatively low effort and costs even for small players. We require therefore that both information and policies are accessible over standard web protocols (e.g., HTTP) and be serialised in standard knowledge representation languages (e.g., RDF, OWL, RIF). Note that web compatibility does not necessarily mean that information and services are publicly available on the Internet, but rather that interoperable technologies are used that are also beneficial in closed (e.g., company-internal) scenarios.

Requirement R2: Formal Semantics
It is desirable that the meaning of usage policies is not dependent on a reference implementation of used algorithms or the human interpretation of a textual specification. We therefore require that the policy language is based on formal logic and has a well-defined semantics. Well-defined formal semantics lead to the advantage, that the meaning of a policy is unam-

Table 2.1: Overview of Requirements

Requirement		Domain
R1	Web Compatibility	Both
R2	Formal Semantics	
R3	Data-centricity of Policies	
R4	Extendable Vocabulary of Computational Model	
R5	Content-based Restrictions on Other Policies	Policy Language
R6	Support for Obligations	
R7	Expressivity for Common Restrictions	
R8	Decidable and Practical Classification	
R9	User Interactions with Hidden Formal Logic	
R10	Decentralised Architecture for Interlinked Information	
R11	Support for Information Services	Information System
R12	Completeness Notions for Queries	

biguously defined, which is very important in scenarios with many heterogeneous entities. System developers can implement automatic verification algorithms based on the formal semantics instead of relying on a reference implementation that may not work with an existing system.

Requirement R3: Data-centricity of Policies
Common to all scenarios is the lack of a central system in which information is created, processed, and consumed. Instead information is transferred between systems under the control of different entities without a complete view on the overall process. Not only is there no complete view of the originally planned process, it is also possible that other processes use the data, including processes that are initiated only after the original process has terminated. Furthermore, the transformation from standardised processes operating on a class of information to individual process instances operating on concrete information artefacts leads to a need for fine-grained policies, which can be individually specified for every data artefact. For example, the energy consumption data of every customer can have a different policy, depending on the customer: while one person wants to share it freely, another person can have very restricting conditions on its use. We thus require that policies are not expressed as restrictions on the overall system behaviour when processing a certain class of informa-

tion, but instead policies should be data-centric, as defined by the following three properties: (i) each artefact has its own policy that is attached to the artefact; (ii) the policy of an artefact employs a local perspective by only restricting the actions immediately using the artefact or directly related to such actions, i.e., performed in the same context (e.g., on the same machine, or by the same user); (iii) the policy of an artefact can restrict the policies that can be assigned to derived or copied artefacts. With data-centric policies the compliance of an isolated data artefact usage is verifiable without the need for a central instance knowing the complete process in which the usage is embedded and the policies can be transferred together with the artefacts between different providers, because they are attached to their protected artefacts. Two basic assumptions for data-centric policies, which policy-aware systems have to enforce, enable the localised view: (i) each used artefact has an attached policy that was either set by the artefact's owner or was assigned in compliance with the policies of the artefacts used to derive the artefact; (ii) produced artefacts will be used in compliance with the assigned policy.

Requirement R4: Extendable Vocabulary of Computational Model
The computational model that is restricted by data-centric policies is based on instances of actions using data artefacts and potentially producing new artefacts, and the relation between such actions. Thus, the usage descriptions are related to descriptions of process instances with a focus on data artefacts and centered around one single usage action, which can only have straightforward relations to other actions. The relation between different action instances, the roles of used and produced artefacts, and the involved actors are also described by approaches for formally modelling provenance. While provenance is concerned with the history of what happened, our model will also apply to planned but not yet executed actions. Nonetheless, the modelled information is similar, and so we require that our vocabulary is aligned to the Open Provenance Model (OPM), an emerging best practice for expressing provenance [MCF+11]. We will extend the OPM vocabulary to model the policies of artefacts and by properties commonly used in usage restrictions, such as the purpose of a usage. We furthermore require that the vocabulary is easily extendable for concrete applications, e.g., by supporting a friends relation between entities in a system including a social network. This is required because no standard model can be built that covers all desired aspects of all possible applications of usage policies.

Requirement R5: Content-based Restrictions on Other Policies
Restricting the policies that can be assigned to derived data enables the localised view of data-centric policies. In the simplest case, derived artefacts inherit the policy of the used artefact (e.g., a copy of a confidential artefact is also confidential). However, in general the policy of the produced artefact can also allow broader usages (e.g., after anonymising an artefact) or allow narrower usages (e.g., an energy producer may use consumption data for billing but is not allowed to share it further). For restricting the allowed policies of produced artefacts there are two possibilities: (i) name-based policy restrictions, and (ii) content-based policy restrictions. Policies using name-based policy restrictions specify an exhaustive list of admissible policies for a produced artefact, which is problematic in scenarios with independent actors that employ policies with different names (i.e., not in the specified list) but with a compatible set of allowed usages (i.e., should be in the list). To overcome such incompatibil-

ities, we require that the policy language supports content-based policy restrictions. Instead of explicitly listing admissible policies for produced artefacts, content-based restrictions describe the admissible policies in terms of the minimal or maximal allowed usages. Content-based restrictions increase compatibility by making policies admissible based on the usages they allow independent of their names. Checking whether a policy fulfills at most or at least the same usages as a target policy corresponds to policy containment, which is well-studied for many policy languages as a tool for policy management (e.g., [PKH05, BM08]). The approach of content-based policy restrictions goes one step further and uses policy containment as part of the policy definitions themselves, which requires meta-modelling (policies are both sets of allowed usages as well as part of usage descriptions) and self-referentiality (a policy can require that derived artefacts have a policy that allows at most the same uses as the original policy). Besides setting an upper bound on the actions allowed by a target policy, the containment condition can also be used to set a lower bound. For example, an individual can decide to share his energy consumption patterns with a statistics institute under the condition that derived artefacts are made available for public use and not only for paying clients.

Requirement R6: Support for Obligations
Obligations are parts of policy conditions that have to be fulfilled only after a certain period of time. Consider for example the obligation that a stored artefact should be deleted within one year: storing the artefact is compliant as long as the deletion within one year can be ensured. In contrast, restricting usage to non-commercial purposes is not an obligation: a commercial usage violates the policy and should be prevented. In case of an unfulfilled obligation, instead of preventing the usage, an obligation handler can either automatically fulfill the obligation (e.g., by scheduling a deletion within a year), or notify the user about missing actions. We thus need an approach to distinguish between policy violations and not yet fulfilled obligations, which then can be passed to the appropriate obligation handlers.

Requirement R7: Expressivity for Common Restrictions
Previous requirements discussed explicit language constructs that are needed for data-centric usage policies. We also need to ensure that the developed policy language, i.e., the formalism and the vocabulary, is expressive enough to formalise usage restrictions that are commonly found in many policies. In the following, we list a number of abstractions of restrictions, which we refer to as policy patterns in the remainder of this work: (i) *rights delegation*: sharing of artefacts is allowed, but rights of the recipient may be restricted, (ii) *attribute-based usage restrictions*: usage can be restricted by conditions on application-specific attributes, (iii) *anonymisation*: after anonymisation the usage restrictions of an artefact may be more lax but still existent, (iv) *required future actions*: certain usages can require that specific actions have to be performed within a specific time span. Additionally, we require that we can capture *domain knowledge*, including hierarchies, from which new facts can be inferred.

Requirement R8: Decidable and Practical Classification
One reason for creating a formal policy language is to enable automated classification of usage descriptions into compliant and non-compliant. To obtain a practical language, the classification procedure should be (i) theoretically decidable, and (ii) in practice implementable as software with acceptable performance levels. We thus require a prototypical implemen-

tation of the classification algorithm that has an appropriate performance for the presented examples in the scenarios.

Requirement R9: User Interactions with Hidden Formal Logic
Formal policies have the advantage of specifying unambiguously a set of restrictions and enabling automated classification of activities into compliant or non-compliant. Human users interacting with such a policy-aware system however are faced with a semantic gap between their understanding of a policy and its formal meaning. The gap is especially large if the users are non-experts. There are two main situations in which users interface with policies: (i) policy specification in order to formalise an intended usage restriction, and (ii) handling of non-compliant actions. For the first case, we require the language to support a conceptually simple but expressive model to compose policies from building blocks modelling common usage restrictions. The building blocks should be described in natural language and be configurable to the concrete needs of a policy specifier. In the second case, it is not sufficient for the user to get a binary decision, whether his intended usage is compliant or not. Instead the user wants to know why the usage is non-compliant (e.g., a missing attribution) and how he can fix this (e.g., add an attribution of the creator of an artefact). Thus, we require algorithms to include a justification mechanism for their decisions. In principal, justifications can be embedded with little effort in reasoning algorithms for many logics by saving a history of logical conclusions. However such logic-based justifications are not easily understandable for human users that cannot be expected to be logic specialists. Therefore it is essential that justifications are translated into natural language explanations that the users can understand.

Requirement R10: Decentralised Architecture for Interlinked Information
The proposed scenarios require a decentralised architecture for hosting the information. Information has to be kept near to its producers and owners instead of in a centralised store for the following reasons: (i) openness: publishing new information should be possible without the need to register with a central authority; (ii) scalability: keeping massive amounts of centrally stored data in sync with highly distributed information sources leads to severe scalability issues; (iii) re-usability: data should be used in different contexts by different entities, a central store shared by all entities is not realistic; (iv) control: data owners should keep control of the data in order to enforce their usage restrictions.

For concrete applications and systems, the relevant information has to be integrated from the distributed data sources. In order to support the discovery of new data sources and for having explicit relations between data stored in different sources, we require an information model that can specify links from one information resource to another. Consider e.g. that the database of the energy producer contains links to the energy consumption data sources of each of its customers.

Requirement R11: Support for Information Services
In the scenarios, we found information sources that cannot be materialised as static data sets for various reasons: (i) data is constantly changing, e.g., stock quotes can have update intervals below one second; (ii) data is generated depending on input from a possibly infinite domain, e.g., the quarterly aggregation of sales data can be applied on arbitrary individual sales data; (iii) the information provider does not want to give arbitrary access to the information, e.g., energy prices may be only available for specific requests in terms of time

and location in order to maintain the possibility for price differentiation. We denote such information sources as information services, as they provide a restricted view on a potentially infinite virtual data set. A requirement for the decentralised information system is the support for information services.

Requirement R12: Completeness Notions for Queries
The interlinked information model supports query processing over the information space by following links between information sources to find further relevant data. However, theoretically every information source in the web could contain relevant data. Querying all information sources is neither feasible (not all sources are interlinked and the size of the web is too enormous) nor desirable (required time and bandwidth are an issue and not every source can be trusted). Instead, we require that there is a completeness notion for queries, which specifies which sources are relevant for a given query. Besides the obvious advantage of limiting the sources that have to be accessed for query evaluation the following benefits arise: (i) users know what to expect from a query evaluation algorithm, e.g., an energy producer can be sure to retrieve all consumption data of a customer; (ii) algorithms can have crisp termination criteria; and (iii) systems can implement operations that rely on checking for the absence of results, such as negation-as-failure.

2.3 Discussion

In the beginning of this chapter, we presented scenarios illustrating the need for decentralised information systems with formalised usage policies. The scenarios work with very different kinds of information (ranging from creative works to personal information) that have to be protected by very different kinds of usage restrictions (ranging from copyright licenses to waivers of privacy rights). Yet, the scenarios share many common features and challenges. We collected a number of requirements that need to be addressed in order to realise systems supporting the proposed scenarios.

In the following, we give a high-level overview of our contributions in this work and discuss how they address the collected requirements:

Language for Data-centric Usage Policies: The policy language consists of two components: an *extendable vocabulary of computational model (R4)* and a formalism to model usage restrictions. The *formal semantics (R2)* is defined on top of first-order logics, which gives the advantage that existing algorithms for reasoning in decidable fragments of first-order logics can be re-used as part of our classification algorithm. In order to support *content-based restrictions on other policies (R5)*, we require meta-modelling and self-referentiality of policies. To retain the *decidability (part of R8)* of the chosen first-order logic fragment, we have to define several restrictions on the allowable axioms, potentially reducing the size of the fragment. By showing how common knowledge representation languages for the web, e.g., OWL can be used as basic first-order logic fragments of our policy language, we show a way to ensure *web compatibility (R1)*. A side effect of web compatibility is that each policy has a URI and a representation that can be transferred via web protocols. Thus, we can attach policies either via reference (their URIs) or via value (their representations) to data artefacts, which together with the support for content-based policy restrictions enables *data-centric policies (R3)*.

Methods for Interacting with Policies: Besides getting a binary answer to the question whether a data usage is compliant or not, there are other ways to interact with policies, respectively a policy-aware system. We present an approach based on abductive reasoning to *support for obligations (R6)* in our policy language. Obligations are identified by system-specific definitions that distinguish unfulfilled obligations from hard violations that should lead to prevention or punishment of non-compliant usages. Unfulfilled obligations on the other hand can be fixed either manually by the user or automatically by an appropriate obligation handler. We furthermore define a conceptually simple structured model for policies that can combine pre-defined building blocks into policies reflecting the intended usage restriction of the policy specifier. The building blocks can be annotated with natural language labels that help the specifier to discover and select blocks for his policy without being exposed to their formal definitions. The structure of policies and their annotations are exploited by an explanation component that helps the user to find out why a usage was classified as non-compliant. The structured model and the explanation component enable the two most common *user interactions with hidden formal logic (R9)*: policy specification and finding reasons for non-compliance.

Extensions to the Linked Data Architecture: Linked Data denotes a set of principles based on *web compatible (R1)* technologies that realise a *decentralised architecture for interlinked information (R10)*. To fully address our collected requirements, we will extend the architecture with two features. On the one hand, we present Linked Data Services (LIDS), a lightweight approach for integrating *information services (R11)* with Linked Data. On the other hand, we will define *completeness notions for queries (R12)* by defining different sets of information sources that have to be accessed in order to completely answer conjunctive SPARQL queries over Linked Data.

Prototypical Implementations and Application to Scenarios: We present a number of prototypes, which implement the algorithms and methods introduced in this work, thus showing that they are *practically implementable (part of R8)*. We apply the prototypes to illustrate how the systems for supporting the proposed scenarios can be built. For the realisation of the scenarios, we have to *extend the vocabularies (R4)* with corresponding domain knowledge. By formalising the required policies for the scenarios we will show that the language has enough *expressivity for common restrictions (R7)* found in usage policies.

We summarise the relation between the contributions and the addressed requirements in Table 2.2.

After introducing preliminaries in Chapter 3, we present the contributions in the subsequent chapters as follows: in Chapter 4 we introduce our data-centric policy language

Table 2.2: Overview of requirements addressed by contributions

Requirement	Contribution			
	Policy Language	Interaction Methods	Linked Data Extensions	Prototypical Implementations
R1: *Web Compatibility*	✓		✓	
R2: *Formal Semantics*	✓			
R3: *Data-centricity of Policies*	✓			
R4: *Extendable Vocabulary of Computational Model*	✓			✓
R5: *Content-based Restrictions on Other Policies*	✓			
R6: *Support for Obligations*		✓		
R7: *Expressivity for Common Restrictions*				✓
R8: *Decidable and Practical Classification*	✓			✓
R9: *User Interactions with Hidden Formal Logic*		✓		
R10: *Decentralised Architecture for Interlinked Information*			✓	
R11: *Support for Information Services*			✓	
R12: *Completeness Notions for Queries*			✓	

including the vocabulary, the semantics and the grounding in concrete knowledge representation languages; the methods for interacting with policies through obligation handling, the structured model, and the explanation component are presented in Chapter 5; Chapter 6 extends the Linked Data architecture with support for information services and completeness notions for queries; as part of Chapter 7, we describe the implementation of the proposed methods and algorithms and their application in the presented scenarios.

Chapter 3

Preliminaries

In this chapter, we introduce the foundation for the work presented in this thesis. A core requirement for our approach is that knowledge is represented in a machine-understandable way, which applies to both the stored and processed information and their usage restrictions. We thus recapitulate formalisms for knowledge representation in Section 3.1. We furthermore require a scalable architecture for communication between different actors, which will be based on the web architecture discussed in Section 3.2. The combination of the web architecture with formal, machine-understandable information is called the Semantic Web. We present relevant Semantic Web technologies in Section 3.3. We discuss the notion of policy as used in computer science and in our work for the formalisation of usage restrictions in Section 3.4.

3.1 Knowledge Representation

The goal of knowledge representation is to make knowledge explicit, which enables its efficient sharing. We are especially interested in formal knowledge representations that computers can understand and from which new knowledge can be automatically inferred. Davis et al. define the notion of knowledge representation (KR) by considering the different roles that a KR plays [DSS93]. Their definition is broad and covers a wide range of possible KR technologies from which we choose logics. Specifically we use first-order logic (FOL) and computationally less expensive FOL fragments. A discussion about the suitability of logics for knowledge representation can be found in [LMP07, pp. 67ff.].

In Section 3.1.1, we describe first-order logic, which is the base for the discussions of Description Logics in Section 3.1.2 and Datalog in Section 3.1.3.

3.1.1 First-Order Logic (FOL)

In the following, we present the definition of first-order logic (FOL) without function symbols on which we base our work. A FOL signature Σ is a set of symbols, which is defined as the union of the disjoint subsets of constants (C) and predicates (P). An arity is assigned to each predicate $p \in P$. Let V be an infinite set of variables, disjoint to the signature. Terms are either variables or constants. An atomic formula is an expression of the form $p(t_1, \ldots, t_n)$, where $p \in P$ is a predicate of arity n, and each $t_i \in C \cup V$ is a term. Formulae are either atomic or if ϕ and ψ are formulae and x is a variable, then $\phi \wedge \psi$, $\phi \vee \psi$, $\phi \rightarrow \psi$, $\neg\phi$, $\exists x.\phi$, and $\forall x.\phi$ are also formulae. Additionally, we allow the formulae $\top$ and $\bot$. A variable x is free in a formula if it occurs outside of the scope of a quantifier ($\forall, \exists$), otherwise it is bound in the formula. A formula is called a sentence, if it has no free variables. A theory is a set of sentences. As special notation, we write $\phi[x]$ with the meaning that ϕ contains no other free variables besides x. We write $\phi[c]$, where $c \in C$ is a constant, to denote the formula, where every free occurrence of x in ϕ is replaced by c.

An FOL interpretation $\mathbf{I}$ for a signature with constants C and predicates P is given by a nonempty set D and a function I. D is the domain, an abstract set of individuals representing the universe in which the symbols in Σ are interpreted. The interpretation function I assigns (i) to every constant $c \in C$ an element $I(c) \in D$ in the domain, and (ii) to every predicate $p \in P$ with arity n a relation $I(p) \subseteq D^n$. An interpretation assigns to every sentence ϕ a truth value $I(\phi)$ in the following way:

- if $\phi = \top$, then $I(\phi) =$ true;
- if $\phi = \bot$, then $I(\phi) =$ false;
- if $\phi = p(t_1, \ldots, t_n)$, then $I(\phi) =$ true, if $(I(t_1), \ldots, I(t_n)) \in I(p)$ and $I(\phi) =$ false otherwise;
- if $\phi = \phi_1 \wedge \phi_2$, then $I(\phi) =$ true, if $I(\phi_1) =$ true and $I(\phi_2) =$ true, and $I(\phi) =$ false otherwise;
- if $\phi = \phi_1 \vee \phi_2$, then $I(\phi) =$ false, if $I(\phi_1) =$ false and $I(\phi_2) =$ false, and $I(\phi) =$ true otherwise;
- if $\phi = \phi_1 \rightarrow \phi_2$, then $I(\phi) =$ true, if $I(\phi_2) =$ true or $I(\phi_1) =$ false, and $I(\phi) =$ false otherwise;
- if $\phi = \neg \psi$, then $I(\phi) =$ true, if $I(\psi) =$ false, and $I(\phi) =$ false otherwise;
- if $\phi = \exists x.\psi[x]$, then $I(\phi) =$ true, if there exists $c \in C$, such that $I(\psi[c]) =$ true. Otherwise $I(\phi) =$ false.
- if $\phi = \forall x.\psi[x]$, then $I(\phi) =$ true, if for all $c \in C$, it holds $I(\psi[c]) =$ true. Otherwise $I(\phi) =$ false.

An interpretation $\mathbf{I}$ satisfies a sentence ϕ, if $I(\phi) =$ true, which is also denoted as $\mathbf{I} \models \phi$. A theory T is satisfied by an interpretation $\mathbf{I}$, if for every $\phi \in T$ it holds $\mathbf{I} \models \phi$. An interpretation $\mathbf{I}$ satisfying a theory T is called a model for T. A theory T is called consistent or satisfiable if there exists a model for T, otherwise it is called inconsistent or unsatisfiable. We say that a theory T_2 is a logical consequence of theory T_1, if every model of T_1 is also a model for T_2. We write this entailment as $T_1 \models T_2$.

3.1.2 Description Logics (DL)

Description Logics (DLs) denote a family of formalisms covering a wide range of expressivity and computational complexity. The language KL-ONE [BS85] became the first DL with well-defined semantics, which however turned out to be undecidable [SS89]. Subsequently, more focus was put on decidability and efficiency of various reasoning tasks. Originally, DLs were developed independent of FOL with the goal of having a precise, model-theoretic semantics for modelling domains of interest. Previous formalisms used for such modelling tasks include semantic networks [Qui67] and frame-based knowledge representations [Min74]. Later, it was found that knowledge expressed in most DLs can be translated into an equivalent FOL theory [Bor96]. For an extensive introduction and discussion of DLs, we refer the reader to [BCM⁺07]. In this section, we restrict our discussion to the special notation, which is commonly used for DLs. The semantics of a DL knowledge base can be given by translating axioms into FOL sentences as given e.g. in [HKR09]. Furthermore, we only discuss the modelling features used in this work, which are given by the DL $\mathcal{ALC}$ [SSS91] extended with inverse roles and nominals.

DLs model a domain in terms of individuals, concepts – unary predicates, i.e., sets of individuals – and roles – binary predicates, i.e., relations between individuals. Let N_I be the set of individual names, N_C be the set of concept names, and N_R be the set of role names. For every named role $R \in N_R$, we also consider its inverse R^- as a role. Besides atomic concepts, we can also describe complex concepts. Let C and D be concepts, R a role, and a an individual then the following are also concepts:

- $\top$: containing all individuals;

- $\bot$: containing no individual;

- $C \sqcap D$: containing the individuals that are both in C and in D;

- $C \sqcup D$: containing the individuals that are in C or in D;

- $\neg C$: containing the individuals that are not in C;

- $\exists R.C$: containing the individuals that are related via the role R to an individual in C;

- $\forall R.C$: containing the individuals that are related via the role R only to individuals in C;

- $\{a\}$: containing exactly the individual a.

A DL knowledge base consists of a set of assertional axioms and a set of terminological axioms. Assertional axioms state knowledge about individuals, i.e., which relations hold between individuals or to which concept an individual belongs. Terminological axioms state knowledge about concepts, i.e., which concept is a subconcept of another concept and which concepts are equivalent. In the following we give the syntax and meaning of axioms, where C is a concept, R is a role, and $a, b \in N_I$ are individuals:

- $C(a)$: assertional axiom stating that a is an instance of C;

- $R(a, b)$: assertional axiom stating that a is related via R to b;

- $C \sqsubseteq D$: terminological axiom stating that C is a subconcept of D, i.e., that every instance of C is also an instance of D;

- $C \equiv D$: terminological axiom stating that C is equivalent to D, i.e., that every instance of C is also an instance of of D and vice versa.

Standard reasoning tasks for DL include:

- Satisfiability: checking whether a knowledge base has a model;

- Subsumption: checking whether a concept is a subconcept of another concept;

- Instance checking: retrieving all individuals that are instance of a concept.

3.1.3 Datalog

Datalog originated as a query and rule language for deductive databases [AHV94], where it is often used with a logic programming semantics, which employs a closed world assumption (CWA). The CWA states that if a statement is not contained in a database then it is not true supporting non-monotonic features such as negations-as-failure. In contrast, we consider Datalog as a fragment of FOL interpreted under FOL semantics implying the open world assumption (OWA). Thus, in this work, Datalog is the rule language consisting of implications with only positive atoms and a single head atom.

We denote a theory in the Datalog fragment as a Datalog program. A Datalog program consists of rules, which are formulae of the following form:

$$\forall x_1, \ldots, \forall x_n.(B_1 \wedge \ldots \wedge B_m \rightarrow H),$$

where each $B_1, \ldots, B_m$ is either $\top$ or an atomic formula, H is an atomic formula, and $\{x_1, \ldots, x_n\}$ is the set of variables in $B_1, \ldots, B_m$ and H.

As all variables in a Datalog rule are universally quantified on the outmost level of the rule, we adopt the convention of omitting them for presentation purposes. Furthermore, we also conform to the convention of starting the rule with the head and using the reversed implication symbol $\leftarrow$. Lastly, for rules that have only the formula $\top$ as condition, we omit the condition and simply write H. Such rules are called facts.

The standard reasoning task for Datalog engines is query answering, i.e., retrieving the content of a relation, which can be defined as the head of a rule.

3.2 Web Architecture

The web is the largest information system ever built. The size of the web is enabled by its scalable architecture, which is decentralised and resistant to inconsistencies and failures. Fielding generalises the architectural patterns of the web into an architectural style known as Representational State Transfer (REST) [Fie00]. In the following, we discuss three properties of the web architecture that are fundamental to the success of the web: information can be referenced, information is accessible, and information is structured.

Referencing information is possible by giving a unique identifier to every resource in form of an *Internationalized Resource Identifier* (IRI [DS05]). IRIs are an extension of *Uniform Resource Identifiers* (URIs [BLFM05]) in that IRIs can include non-ASCII characters. IRIs identify objects including web-accessible resources, real world objects such as persons,

Table 3.1: HTTP response codes

Code	Meaning
200	Success; the server returns a representation of the requested resource.
303	See other; the server returns the IRI under which the resource can be found. Also known as redirect.
400	Bad request; the request of the client has malformed syntax and thus cannot be served.
404	Not found: the resource is not managed by the server.
500	Internal server error: although the request of the client might be valid, the server is not able to respond to it in the expected fashion at the current time.

and abstract concepts and relations such as the class of all persons. We mainly use Hypertext Transfer Protocol (HTTP [FGM+99]) IRIs, which do not only identify resources but also embody enough information to access their representations. An example IRI identifying the relation between a person and its name is: http://xmlns.com/foaf/0.1/name. As IRIs are often long and repetitive we use the QName syntax, which replaces common IRI prefixes by abbreviations. The abbreviated prefix is followed by a colon and a local part, and stands for the IRI obtained by concatenating the expanded prefix and the local part. For example we use the prefix foaf for http://xmlns.com/foaf/0.1/ and can then abbreviate the IRI for the name relation as foaf:name.

Information is accessible over the Hypertext Transfer Protocol (HTTP), which is an open protocol for accessing and managing resources hosted on a server. HTTP IRIs consist of two parts: the server address, which can be a logical host name, and the path component, which refers to a specific resource on the server. The domain name system (DNS) resolves logical host names in an IRI into the physical Internet addresses of the corresponding servers. The simplest interaction with an HTTP server is the GET request where a client requests a resource managed by the server, which is identified by the path component of an IRI. The server responds with a code, and in case of a successful request with a representation of the corresponding resource. Table 3.1 lists the most common response codes and their meaning.

Information structure on the web is given by links between resources. Links are unidirectional, not necessarily reciprocal references from one resource to another resource using its IRI. Links can be specified without the requirement of consent of the owner of the destination resource. Having links allows an information consumer to follow the links to further relevant information. Links are an integral part of HTML (HyperText Markup Language [W3C99]) – the initial resource representation format on the web – but are missing from subsequently developed representation formats for structured information such as XML and later JSON. Links are explicitly supported in RDF – the representation format used in the Semantic Web – which will be discussed in Section 3.3.

3.3 Semantic Web Technologies

The Semantic Web aims at making the information available on the web understandable for machines. The foundation is given by the Resource Description Framework (RDF) – a graph-based data model [W3C04c]. The nodes of an RDF graph are either resources or literals, e.g., strings, numbers or dates. Resources are connected via directed and labelled edges to other resources and literals. Both edge labels and resources are given as IRIs, which makes RDF suitable for information integration by simply merging graphs, which can use globally unique identifiers (IRIs) across different data sources. Alternatively instead of an IRI also blank nodes, i.e., identifiers local to a graph, can be used as node names whenever it is not required or desired to assign a global identifier.

Edges are specified as triples, each consisting of a subject (the source of the edge), a predicate (the edge label) and an object (the destination of the edge). Edge labels are called properties.

RDF comes with an XML-based serialisation, which makes it suitable for exchanging RDF graphs over the web. For easier presentation, we use the N3 [BLC11] serialisation when giving examples in this work. RDF graphs are specified in N3 as list of triples, which we write using the verbatim font. A triple is written as subject, predicate, and object separated by whitespaces and is ended by a dot (.). IRIs are written in angle brackets (< + IRI + >) and literals are written in quotes (" + literal value + "). For example, the following triple states that Queen Elizabeth II. has the name "Elizabeth II":

```
<http://dbpedia.org/resource/Elizabeth_II>
                <http://xmlns.com/foaf/0.1/name> "Elizabeth II" .
```

IRIs can also be serialised as QNames if the prefix has been declared previously using the @prefix keyword. For example the graph

```
@prefix dbp: <http://dbpedia.org/resource/> .
@prefix dbpo: <http://dbpedia.org/ontology/> .
dbp:Anne,_Princess_Royal dbpo:parent  dbp:Elizabeth_II .
```

corresponds to

```
<http://dbpedia.org/resource/Anne,_Princess_Royal>
                <http://dbpedia.org/ontology/parent>
                        <http://dbpedia.org/resource/Elizabeth_II> .
```

A list of prefixes that we use in this work without specifying them explicitly in N3 is given in Table 3.2. If a triple is ended with a semicolon (;) instead of a dot, then only a 2-tuple is following that is treated as predicate and object of a new triple inheriting the previous subject. Similarly, ending a triple with a comma (,) means that only an object is following and subject and predicate are inherited. A blank node is denoted by square brackets ([ ]). Inside of the brackets there can be 2-tuples, which then stand for the predicate and object of a triple with the blank node as subject. Brackets can be nested, e.g., one can express that somebody knows somebody named "Prince Charles" as follows:

Table 3.2: IRI prefixes used throughout this work.

Prefix	IRI
`rdf:`	`http://www.w3.org/1999/02/22-rdf-syntax-ns#`
`rdfs:`	`http://www.w3.org/2000/01/rdf-schema#`
`owl:`	`http://www.w3.org/2002/07/owl#`
`foaf:`	`http://xmlns.com/foaf/0.1/`
`geo:`	`http://www.w3.org/2003/01/geo/wgs84_pos#`
`dbp:`	`http://dbpedia.org/resource/`
`dbpo:`	`http://dbpedia.org/ontology/`
`opmv:`	`http://purl.org/net/opmv/ns#`
`cc:`	`http://creativecommons.org/ns#`

```
[foaf:knows [foaf:name "Prince Charles"]] .
```

The meaning of concepts and properties used in an RDF graph can be formally defined with several web-compatible knowledge representation languages. These languages include RDF Schema (RDFS) [W3C04b], the Web Ontology Language (OWL) [W3C09a], and the Rule Interchange Format (RIF) [W3C12b]. RDFS is a simple language allowing to specify subconcept relationships and domains and ranges of properties. The foundation of OWL are description logics. There exist several profiles of OWL, each based on a different DL with a specific tradeoff between modelling features and reasoning complexity. RIF defines multiple rule-based languages, including RIF Core, which corresponds to Datalog. The benefits of the RIF and OWL standards are mainly that they (i) provide standardised serialisation as web compliant documents, (ii) define the features and semantics of the KR formalisms, which is important for interoperability, when considering the differences in the formalisms found in the literature and used by systems. Using one of the KR languages, new information can be inferred from RDF graphs.

The standard technology for querying RDF information is the SPARQL Protocol And RDF Query Language (SPARQL) [W3C08]. We discuss here only the subset of SPARQL used throughout this work. SPARQL queries include conditions, which we restrict to basic graph patterns (BGP) in this work. BGPs are RDF graphs that allow variables instead of resources, edge labels, and literals. A BGP can be matched to a graph if a mapping of the variables in the BGP to IRIs and literal values can be found such that the mapped BGP is a subgraph of the RDF graph. The notation for BGPs in SPARQL corresponds to N3 as discussed above, where variables are marked with a question mark (?) in the beginning, e.g., `dbp:Elizabeth_II dbpo:parent ?x` matches all triples describing the parents of Elizabeth II. SPARQL queries come in two forms, either as SELECT or as CONSTRUCT queries. A SELECT query specifies a subset of the variables in the condition and returns a set of variable bindings. The syntax is as follows (`CONDITION` stands for a BGP that binds the variables $?v1, \ldots, ?vn$):

```
SELECT ?v1, ..., ?vn WHERE { CONDITION }
```

A CONSTRUCT query specifies a head BGP using a subset of the variables in the condition and returns a graph containing the triples obtained by replacing the variables in the head BGP using each found variable binding. The syntax is as follows (CONDITION and HEAD stand for BGPs, where the variables in HEAD are a subset of the variables in CONDITION):

```
CONSTRUCT HEAD WHERE { CONDITION }
```

IRI prefixes are specified as in N3.

After having introduced how we can express and query semantic data, we discuss in the following the Linked Data principles, which provide a guideline for publishing semantic data in an accessible way on the web [BL06]:

1. Use URIs as names for things.
2. Use HTTP URIs so that people can look up those names.
3. When someone looks up a URI, provide useful information, using the standards (RDF, SPARQL).
4. Include links to other URIs. So that they can discover more things.

For a more extensive discussion about Linked Data and its history, we refer the reader to [BHBL09]. In the remainder of this section, we give a formalisation of RDF, Linked Data, and BGPs. Additionally, we discuss vocabularies and datasets used throughout this work.

3.3.1 Resource Description Framework (RDF)

We introduce basic notation to clarify our understanding of RDF, Linked Data and queries. We stay close to similar definitions as found in [PAG09].

Definition 1 (RDF Terms, Triple, Graph). *The set of RDF terms consists of the set of IRIs $\mathcal{I}$, the set of blank nodes $\mathcal{B}$ and the set of literals $\mathcal{L}$. The sets $\mathcal{I}, \mathcal{B},$ and $\mathcal{L}$ are pairwise disjoint. A triple $(s, p, o) \in \mathcal{T} = (\mathcal{I} \cup \mathcal{B}) \times \mathcal{I} \times (\mathcal{I} \cup \mathcal{B} \cup \mathcal{L})$ is called an RDF triple, where s is the subject, p is the predicate and o is the object. We denote by $\mathsf{s}(t)$ the subject, $\mathsf{p}(t)$ the predicate and $\mathsf{o}(t)$ the object of a triple t. We denote by $\mathsf{iris}(t)$ all IRIs from a triple t, and by $\mathsf{terms}(t)$ all RDF terms. A set of triples is called RDF graph; $\mathcal{G} = 2^{\mathcal{T}}$ is the set of all graphs.*

3.3.2 Linked Data

Next, we define ways for accessing RDF graphs published on the web as Linked Data. A key characteristic of Linked Data is the correspondence between an identifier and a source; i.e., the name for a thing (non-information resource) is associated with the document where one can find related information (information resource).

Definition 2 (Information Resource, Lookup). *Let $\mathcal{I}_I \subseteq \mathcal{I}$ be the set of all information resources. The set of all non-information resources is defined as $\mathcal{I}_N = \mathcal{I} \setminus \mathcal{I}_I$. The function $\mathsf{deref}: \mathcal{I}_I \mapsto \mathcal{G}$ models a Linked Data lookup and returns the graph represented in a document, or the empty set if none found, e.g., if there is a timeout or the document returns non-RDF content.*

We use Information Resource and document interchangeably. To be able to model the association between Non-Information Resources and Information Resources we introduce the concept of correspondence.

Definition 3 (Correspondence). *The function* $co: I \mapsto I_I$ *associates to a resource its information resource. For inputs from* I_I, co *behaves as the identity function.*

It is not always possible to determine the kind of an IRI from the outset; an HTTP lookup clarifies the kind of IRI. We define a high-level function which provide abstractions on low-level functionality pertaining to protocol-level issues. Thus, in co we abstract away the following cases:

1. remove the local identifier from an IRI;

2. dereference the IRI and follow redirects (HTTP status codes 30x);

3. dereference the IRI and parse the `Content-Location` header to yield the canonical name;

4. no-op: do nothing if the IRI is an information resource.

Options 1-3 may be called never or repeatedly, to ultimately arrive at 4. The co function may never return due to infinite redirects; in practice, one sets a limit on how often co can be applied.

3.3.3 Basic Graph Pattern (BGP)

Definition 4 (Variable, Triple Pattern). *Let* V *be the set of variables; variables bind to RDF terms from* $I \cup B \cup L$. *A triple* $p \in (I \cup V) \times (I \cup V) \times (I \cup L \cup V)$ *is called triple pattern. We omit blank nodes from triple patterns for ease of exposition.* P *is the set of all triple patterns. We denote by* $vars(p)$ *all variables occurring in a triple pattern p.*

Definition 5 (Variable Binding). *We define* M *as the set of all partial functions* $\mu: V \mapsto I \cup B \cup L$. *A function* $\mu \in M$ *is called a variable binding.*

Definition 6 (Basic Graph Pattern (BGP)). *A BGP (or just query) is a set* $Q \subset P$. *The set of all queries is* $Q = 2^P$.

BGP queries are important as they present a large subset of SPARQL.

Definition 7 (Query Binding). *The bindings of a query* $Q \in Q$ *on an RDF graph* $G \in G$ *consisting of the triples obtained by dereferencing a set of information resources* $I \subset I_I$, *denoted as* $bindings: Q \times 2^{I_I} \mapsto 2^M$, *is the set of minimal variable bindings which map* Q *to a subgraph of* G:

$$bindings(Q, I) = \{\mu \in M \mid dom(\mu) = vars(Q) \wedge \forall p \in Q.\mu(p) \in \cup_{u \in I} deref(u)\}.$$

3.3.4 Datasets and Vocabularies

After having discussed Linked Data from a formal viewpoint, we give in the following an overview of the datasets and vocabularies used throughout this work. The two main datasets used are:

- **DBpedia**, which is the result of an ongoing effort to expose information in Wikipedia as a structured data source according to the Linked Data principles [BLK+09]. The data, like Wikipedia, covers a wide range of domains. Information is described using both existing vocabularies and terms from a large manually modelled ontology. DBpedia serves as a link hub for much of the available Linked Data. DBpedia exposes more than 270 million triples describing more than 2.6 million resources [BLK+09].

- **GeoNames**, which contains geographical information including latitude and longitude for more than eight million geographic features[1]. Further information includes a classification into different feature types and if applicable population numbers and relation to administrative areas. Each feature is identified by an IRI, which can be resolved according to the Linked Data principles.

In the following, we shortly describe the vocabularies and terms that we use in this work. For presentation purposes, we abbreviate IRIs using the prefixes listed in Table 3.2.

- RDF, RDFS, and OWL define vocabularies to express data and schematic information. Particularly useful is `rdf:type` for stating that an individual is an instance of a concept. The subconcept relationship can be expressed using `rdfs:subClassOf`. The property `rdfs:label` gives a standard way to assign natural language labels to resources. With `owl:sameAs`, we can express equivalence between two resources, i.e., all descriptions of one resource also hold for the other resource and vice versa.

- The Friend of a Friend (FOAF) vocabulary provides terms for describing people, their activities, and their relations [BM10]. A central concept in FOAF is `foaf:Person`, which includes human beings and is a subclass of the more general `foaf:Agent`, which also includes organisations and groups. Names of things are specified with the `foaf:name` property, whereas pictures of things are given by the `foaf:depiction` property. Spatial things, which includes persons, can be `foaf:based_near` some other spatial thing, e.g., a geographical feature with a latitude and longitude. An important property in FOAF is `foaf:knows`, which relates one person to another person in a very generic way. The meaning of `foaf:knows` can vary for different applications.

- The basic geo vocabulary of the W3C Semantic Web Interest Group defines a standard namespace for representing spatial information [Gro03]. The basic feature is a geographic `geo:Point`, which relates via `geo:lat` to its latitude and via `geo:long` to its longitude.

---

[1] `http://www.geonames.org/`, accessed July 20th 2012

- DBpedia defines its own vocabulary identified by the prefix `dbpo:` modelling the information retrieved from Wikipedia. As an example the property `dbpo:parent` relates a child to its parents. Additionally, we use the prefix `dbp:` for resources described by DBpedia, e.g., `dbp:Elizabeth_II` represents Queen Elizabeth II.

- The Open Provenance Model (OPM [MCF⁺11]) provides a way to specify provenance information, i.e., from where artefacts originated and how they are used and processed. A lightweight ontology realising the OPM is realised in OPMV – the Open Provenance Model Vocabulary [Zha10]. A central concept in OPMV is the `opmv:Artifact`, which represents the immutable state of some entity, e.g., a specific digital representation of some information. The artefacts can be used in `opmv:Processes`, which are controlled (modelled as property `opmv:wasConrolledBy`) by `opmv:Agents`, which are equivalent to `foaf:Agents`.

- Creative Commons (CC) defines IRIs for each of its licenses. For example, `http://creativecommons.org/licenses/by-nc/3.0/` stands for version 3.0 of the CC Attribution-NonCommercial license. Furthermore, [AALY08] provides an RDF vocabulary (with the prefix `cc:`) for describing licenses in terms of what they `cc:permit` (e.g., `cc:Sharing`), `cc:prohibit` (e.g., `cc:CommercialUse`), and `cc:require` (e.g., `cc:ShareAlike`). Note, that the terms have no formally defined meaning, e.g., it is not modelled that `cc:ShareAlike` corresponds to a `cc:Sharing` under equivalent license terms.

3.4 Usage Policies

In computer science, the notion of a *policy* refers to a formal description of the actions and behaviors that are allowed or required in a protected context. The context can be characterised for example by the data artefacts that are used, the agents involved in performing the action, or temporal constraints. Formal specifications enable the automated detection of policy violations of systems or agents that are formally described. Additionally in many applications, required adoptions to transit from violation to compliance, can be automatically computed and realised by the corresponding system or agent. In this sense, policies can be used to formalise laws, norms and regulations that apply to a computer system, or a process realised or supported by such a system.

In our approach, we consider goal-based policies as defined in [KW04]. Goal-based policies are on a high conceptual level as they only describe the desired states of (the modelled) world, instead of specifying how such a state can be reached.

We assume that the state of the world is described by the FOL theory T of the signature consisting of constants C and predicates P. A policy p is applicable to a set $S_p \subseteq C$ of policy subjects. Policy subjects can either be compliant or non-compliant with p, all other constants $c \in C \setminus S_p$ are called inapplicable. A policy p is defined by a formula $\phi_p[x]$ with one free variable. The compliant subjects are given by the set of constants that when replacing x in ϕ establish $T \models \phi$.

The modelled world in our work is the one of information usages. Usage policies go further than traditional access policies, which basically specify who can access what information [Lam71]. Usage policies restrict what can be done with the information after access was gained. Restricting access was a working paradigm when collecting, communicating, and processing on a large scale was a privilege of few corporations and government agencies [Wei07], i.e., before the advent of cheap computing power and the Internet. Dating back to this time is also Westin's definition of privacy in terms of control over the communication of personal information ([Wes67] according to [Wei07]). Today, much information is published intentionally, i.e., communicated to the public, but without the intent to allow arbitrary usage for any purpose, which applies not only to privacy relevant data, but e.g., also for copyright-protected information [WABL+08]. Thus, effective policies have to shift from access restrictions to usage restrictions.

Usage policies can be enforced in two principal ways: usage control and information accountability. Usage control means technically preventing non-compliant usages [PS02, PS04], usually relying on cryptographic technologies. Digital Rights Management (DRM) systems are examples of usage control systems mainly used for copyright-protected information. There are theoretical arguments why DRM systems will fail in principle [BEPW03, Doc04]. Information accountability builds on making information usage transparent by recording relevant usages in logs [WABL+08]. With such logs information usages can be checked for compliance to usage restrictions and in case of non-compliance the policy violator can be held accountable. We consider enforcement as complementary issue to our work, but propose that for most systems it is appropriate that access is controlled and subsequent usages have to be enforced via accountability.

Chapter 4

A Data-centric Usage Policy Language

In this chapter, we introduce a language for data-centric usage policies, consisting of a vocabulary for modelling the information usages of systems, and a formal language to specify usage restrictions. The formal language is defined as a fragment of first-order logic with an extended semantics for modelling containment relations between policies. For practical applications, we show how existing knowledge representation languages can be aligned with our proposed language and semantics, so that existing reasoner implementations can be reused when creating policy engines. This chapter describes the classification of information usages into compliant or non-compliant to a given policy. Other interactions with policies, respectively policy-aware systems, are discussed in Chapter 5.

In Section 4.1, we describe how we model the relevant system behaviour that we want to restrict, i.e., the usage of information artefacts, and present a compatible formalisation for policies. The basic behaviour and policy model is defined based on first-order logic (FOL). In Section 4.2, we motivate the need for additional expressivity in the form of a predicate representing the containment relation between policies in order to support content-based policy restrictions. Defining such a containment predicate with meaningful semantics brings up a number of challenges, which we discuss in Section 4.3. In order to address the challenges, we define in Section 4.4 a first-order logic fragment for which the containment predicate is well-behaved, i.e., does not lead to unwanted conclusions. To build practicable systems, we want to base our policies in decidable knowledge representation languages with efficient implementations of reasoning procedures. Therefore, we show in Section 4.5 how the proposed semantics can be applied to the Web Ontology Language (OWL) and to Datalog to create practical policy languages. In Section 4.6, we describe how policies can be attached to information artefacts. In Section 4.7, we show a number of policy patterns realising restrictions commonly found in usage policies. Section 4.8 discusses related work before we conclude the chapter in Section 4.9.

A basic version of the policy language, which introduced content-based policy restrictions, is published in [SS10a]. The generalised language with support for self-referential policy restrictions is presented in [KS11b] and the accompanying technical report [KS11a]. The notion of data-centric policies as well as the policy patterns are published in [SH12] which builds on the extended technical report [Spe12a].

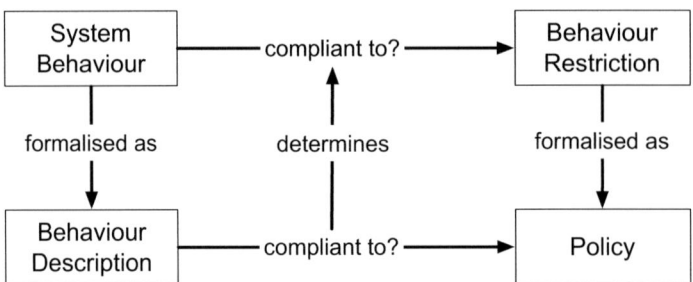

Figure 4.1: Relations between system behaviour, behaviour description, behaviour restrictions and policies

4.1 Modelling System Behaviour and Behaviour Restrictions

One goal of our work is to formally express restrictions on the allowed behaviour of systems, particularly constraining the usages of specific information artefacts. We denote the formal restrictions as policies. Checking compliance of an actual system in general is not feasible because practical information processing systems are implemented in Turing-complete languages such as Java or the Business Process Execution Language (BPEL), and thus too complex. Thus, we abstract from the actual system behaviour by creating a formal description of the behaviour. For the formal description, we can then show via formal proof, whether the described behaviour is compliant to a policy expressed in a compatible formalism or not. A policy-aware tool or system therefore always needs a component, which creates a description in our model of any planned or actual behaviour for which compliance has to be determined. The description can then be checked for compliance to one or more policies by a general purpose policy engine. The result is returned to the policy-aware system. The relations between system behaviour, behaviour descriptions, behaviour restrictions and policies are visualised in Figure 4.1. The separation between system behaviour and behaviour restrictions on the one hand, and formal behaviour descriptions and policies on the other hand is important for building a general purpose solution, which can be applied in many different systems and applications. The separation is however often clear from the context and thus for reasons of readability we say, e.g., that "the system is compliant to a policy" instead of saying that "the description of the system's behaviour is compliant to a policy".

In Section 4.1.1, we present our model for describing the aspects of system behaviour that we want to restrict, i.e., a model for describing usages of information artefacts. Based on the model, we define in Section 4.1.2 how policies are described. We furthermore describe how compliance of a behaviour description to a policy is defined.

4.1.1 Behaviour Description

The behaviour of a system is given by a trace of actions that it performs. Such a trace is an ordered collection of actions and can both describe the past and the future behaviour of a system. The program code of a system, e.g. specified in an object-oriented programming language like Java or a process specification language like BPEL, determines the possible traces of actions that the system can perform. Process algebras, e.g., the π-calculus [Mil99], can formally model such sets of possible traces including the communication between different subsystems. The set of possible behaviours can be very large (state-space explosion), especially in a decentralised environment whose behaviour is composed from the behaviour of a potentially large number of systems. Furthermore, due to the lack of a central controlling entity it is infeasible to collect and integrate all such behaviour descriptions. As argued before, usage restrictions are attached to information artefacts so instead of checking the compliance of the process performed by a system for all possible inputs, we can focus on the process instance, i.e., the trace of actions, which are executed when given the protected information artefact as an input.

However, even the single process instance may not be fully known when checking compliance either because systems do not reveal their actions performed in the past or planned for the future, or because the future actions in the process instance are not fully specified because of dependencies on other unknown inputs or context parameters. Consider that we want to check the compliance of a usage action U to the policy P of the used artefact A. Reasons for not having access to the history, i.e., the actions performed before U, can include: (i) the history is sensitive, e.g., A may be the anonymised version of an artefact A' whose identity must not be revealed; (ii) the producer of A does not want to reveal information about his processes; (iii) representing the history means too much data, which is amplified by the lack of clear constraints about what belongs to the relevant history: theoretically relevant are all actions that produced A or produced artefacts from which A was directly or indirectly derived. Reasons for not knowing about the future, i.e., the actions that will be performed after U, can include: (i) same lack of clear constraints as with the history: theoretically all future actions using products of U or their derivations would be relevant; (ii) the future is simply not yet known, because unanticipated usages of the information might become desirable; (iii) same as with the history, not all information processors want to reveal their processes; (iv) the future execution is not yet known as decisions on which possible future processing branch to take will depend on not yet known context information or other information artefacts.

Instead, we need to model a local view on information artefact usages that can be checked for compliance without having a global overview of the whole processes or process instances in which the usage is embedded. The local view does not necessarily mean that only an isolated usage action is modelled, e.g., for ensuring that a stored artefact is deleted within a time span, we have to model both the storage and the deletion action. Instead, we define locality as only restricting the usage action and the actions that must be performed in order to fulfill the obligations that are needed for the usage action to be allowed. For example, the deletion of an artefact within a time span is local to the storage action, whereas the

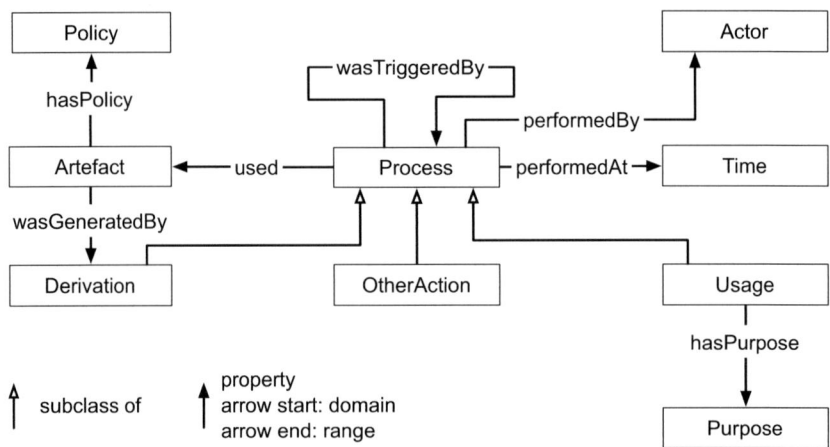

Figure 4.2: Vocabulary for modelling a local view on information usages

subsequent sharing of the stored artefact is not local to the storage action[1]. The locality is achieved by only regarding used and produced artefacts and their policies instead of the actions that produced the used artefacts and the actions that use the produced artefacts. In order to determine usage compliance based on the local view, we establish two assumptions: (i) each used artefact has an attached policy, that was either set by the artefact's owner or was assigned in compliance with the policies of the artefacts used to derive the artefact; (ii) produced artefacts will be used in compliance with the assigned policy.

A model for the local view on information usages, in particular, must represent the origin of the artefact, and the context in which it has been published. Such *provenance* information can be described in various ways, e.g. with a provenance graph that specifies the dependencies between processes and the artefacts they use and generate. In the following, we present a vocabulary for modelling a local view of information usages in first-order logic (FOL). For describing the vocabulary we use the terms *class* – a FOL predicate of arity 1 – and *property* – a FOL predicate of arity 2. The vocabulary is aligned to the Open Provenance Model (OPM) [MCF+11], a specification developed in the spirit of open source software[2]. The core of our model is illustrated in Figure 4.2, where rectangles represent classes, solid lines with filled arrows are properties between instances of the connected classes, and solid lines with unfilled arrows denote a subclass relationship. The model can of course be further specialised for specific applications and use cases. The model re-uses the vocabulary elements *Artefact*, *Process*, *used*, *wasGeneratedBy*, and *wasTriggeredBy* from the Open Provenance Model.

An *Artefact* is an immutable physical manifestation of an abstract information object with a fixed *Policy*. A *Process* represents an action, which can be performed by a system. For our

---

[1]Assuming that the deletion is required by the policy and the sharing is allowed but not required.
[2]http://twiki.ipaw.info/bin/view/OPM/, accessed 14th March 2012

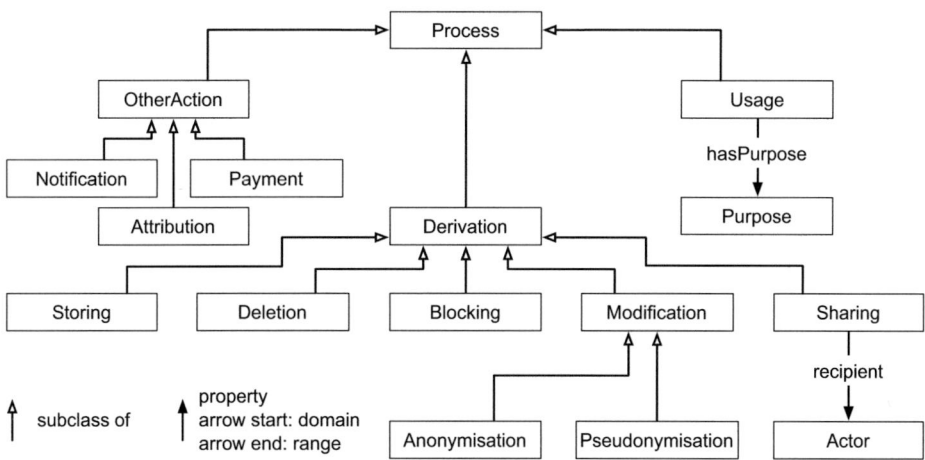

Figure 4.3: Basic set of action types

particular application, we further split processes into *Derivation*s (processes that generate a new artefact), *Usage*s that only use artefacts without change, and *Other Action*s that do not use artefacts. We consider derivations, usages, and other actions as pairwise disjoint. The relations between processes and artefacts are modelled by the *used* and *wasGeneratedBy* properties. The *hasPolicy* property assigns to an artefact a *Policy*, which means that all processes using the artefact are (legally) required to comply to its policy. The *hasPurpose* property relates a usage to its *Purpose*, e.g., stating that a usage was non-commercial. According to OPM, a process p_1 *wasTriggeredBy* another process p_2, if p_1 can only have started after p_2 started. So, somewhat contrary to intuition, the "triggering" is rather a precondition but not a necessary cause of the triggered one. A usage restriction that requires attribution would thus be formalised as a policy requiring that the usage process *wasTriggeredBy* an attribution process, and not the other way around. Processes are *performedAt* specific *Time* points and are *performedBy* an *Actor*.

In Figure 4.3, we introduce a basic set of action types as subclasses of process. Derivations include: *Storing* a new copy of an artefact, *Deletion* of an artefact, *Blocking* of an artefact, i.e., denying any further access, *Sharing* of an artefact with a *recipient*, i.e., giving a new copy to another entity, and a general class of *Modification*s, with the examples of *Anonymisation* and *Pseudonymisation* of an artefact. Usages are a general class of actions, which include all actions that use artefacts but are no derivations. A usage is described by its purpose. Other actions include: *Attribution*s, i.e., giving credit to the original creator or owner of an artefact, *Payment*s, and giving *Notification*s about data usages.

Example 1. *In the following we formalise the description of an action* d_1 *that takes an image* a_1 *with a policy BY-SA representing the Creative Commons Attribution ShareAlike license* *and produces a black and white version* a_2 *that also is assigned policy BY-SA:*

$$Derivation(d_1) \wedge used(d_1, a_1) \wedge wasGenBy(a_2, d_1) \wedge$$
$$hasPolicy(a_1, BY\text{-}SA) \wedge hasPolicy(a_2, BY\text{-}SA).$$

Example 2. *We formalise the action* d_1 *of storing a new copy* a_2 *of the data artefact* a_1, *where the new copy is deleted after one year:*

$$Storing(d_1) \wedge used(d_1, a_1) \wedge wasGenBy(a_2, d_1) \wedge$$
$$Deletion(d_2) \wedge used(d_2, a_2) \wedge$$
$$performedAt(d_1, t_1) \wedge performedAt(d_2, t_1 + 1y).$$

4.1.2 Policies

In computer science, the notion of a policy refers to a formal description of the actions and behaviors that are allowed or required in a protected context. In our approach, we consider goal-based policies as defined in [KW04]. Goal-based policies are on a high conceptual level, as they only describe the desired states of (the modelled) world, instead of specifying how such a state can be reached. A policy that represents a set of allowed processes then corresponds to a formula $\varphi[x]$ with one free variable x, representing the set of individuals that make $\varphi[x]$ true when assigned as values to x.

Example 3. *A policy P that allows no uses other than derivations that generate artefacts with policy P can be described as:*

$$P : Derivation(x) \wedge \exists y.(wasGenBy(y, x) \wedge hasPolicy(y, P)).$$

A set of such policy definitions $p : \varphi_p[x]$ will be called a *policy system*. Let N_P be a set of policy names. Given a policy system with definitions $p : \varphi_p$ for all policy names $p \in N_P$, we can formalise a predicate to capture the compliance of a process to a policy:

$$\forall x.compliantTo(x, p) \leftrightarrow \varphi_p[x] \qquad \text{for all } p \in N_P. \tag{4.1}$$

Formula (4.1) defines compliantTo to relate processes to the policies they are compliant to. Please note the difference between compliantTo (actual semantic conformance) and the property chain used ∘ hasPolicy (legally required conformance).

Example 4. *Consider policy P from Example 3 and the following description of a derivation of artefact* a_1:

$$Derivation(d_1) \wedge used(d_1, a_1) \wedge wasGenBy(a_2, d_1) \wedge$$
$$hasPolicy(a_1, P) \wedge hasPolicy(a_2, P).$$

The derivation d_1 *has to be compliant to P, because this is the policy of the used artefact* a_1. *As* d_1 *makes the defining formula of P true, it follows that* d_1 *is compliant and thus holds:*

$$compliantTo(d_1, P).$$

4.2 The Need for Content-based Policy Restrictions

In previous examples, we restricted the admissible policies for generated artefacts by directly specifying their identity (e.g., $\mathsf{hasPolicy}(x, \mathrm{P})$). We call such a modelling *name-based* policy restrictions, because we can specify an exhaustive list of all policy names that can be assigned to derived artefacts. Name-based restrictions are more powerful than simple policy inheritance, were derived artefacts have to have the same policy as the used artefacts. With name-based restrictions the policy of a derived artefact can differ arbitrarily from the policy of the original artefact. Depending on the actions performed on an artefact, the restrictions on the resulting artefact can be both laxer or stricter. Consider the example of sharing a data artefact, but in this case the recipient is only allowed to use the artefact for a specified purpose but not to share it with a third party, i.e., the restrictions on the resulting artefact are stricter. Another example is a zip code, which can be freely used and shared by the provider for statistical purposes. However, an artefact derived from both the zip code and the birth date of an individual, cannot be shared anymore, as it possibly allows the identification of the individual. More relaxed restrictions can for example be applicable after an anonymisation action. Additional rights can be admitted on the anonymised artefact, while still some restrictions can apply, e.g. it can only be used for research purposes. However, name-based policy restrictions have considerable impact on the interoperability between different providers, respectively between different policies with the same or similar intention.

Example 5. *Consider a policy that allows a provider to store an artefact with policy P1, which allows arbitrary usages of the artefact. The provider that wants to store the artefact, however specifies that he wants to assign policy P2, which only allows usages for statistical purposes. The storage action is classified as non-compliant, because the provider wants to use policy P2 instead of policy P1. However, the intention of the owner of the artefact is most certainly that the storage is also allowed under a policy that allows a restricted set of usages. Even for policies with exactly the same set of allowed usages, a non-compliant classification can be made because different policy names were used. In a scenario with a multitude of heterogeneous providers, it is not realistic to assume canonical names for policies with the same set of compliant usages.*

Example 6. *Suppose you want create a homepage about your planned trip to Japan. You found interesting information from Wikipedia that you want to integrate and which is available under the Creative Commons Attribution, ShareAlike (CC BY-SA) license. Furthermore, you want to illustrate the text with pictures you found on Flickr and which are licensed under the GNU Free Documentation License (GFDL). Technically it is no problem to integrate the contents, and both license terms in isolation are suitable for you: you would anyway attribute the sources and publish the homepage under an open license. The problem is that although the intentions behind the licenses are very similar, both include a condition that requires to use the same license for derived work (the homepage). This is not possible, because if you choose either CC BY-SA or GFDL for your homepage, you will violate the other. At least for Creative Commons this incompatibility is not intended as it obstructs creativity [Les05]. Instead, it should be possible to require in the ShareAlike clause of a CC license that derived* *content must be published under a license allowing and requiring the same conditions as the CC license.*

To overcome this interoperability problems, we introduce *content-based* policy restrictions that are based on the usages allowed by policies. Namely, we enable the use of policy containment conditions in restrictions of allowed usages. A policy p_a is contained in a policy p_b, if every usage compliant to p_a is also compliant to p_b.

Example 7. *With the containment conditions, the Example 5 can be modified in the following way: the policy allows a provider to store an artefact with a policy that is contained in policy P1 (which allows arbitrary usages). Now, the storage of the artefact with policy P2 is compliant, as every usage for statistical purposes, i.e., every usage compliant to P2, qualifies as an arbitrary usage, i.e., is also compliant to P1 and thus P2 is contained in P1.*

Besides setting an upper bound on the actions allowed by a target policy, the containment condition can also be used to set a lower bound.

Example 8. *The ShareAlike clause of a Creative Commons policy can be modelled as a requirement that the policy of a derived artefact allows at least the same usages as the original policy.*

We introduce a new predicate containedIn that represents the containment relation between two policy names based on their definitions:

$$\forall x, y.\text{containedIn}(x, y) \leftrightarrow \forall z.(\text{compliantTo}(z, x) \rightarrow \text{compliantTo}(z, y)). \qquad (4.2)$$

For a given set of policy names N_P, the set of sentences defined by Formula 4.2 and Formula 4.1 (the definition of compliantTo) is denoted by T_{ct}. Informally speaking, the fact containedIn(p, q) can also be read as: any process that complies with policy p also complies with policy q. When allowing policy conditions to use containedIn, the question whether or not a process complies to a policy in turn depends on the evaluation of containedIn. Our goal therefore is to propose a formal semantics that resolves this potentially recursive dependency in a way that corresponds to our intuitive understanding of the policies that occur in practice. In Section 4.3, we will discuss specific challenges that arise when defining such a semantics, which then in turn motivates the solution that we present in Section 4.4.

4.3 Challenges of Defining a Semantics for Policies

We already introduced the theory T_{ct}, which comprises the set of sentences given for a set N_P of policy names by the Formulae 4.1 and 4.2, which we repeat in the following:

$$\forall x.\text{compliantTo}(x, p) \leftrightarrow \varphi_p[x] \qquad \text{for all } p \in N_P,$$
$$\forall x, y.\text{containedIn}(x, y) \leftrightarrow \forall z.(\text{compliantTo}(z, x) \rightarrow \text{compliantTo}(z, y)).$$

Unfortunately, these formulae under first-order semantics do not lead to the intended interpretation of policies. Consider the policy P given by

$$P : \text{Derivation}(x) \land \exists y.(\text{wasGeneratedBy}(y, x) \land$$
$$\exists z.(\text{hasPolicy}(y, z) \land \text{containedIn}(z, P))). \tag{4.3}$$

Furthermore, consider a second policy Q that is defined by exactly the same Formula (4.3), but with P replaced by Q. Intuitively, P and Q have the same conditions but merely different names, so they should be in a mutual containedIn relationship. Indeed, there are first-order models of T_{ct} where this is the case: if containedIn(P, Q) holds, then $\forall x.\varphi_P[x] \rightarrow \varphi_Q[x]$ is also true. However, this is not the only possible interpretation: if containedIn(P, Q) does not hold, then $\forall x.\varphi_P[x] \rightarrow \varphi_Q[x]$ is not true either. First-order logic does not prefer one of these interpretations, so in consequence we can conclude neither containedIn(P, Q) nor ¬containedIn(P, Q).

Working with first-order interpretations still has many advantages for defining a semantics, in particular since first-order logic is widely known and since many tools and knowledge representation languages are using it. This also enables us to specify additional background knowledge using first-order formalisms of our choice, e.g. the OWL DL ontology language. However, we would like to restrict attention to first-order models that conform to our preferred reading of containedIn. Logical consequences can still be defined as the statements that are true under all of the preferred interpretations, but undesired interpretations will be ignored for this definition. Our goal of defining the semantics of self-referential policies thus boils down to defining the "desired" interpretations of a given first-order theory that uses containedIn. To do this, we propose a semantics for policy containment that, intuitively speaking, always prefers containedIn(P, Q) to hold if this is possible without making additional unjustified assumptions. For illustration, consider the following policy Q that further restricts P from (4.3) to non-commercial uses:

$$Q : \text{Derivation}(x) \land \forall w.(\text{hasPurpose}(x, w) \rightarrow \text{NonCommercial}(w)) \land$$
$$\exists y.(\text{wasGeneratedBy}(y, x) \land \exists z.(\text{hasPolicy}(y, z) \land \text{containedIn}(z, Q))). \tag{4.4}$$

Though the policy Q is clearly more restrictive than P, there still is a first-order interpretation that satisfies containedIn(P, Q) by simply assuming that all things that conform to P happen to have non-commercial uses only. Nothing states that this is not the case, yet we do not want to make such assumptions to obtain more containedIn conclusions.

We thus distinguish *basic predicates* such as NonCommercial and hasPolicy from the two "special" predicates containedIn and compliantTo. Basic predicates are given by the data, and represent the available information, and their interpretation should not be considered a matter of choice. Special predicates in turn should be interpreted to reflect our intended understanding of policy containment, and as shown in the above example it is often desirable to maximise containedIn entailments. In other words, we would like to ensure that the consideration of a policy system does not lead to new logical consequences over basic predicates – merely defining license conditions should not increase our knowledge of the world. More formally: the policy semantics should be *conservative* over first-order semantics w.r.t. sentences that use only basic predicates.

Unfortunately, this is not easy to accomplish, and we indeed can only achieve a limited version of this (as captured in Theorem 1 on page 47). One reason is that even T_{ct} may entail undesired consequences. Consider policies as follows (we use abstract examples to highlight technical aspects):

$$P:\ A(x) \land \mathsf{containedIn}(P, Q) \qquad\qquad Q:\ B(x). \qquad\qquad (4.5)$$

This policy system entails $\mathsf{containedIn}(P, Q)$. Indeed, if $\mathsf{containedIn}(P, Q)$ would not hold, then nothing would conform to P by (4.1). But then the set of usages compliant to P is the empty set, which is clearly a subset of every other set, hence $\mathsf{containedIn}(P, Q)$ would follow by (4.2). Thus all interpretations that satisfy T_{ct} must satisfy $\forall x.A(x) \land \mathsf{containedIn}(P, Q) \to B(x)$, and thus $\forall x.A(x) \to B(x)$ is a consequence over basic predicates. Clearly, the mere definition of licenses should not entail that some otherwise unrelated class A is a subclass of B.

4.4 A Formalism for Policy Languages

In order to address the challenges discussed in the previous section, we now formally define a policy language. More precisely, we define a language for policies *and* a first-order language that is to be used for background theories. These definitions are intended to be very general to impose only those restrictions that we found necessary to obtain a well-behaved semantics. Section 4.5 shows how this general framework can be instantiated in various well-known modelling languages.

The basic restriction that we impose on the logic is *connectedness*. Intuitively, this ensures that a formula can only refer to a connected relational structure of individuals. In our setting the conformance of a process to a policy thus only depends on the characteristics of individuals directly or indirectly reachable from the process. We argue that this is a small restriction. It might even be a best practice for "controlled" modelling in an open environment like the web, as it ensures that the classification of any object is based only on its "environment" and not on completely unrelated individuals.

Our formal definition is reminiscent of the *Guarded Fragment* (GF) of first-order logic [AvBN95] and indeed it can be considered as a generalisation of GF, though without the favourable formal properties that motivated GF. We first define open connected formulae (with free variables) and then closed ones. We write $\varphi[\vec{x}]$ to indicate that φ has at most the free variables that occur in $\vec{x}$ (or possibly less). For technical reasons, our first definition distinguishes "guard predicates" that must not use constant symbols from "non-guard predicates" where constants are allowed:

Definition 8. *Consider a first-order signature Σ where each predicate in Σ is marked as a* guard predicate *or as a* non-guard predicate. *The connected open fragment COF of first-order logic over Σ is the smallest set of formulae over Σ that satisfies the following properties:*

> *1. Every atomic formula $p(\vec{t})$ with $\vec{t}$ a vector of terms that contain at least one variable belongs to COF, provided that $\vec{t}$ contains only variables if p is a guard predicate.*

2. *If φ_1 and φ_2 are in COF then so are $\neg\varphi_1$, $\varphi_1 \wedge \varphi_2$, $\varphi_1 \vee \varphi_2$, and $\varphi_1 \rightarrow \varphi_2$.*

3. *Consider a formula $\varphi[\vec{x},\vec{y}]$ in COF, and a conjunction $\alpha[\vec{x},\vec{y}] = \alpha_1[\vec{x},\vec{y}] \wedge \ldots \wedge \alpha_n[\vec{x},\vec{y}]$ of atomic formulae α_i that contain only guard predicates and variables, such that $\vec{x}$, $\vec{y}$ are both non-empty and do not share variables. Then the formulae*

$$\exists \vec{y}.\alpha[\vec{x},\vec{y}] \wedge \varphi[\vec{x},\vec{y}] \qquad \forall \vec{y}.\alpha[\vec{x},\vec{y}] \rightarrow \varphi[\vec{x},\vec{y}],$$

are in COF provided that for each variable y in $\vec{y}$, there is some variable x in $\vec{x}$ and some atom $\alpha_i[\vec{x},\vec{y}]$ where both x and y occur.

The distinction of guard and non-guard predicates is important, but a suitable choice of guard predicates can be easily made for a given set of formulae in COF by simply using exactly those predicates as guards that do not occur in atomic formulae with constants. The only predicate that we really need to be a non-guard is containedIn. Therefore, we will omit the explicit reference to the signature Σ in the following and simply assume that one signature has been fixed.

Definition 9. *The* connected fragment *CF of first-order logic consists of the following sentences:*

- *Every formula without variables is in CF.*

- *If $\varphi[x]$ is a COF formula with one free variable x, then $\forall x.\varphi[x]$ and $\exists x.\varphi[x]$ are in CF.*

We will generally restrict to background theories that belong to CF. As discussed in Section 4.5 below, large parts of OWL DL and Datalog fall into this fragment. A typical example for a non-CF sentence is the formula $\neg\exists x.A(x) \vee \neg\exists x.B(x)$. Also note that the formulae (4.1) and (4.2) of T_{ct} are not in CF – we consider them individually in all our formal arguments. On the other hand, the policy conditions (4.3), (4.4), and (4.5) all are in COF. Using the terminology of connected formulae, we can define policy conditions, policy descriptions, and policy systems that we already introduced informally above:

Definition 10. *Let N_P be a set of* policy names. *A* policy condition *φ for N_P is a formula that may use an additional binary predicate containedIn that cannot occur in background theories, and where:*

- *φ is a COF formula with one free variable,*

- *φ contains at most one constant symbol $p \in N_P$ that occurs only in atoms of the form containedIn(y, p) or containedIn(p, y),*

- *every occurrence of containedIn in φ is positive (i.e. not in the scope of a negation) and has the form containedIn(y, p) or containedIn(p, y).*

A policy description *for a policy $p \in N_P$ is a pair $\langle p, \varphi \rangle$ where φ is a policy condition. A* policy system *P for N_P is a set of policy descriptions that contains exactly one description for every policy $p \in N_P$.*

This definition excludes the problematic policy p in (4.5) above while allowing (4.3), and (4.4). Moreover, it generally requires containedIn to be a non-guard predicate.

We define the semantics of policy containment as the greatest fixed point of an operator introduced next. Intuitively, this computation works by starting with the assumption that all named policies are contained in each other. It then refers to the policy definitions to compute the actual containments that these assumptions yield, and removes all assumptions that cannot be confirmed. This computation is monotone since the assumptions are reduced in each step, so it also has a greatest fixed point.

Definition 11. *Consider a set of CF sentences T (background theory), a set of policy names N_P that includes the top policy $p_\top$ and the bottom policy $p_\bot$, and a policy system P for N_P such that $\langle p_\top, \top(x)\rangle, \langle p_\bot, \bot(x)\rangle \in P.$[3] Let T_{ci} be the following theory:*

$$T_{ci} = \{\forall x, y, z.\mathsf{containedIn}(x, y) \wedge \mathsf{containedIn}(y, z) \to \mathsf{containedIn}(x, z),$$

$$\forall x.\mathsf{containedIn}(x, p_\top), \forall x.\mathsf{containedIn}(p_\bot, x)\}.$$

For a set $C \subseteq N_P^2$, define $\mathsf{Cl}(C) := \{\mathsf{containedIn}(p, q) \mid \langle p, q\rangle \in C\}$. An operator $P_T : \mathcal{P}(N_P^2) \to \mathcal{P}(N_P^2)$, where $\mathcal{P}(N_P^2)$ is the powerset of N_P^2, is defined as follows:

$$P_T(C) = \{\langle p, q\rangle \mid \langle p, \varphi_p\rangle, \langle q, \varphi_q\rangle \in P \text{ and } T \cup T_{ci} \cup \mathsf{Cl}(C) \models \forall x.\varphi_p[x] \to \varphi_q[x]\}.$$

Proposition 1. *The operator P_T has a greatest fixed point $\mathsf{gfp}(P_T)$ that can be obtained by iteratively applying P_T to N_P^2 until a fixed point is reached. More concretely, the greatest fixed point is of the form $P_T^n(N_P^2)$ for some natural number $n \leq |N_P|^2$ where P_T^n denotes n-fold application of P_T.*

The fact that P_T requires the existence of policies $p_\top$ and $p_\bot$ is not restricting the applicability of our approach since the according standard policy declarations can always be added. Using the greatest fixed point of P_T, we now define what our "preferred" models for a policy system and background theory are.

Definition 12. *Given a policy system P, a P-model for a theory T is a first-order interpretation $\mathcal{I}$ that satisfies the following theory:*

$$\mathcal{I} \models T \cup T_{ci} \cup \mathsf{Cl}(\mathsf{gfp}(P_T)) \cup T_{ct}, \tag{4.6}$$

where T_{ci} and $\mathsf{Cl}(\mathsf{gfp}(P_T))$ are as in Definition 11, and where T_{ct} is the collection of all sentences of the form (4.1) and (4.2). In this case, we say that $\mathcal{I}$ P-satisfies T. A sentence φ is a P-consequence of T, written $T \models_P \varphi$, if $\mathcal{I} \models \varphi$ for all P-models $\mathcal{I}$ of T.

It is essential to note that the previous definition uses a fixed point computation only to obtain a minimal set of containments among named policies that must be satisfied by all P-models. It is not clear if and how the semantics of P-models could be captured by traditional fixed point logics (cf. Section 4.8). At the core of this problem is that policy conformance is

---

[3]As usual, we consider $\top/\bot$ as unary predicates that are true/false for all individuals.

inherently non-monotonic in some policies that we want to express. A policy p might, e.g., require that the policy of all derived artefacts admits *at least* all uses that are allowed by p. Then the fewer uses are allowed under p, the more policies allow these uses too, and the more uses conform to p. This non-monotonic relationship might even preclude the existence of a model.

The policy semantics that we defined above is formal and well-defined for all policy systems and background theories, even without the additional restrictions of Definition 9 and 10. However, three vital questions have to be answered to confirm that it is appropriate for our purpose: (1) How can we compute the entailments under this new semantics? (2) Does this semantics avoid the undesired conclusions discussed in Section 4.3? (3) Does the semantics yield the intended entailments for our use cases? The last of these questions will be discussed in Chapter 7. Questions (1) and (2) in turn are answered by the following theorem:

Theorem 1. *Consider a theory T and a policy system P. For every φ that is a CF formula over the base signature, or a variable-free atom (fact) over the predicates* containedIn *or* compliantTo *we have:*

$$T, T_{ci}, \mathrm{Cl}(\mathrm{gfp}(P_T)), T_{ct}^- \models \varphi \qquad iff \qquad T \models_P \varphi, \qquad (4.7)$$

where T_{ci} and $\mathrm{Cl}(\mathrm{gfp}(P_T))$ are defined as in Definition 11, and where T_{ct}^- is the collection of all sentences of the form (4.1).

Let us first discuss how Theorem 1 answers the above questions.

1. The theorem reduces P-entailment to standard first-order logic entailment. Since $\mathrm{gfp}(P_T)$ can be computed under this semantics as well, this means that reasoning under our semantics is possible by re-using existing tools given that one restricts to fragments of (CF) first-order logic for which suitable tools exist. We pursue this idea in Section 4.5.

2. The theorem asserts that all CF formulae that are P-entailments are entailed by the first-order theory $T \cup T_{ci} \cup \mathrm{Cl}(\mathrm{gfp}(P_T))$. It is easy to see that T_{ci} and $\mathrm{Cl}(\mathrm{gfp}(P_T))$ only affect the interpretation of formulae that use containedIn. All other CF formulae are P-entailments of T if and only if they are first-order entailments of T. Thus, new entailments over base predicates or even inconsistencies are not caused by considering a policy system.

The proof of Theorem 1 is not straightforward. At its core, it hinges on the fact that every model $\mathcal{I}$ of $T \cup T_{ci} \cup \mathrm{Cl}(\mathrm{gfp}(P_T))$ can be extended into a P-model $\hat{\mathcal{I}}$ of T that satisfies no containedIn or compliantTo facts that have not already been satisfied by $\mathcal{I}$. Constructing this P-model requires a number of auxiliary constructions centred around the idea that, for every policy containment not in $\mathrm{Cl}(\mathrm{gfp}(P_T))$, one can find a witness (a process conforming to the one policy but not to the other) in some model of $T \cup T_{ci} \cup \mathrm{Cl}(\mathrm{gfp}(P_T))$. This witness (and all of its environment) is then copied into the P-model that we want to construct. This is only feasible since the CF formulae in T are inherently "local" and will not change their truth value when extending the model by new (disjoint) individuals. After enough witnesses have been included to refute all non-entailed containedIn facts, the construction of $\hat{\mathcal{I}}$ is completed by defining suitable extensions for compliantTo where care is needed to do this for "unnamed" policies so that T_{ct} is satisfied. A full formal argument is found in the technical report [KS11a].

4.5 Practical Policy Languages and Reasoning

In this section, we provide concrete instantiations of the general formalism introduced above. The CF fragment still is overly general for practical use, in particular since the computation of entailments in this logic is undecidable which precludes many desired applications where policy containment would be checked automatically without any user interaction.[4] However, Theorem 1 asserts that we can generally evaluate formal models under the semantics of first-order logic which is used in many practical knowledge representation languages. By identifying the CF fragments of popular modelling formalisms, we can therefore obtain concrete policy modelling languages that are suitable for specific applications.

There are various possible candidates for knowledge representation languages that can be considered under a first-order semantics and for which good practical tool support is available. Obvious choices include the Web Ontology Language OWL under its Direct Semantics [W3C09a], and the rule language Datalog under first-order semantics [AHV94] which we will discuss in more detail below.

As we will explain for the case of Datalog, one can also model policy conditions as (conjunctive/disjunctive) queries with a single result, given that the query language uses a first-order semantics. Query evaluation is known to be difficult for expressive modelling languages, but can be very efficient when restricting to a light-weight background theory. A possible example is the combination of SPARQL for OWL [GK10] with the lightweight OWL QL or OWL RL languages [W3C09a]. The cases below thus can only serve as an illustration of the versatility of our approach, not as a comprehensive listing.

4.5.1 Modelling Policies in OWL DL

The Direct Semantics of OWL 2 is based on description logics which in turn are based on the semantics of first-order logic [W3C09a]. The ontology language OWL 2 DL for which this semantics is defined can therefore be viewed as a fragment of first-order logic to which we can apply the restrictions of Section 4.4. The standard translation to first-order logic (see, e.g., [HKR09]) produces formulae that are already very close to the syntactic form of CF sentences described above. Moreover, OWL class expressions are naturally translated to first-order formulae with one free variable, and are thus suitable candidates for expressing policies. Policy containment then corresponds to class subsumption checking – a standard inferencing task for OWL reasoners. The binary predicates of our simple provenance model, as well as the special predicates containedIn and compliantTo can be represented by OWL

---

[4]This is easy to see in many ways, for example since (as noted below) CF allows us to express description logics like $\mathcal{SRIQ}$, whereas CF does not impose the regularity or acyclicity conditions that are essential for obtaining decidability of reasoning in these logics [HS04].

properties, whereas unary predicates from the provenance model correspond to primitive OWL classes.

Some restrictions must be taken into account to ensure that we consider only ontologies that are CF theories, and only classes that are valid policy conditions. Nominals (enumerated classes as provided by ObjectOneOf in OWL) are expressed in first-order logic using constant symbols, and must therefore be excluded from background ontologies. On the other hand nominals must be used in containedIn in policy descriptions (in OWL this particular case can conveniently be expressed with ObjectHasValue). Besides nominals, the only non-connected feature of OWL 2 that must be disallowed is the universal role (owl:topObjectProperty). On the other hand, cardinality restrictions are unproblematic even though they are usually translated using a special built-in equality predicate $\approx$ that we did not allow in Section 4.4. The reason is that $\approx$ can easily be emulated in first-order logic using a standard equality theory as shown in [KS11a], so that all of our earlier results carry over to this extension.

To apply Theorem 1 for reasoning, we still must be able to express T_{ci} of Definition 11 in OWL. Transitivity of containedIn is directly expressible, and the remaining axioms can be written as follows:[5]

$$\top \sqsubseteq \exists \text{containedIn}.\{p_\top\} \qquad \top \sqsubseteq \exists \text{containedIn}^-.\{p_\bot\}$$

Note that the represented axioms are not in CF, and likewise the restriction to nominal-free OWL is not relevant here.

Concrete policies are now easily modelled. The public domain (PD) policy that allows every type of usage and derivation is expressed as:

$$\text{PD}: \text{Usage} \sqcup \text{Derivation} .$$

Processes compliant to CC BY are either usages that were triggered by some attribution, or derivations for which all generated artefacts have only policies that also require attributions, i.e., which are contained in BY:

$$\text{BY}: (\text{Usage} \sqcap \exists \text{wasTriggeredBy.Attribution}) \sqcup$$
$$(\text{Derivation} \sqcap \forall \text{wasGeneratedBy}^-.\forall \text{hasPolicy}.\exists \text{containedIn}.\{\text{BY}\}).$$

To account for the modular nature of CC licenses, it is convenient to re-use class expressions as the one for BY. Thus, we will generally write C_{BY} to refer to the class expression for BY, and similarly for the other policies we define. To define NoDerivs (ND) licenses that allow all processes that are not derivations, we introduce C_{ND} as an abbreviation for Process $\sqcap$ $\neg$Derivation. We can thus express CC BY-ND as

$$\text{BY-ND}: C_{\text{BY}} \sqcap C_{\text{ND}}.$$

The ShareAlike (SA) condition cannot be modelled as a general component, as it refers directly to the policy in which it is used. In Section 5.1, we present a structured model for

---

[5]Throughout this section we use the usual DL notation for concisely writing OWL axioms and class expressions; see [HKR09] for an extended introduction to the relationship with OWL 2 syntax.

exposing such components as parameterised building blocks. As an example, we model the condition for the CC BY-SA policy as a requirement that all policies of all generated artefacts are equivalent to BY-SA, i.e., they are contained in BY-SA and BY-SA is contained in them:

$$\text{BY-SA}: C_{\text{BY}} \sqcap \forall \, \text{wasGeneratedBy}^-.\forall \, \text{hasPolicy}.(\exists \, \text{containedIn}.\{\text{BY-SA}\} \sqcap$$
$$\exists \, \text{containedIn}^-.\{\text{BY-SA}\}).$$

4.5.2 Modelling Policies in Datalog

Datalog is the rule language of function-free definite Horn clauses, i.e., implications with only positive atoms and a single head atom. It can be interpreted under first-order semantics [AHV94]. The syntax corresponds to first-order logic with the only variation that quantifiers are omitted since all variables are understood to be quantified universally. Datalog rules can thus be used to express a background theory. Policies can be expressed by conjunctive or disjunctive queries, i.e., by disjunctions and conjunctions of atomic formulae where one designated variable represents the free variable that refers to the conforming processes, while the other variables are existentially quantified.

Again we have to respect syntactic restrictions of Section 4.4. Thus we can only use rules that are either free of variables, or that contain no constants. In the latter case, all variables in the rule head must occur in its body (this is known as *safety* in Datalog), and the variables in the rule body must be connected via the atoms in which they co-occur. For policy queries, we also require this form of connection, and we allow constants in containedIn. The (non-CF) theory T_{ci} of Definition 11 is readily expressed in Datalog.

Containment of conjunctive and disjunctive queries is decidable, and can be reduced to query answering [AD98]. Namely, to check containment of a query q_1 in a query q_2, we first create for every conjunction in q_1 (which is a disjunction of conjunctive queries) a grounded version, i.e., we state every body atom in the conjunction as a fact by uniformly replacing variables with new constants. If, for each conjunction in q_1, these new facts provide an answer to the query q_2, then q_1 is contained in q_2. Note that Datalog systems that do not support disjunctive query answering directly can still be used for this purpose by expressing disjunctive conditions with multiple auxiliary rules that use the same head predicate, and querying for the instances of this head.

As above, the simplest policy is the public domain (PD) license:

$$\text{PD}: \text{Usage}(x) \vee \text{Derivation}(x).$$

Here and below, we always use x as the variable that represents the corresponding process in a policy description. CC BY can now be defined as follows:

$$\text{BY}: (\text{Usage}(x) \wedge \text{wasTriggeredBy}(x, y) \wedge \text{Attribution}(y)) \vee$$
$$(\text{Derivation}(x) \wedge \text{wasGeneratedBy}(z, x) \wedge \text{hasPolicy}(z, v) \wedge \text{containedIn}(v, \text{BY})) \, .$$

This formalisation alone would leave room for derivations that are falsely classified as compliant, since the condition only requires that there exists one artefact that has one contained policy. Further artefacts or policies that violate these terms might then exist. We can prevent this by requiring hasPolicy to be *functional* and wasGeneratedBy to be *inverse functional* (as before, we assume that $\approx$ has been suitably axiomatised, which is possible in Datalog):

$$v_1 \approx v_2 \leftarrow \mathsf{hasPolicy}(x, v_1) \wedge \mathsf{hasPolicy}(x, v_2),$$
$$z_1 \approx z_2 \leftarrow \mathsf{wasGeneratedBy}(z_1, x) \wedge \mathsf{wasGeneratedBy}(z_2, x) \,.$$

Using this auxiliary modelling, we can easily express CC BY-ND and CC BY-SA:

$$\text{BY-ND}: \mathsf{Usage}(x) \wedge \mathsf{wasTriggeredBy}(x, y) \wedge \mathsf{Attribution}(y)$$
$$\text{BY-SA}: (\mathsf{Usage}(x) \wedge \mathsf{wasTriggeredBy}(x, y) \wedge \mathsf{Attribution}(y)) \vee$$
$$(\mathsf{Derivation}(x) \wedge \mathsf{wasGeneratedBy}(z, x) \wedge \mathsf{hasPolicy}(z, v) \wedge$$
$$\mathsf{containedIn}(v, \text{BY-SA}) \wedge \mathsf{containedIn}(\text{BY-SA}, v)) \,.$$

4.6 Attaching Policies to Information Artefacts

To attach policies to information artefacts, we have two possibilities: attaching by value, and attaching by reference. By value means, that we want to store and transport the policy together with an artefact. For this we need a serialisation that can be processed on a wide range of systems and particularly is compatible with web protocols that underly our decentralised information system architecture. Ideal candidates for such a serialisation are XML and the various serialisations of RDF, including RDF/XML. For the two proposed practical languages, i.e., OWL and Datalog, these serialisations already exist. OWL 2 comes with mappings to both XML [W3C09d] and RDF [W3C09b]. The W3C standard Rule Interchange Format (RIF, [W3C12b]) defines a core dialect corresponding to Datalog [W3C10b]. For RIF there exist both serialisations in XML [W3C10a] and in RDF [W3C11].

Both OWL and RIF allow to identify policies (i.e., classes, respectively rules) by IRIs. We adopt the Linked Data principle that IRIs of policies should be HTTP URIs and if they are dereferenced a corresponding description of the policy should be returned, i.e., an OWL or RIF document defining the policy. By having identifiers and a mechanism to get policies from identifiers, we can support attaching by reference: attaching the IRI of a policy to an artefact is sufficient to enable the user of the artefact to retrieve the policy and check compliance of his actions using the artefact.

HTTP as the information access protocol of our architecture supports the link header, which can be used to communicate a reference to related information about the served resource [Not10]. We can use the link header to specify the corresponding policy. The link header not only gives a reference as a URI, but also specifies the relation to the served resource, which we will set to *policy*. An example header when serving an artefact with a policy formalising the CC Attribution, ShareAlike license will look like:

```
Link: <http://example.org/policies/CC/BY-SA#policy>; rel=policy
```

When serving information represented in RDF via the Linked Data architecture, the returned graph is identified by an URI and so is a normal resource that we can further describe

Table 4.1: List of Patterns for Common Policy Restrictions

Pattern	
P1	ShareAlike
P2	Attribute-based Usage Restrictions
P3	Data Sharing / Rights Delegation
P4	Hierarchies and other Domain Knowledge
P5	Anonymisation / Pseudonymisation
P6	Opt-in and Opt-out
P7	Obligations
P8	Time Spans

with RDF triples. Via the *hasPolicy* property of the proposed vocabulary we can assign a policy to an identified graph. Such identified graphs are similar to named graphs for RDF, whose development was motivated by a need for expressing metadata, including usage restriction [CBHS05]. When locally storing triples, one can extend them to quads to keep track of the graph that contained them and thus the link to the applicable policy. Quads extend triples by a fourth element containing the IRI of the graph.

4.7 Patterns for Common Policy Restrictions

We already defined several example policies, mainly for the Creative Commons use case. In the following, we list a number of common types of usage restrictions and show for each a concrete example formalised in our policy language that can be easily generalised into a re-usable pattern. The patterns can serve as an initial set of policy building blocks for the structured policy model that we present in Section 5.1. In Table 4.1 we list the patterns that we discuss in detail in the remainder of the section. We formalise the patterns using the Datalog-based policy language and omit the OWL-based version, which can be obtained by trivial translation.

Pattern P1: ShareAlike
In our Creative Commons examples we already used ShareAlike clauses, meaning a requirement to assign a policy to a derived artefact that is equivalent to the policy of the original artefact. Here, we define two minimal examples: NB-SA for name-based ShareAlike, meaning that exactly the same policy is required, and CB-SA for content-based ShareAlike, meaning that a policy is required that allows the same usages:

$$\text{NB-SA}: \text{Derivation}(x) \wedge \text{wasGenBy}(a, x) \wedge \text{hasPolicy}(a, \text{NB-SA}).$$

$$\text{CB-SA}: \text{Derivation}(x) \wedge \text{wasGenBy}(a, x) \wedge \text{hasPolicy}(a, p) \wedge$$
$$\text{containedIn}(p, \text{CB-SA}) \wedge \text{containedIn}(\text{CB-SA}, p).$$

Pattern P2: Attribute-based Usage Restrictions

The policy vocabulary can be extended with application-specific properties, that can be used for modelling compliant actions. For example a social network can model the hasFriend property between agents participating in the network. Restricting usage to agents that have the attribute "friend of Carol" can be modelled as follows:

$$\text{U-FRIEND}: \text{Usage}(x) \wedge \text{performedBy}(x, f) \wedge \text{hasFriend}(\text{Carol}, f).$$

Each data artefact has its own policy attached, however it can make sense to specify policies that can be attached to a whole class of artefacts and specify compliant usages in terms of attributes of the concrete protected artefact. Consider for example the following policy, which specifies that only a person depicted on a picture can share it with others:

$$\text{U-DEPICT}: \text{Sharing}(x) \wedge \text{performedBy}(x, pers) \wedge \text{used}(x, pic) \wedge \text{depicts}(pic, pers).$$

Pattern P3: Data Sharing / Rights Delegation

One key feature of our proposed approach is the ability to express powerful restrictions on the policies of shared data. Rights delegation can be allowed by enabling the rights holder to share the data with further parties under the same or more restricted conditions. The following example policy DLG allows arbitrary usage and the free delegation of this right:

$$\text{DLG}: \text{Usage}(x) \vee$$
$$(\text{Sharing}(x) \wedge \text{wasGenBy}(a, x) \wedge \text{hasPolicy}(a, p) \wedge \text{containedIn}(p, \text{DLG})).$$

Of course, the delegation can be further constrained e.g. on the attributes of the actor or the artefact as shown before.

One common aspect of rights delegation is limiting the depth upto which rights receivers can further delegate the rights. This can be implemented by sharing an artefact with policies allowing a decreasing number of further sharings. A general set of policies, which allows n delegations is described in the following, where DLG-1 is assigned to the original artefact (for $i \in [2, n-1]$):

$$\text{DLG-1}: \text{Usage}(x) \vee$$
$$(\text{Sharing}(x) \wedge \text{wasGenBy}(a, x) \wedge \text{hasPolicy}(a, p) \wedge \text{containedIn}(p, \text{DLG-2})).$$
$$\text{DLG-i}: \text{Usage}(x) \vee$$
$$(\text{Sharing}(x) \wedge \text{wasGenBy}(a, x) \wedge \text{hasPolicy}(a, p) \wedge \text{containedIn}(p, \text{DLG-(i+1)}))).$$
$$\text{DLG-n}: \text{Usage}(x).$$

Pattern P4: Hierarchies and other Domain Knowledge

Hierarchies are widespread when modelling usage restrictions:

- Users groups. E.g., managers are a subclass of employees; rights granted to acquaintances should automatically also granted to friends.

- Artefacts. E.g., usage of a birthday implies usage of personal information; allowing the sharing of location data includes allowing the sharing of latitude and longitude.

- Purposes. E.g., marketing is a commercial purpose.

Such hierarchies can be modelled as background knowledge in the Datalog formalism used as a basis for the proposed policy language. E.g. the following rules express that every friend of a person is also an acquaintance and that every manager is also an employee:

$$hasAcquaintance(p, f) \leftarrow hasFriend(p, f).$$
$$Employee(m) \leftarrow Manager(m).$$

Furthermore, background theories can express domain knowledge, e.g. that a selling action has per definition a commercial purpose:

$$Commercial(c).$$
$$hasPurpose(x, c) \leftarrow Selling(x).$$

Another example is that a disk failure can be regarded as a deletion action of the artefacts stored on the disk:

$$Deletion(x) \land used(x, a) \leftarrow DiskFailure(x) \land affected(x, d) \land isStoredOn(a, d).$$

Pattern P5: Anonymisation / Pseudonymisation

The extension of rights after an artefact is anonymised or pseudonymised is modelled in a similar way as rights delegation. A corresponding policy condition allows the transformation action and restricts the generated artefact's policy accordingly. Consider for example a policy ORG that allows arbitrary usage (but no sharing) of an anonymised artefact:

$$ORG: Anonymisation(x) \land wasGenBy(a, x) \land hasPolicy(a, p) \land containedIn(p, ANO).$$
$$ANO: Usage(x).$$

Pattern P6: Opt-in and Opt-out

Opt-in means that a user has to explicitly agree to a data usage, whereas opt-out means that data usage is done by default if the user does explicitly disagree with it. A basic assumption of our policy model is that usages are only allowed if they are explicitly described as compliant to a policy. This corresponds to opt-in. Data usages for which a user can decide, whether he wants to allow it to a service provider, often affect other attributes of the service such as costs or performance. In this case, a provider can offer several configurations of his service for which he specifies data requests with different desired policies. Depending on the requested policies and corresponding configuration, a user can decide whether he wants to provide specific data artefacts or not.

Pattern P7: Obligations

Obligations are parts of policy conditions that can be temporarily unfulfilled. Typically, obligations require actions that are related via the wasTriggeredBy predicate to the restricted action. As example take a policy P1 that has the obligation to notify an artefact's owner whenever it is used:

$$P1: Usage(x) \land used(x, a) \land owner(a, o) \land$$
$$wasTriggeredBy(x, n) \land Notification(n) \land recipient(n, o).$$

If we consider an action that uses an artefact with policy P1, it will be classified as non-compliant as long as it is not triggered by a notification. In Section 5.3, we present a method to distinguish between policy violations that should prevent the execution of an action and temporary violations that can be executed under the condition that the corresponding obligation will be fulfilled.

Pattern P8: Time Spans

A common condition of obligations is that they have to be fulfilled within a limited time span. Without a time restriction requiring a notification or deletion is not very valuable, because the obliged agent can postpone the fulfillment forever. The following policy requires that a stored artefact is deleted before the end of the year 2012:

$$\text{TIME}: \text{Storing}(x) \wedge \text{wasGenBy}(a, x) \wedge \text{wasTriggeredBy}(x, d) \wedge$$
$$\text{Deletion}(d) \wedge \text{performedAt}(d, t) \wedge t \leq \text{"2012-12-31 23:59:59"}.$$

Absolute time restrictions are used, as the policies refer to concrete artefacts that are passed to concrete providers. To see the advantage of absolute times, consider a policy with a relative time restriction that would allow storage, if it triggers a deletion one year after the storage, and allows the same terms for the stored artefact. The deletion obligation could be circumvented by always storing a new copy of the artefact, which again can be kept for one further year.

However, in case of a data owner who gives away his artefacts with the requirement to delete them after one year, it is inconvenient to update the absolute times in his policy every second. Instead, he can specify a template policy using time arithmetic expressions including the now() function. Whenever the compliance of a data request is checked or an artefact given away, the arithmetic expressions are replaced by the absolute time values to which the expressions evaluate. An example for such a template policy allowing one year of storage is given as follows:

$$\text{TIME-REL}: \text{Storing}(x) \wedge \text{wasGenBy}(a, x) \wedge \text{wasTriggeredBy}(x, d) \wedge$$
$$\text{Deletion}(d) \wedge \text{performedAt}(d, t) \wedge t \leq \text{now}() + 1y.$$

4.8 Related Work

For the following discussion, we split the work related to our proposed policy language into two parts: (i) other policy languages for usage restrictions and related problems such as access control, and (ii) formalisms with meta-modelling capabilities that are not specially targeted at policies. We exclude policy languages focusing on other domains, such as preferences on the configuration of services (e.g., [Lam07, W3C07, Spe10]), information trust (e.g., [BCGM05]), or service licensing ([GD11, BL10]).

Policy Languages

Access control policies regulate who can access protected information or services. The basic model is the access control matrix, which specifies for each combination of user and type of access, whether it is allowed or not [Lam71]. There exist also approaches that specify allowed accesses not for user identities but for roles [FK92] or possessors of credentials [AS05]. XACML is a widely-used industry standard for policies [OAS05], but lacks a formal, declaratively defined semantics. Mankai and Logrippo define a formal semantics for XACML based on first-order logic [ML05]. Several approaches employ semantic technologies to formally model access control policies, e.g., [FJK$^+$08, WHBLC05].

Besides approaches that use semantic technologies to realise access control languages, there also exist policy languages for protecting semantic data, e.g., [ACH$^+$07, RFJ05, JF06, DA06]. Such works define subgraphs of an RDF graph to which certain users have access. The subgraphs are defined by triple patterns and can also depend on contextual information, such as user identity or the current time. In our approach, we regard one or more RDF triples as an information artefact to which then a specific policy applies. We propose to realise the correlation of triples to artefacts by extending triples with an artefact identifier to quads or using named graphs. Several works provide solutions for access control for Linked Data [MKF10, VDGG11, SPD11, CVDG12].

Approaches that realise privacy through access control (e.g., [BBL05, NTBL07, SP11a, SP11b] or the PrimeLife^6 project) have limited applications due to the fact that users often publish information on purpose but still want to restrict usage. The omnipresence of such published information with restricted usages (e.g., in social networks) lead to the opinion that access control is not a good approach for realising usage restrictions [Wei07, WABL$^+$08, KA10]. We share this opinion as it is evident from our scenarios, where, e.g., pictures with a Creative Commons Attribution NonCommercial license are published on the web but usage is restricted to non-commercial purposes. Access control cannot deal with situations where information is published on purpose but should still have restricted usages.

Usage control thus goes further than access control by regulating usage of information after initial access was granted [PS02, PS04]. Park and Sandhu observe that digital rights management (DRM), privacy policies and access control are developed independently despite their similarity and propose the UCON model as a theoretical foundation for usage control, which encompasses the mentioned areas [PS04]. The UCON model regards systems as closed environments in which all data usages take place (no sharing of the data with further parties is considered) and can thus be considered as a system-level approach. The conceptual model was formalised using temporal logics by Janicke et al. [JCZ07] and Zhang et al. [ZPPPS04].

Pretschner et al. give an overview of enforcement of usage control [PHS$^+$08] and also present a corresponding language [HPB$^+$07] and enforcement mechanisms [PHB$^+$08].

In the area of digital rights management (DRM), there exist several rights expression languages (REL), e.g. ODRL [Ian02] and XrML [WLD$^+$02], which are both XML-based languages with a lack of formal semantics. Several semantics are proposed in independent subsequent works, e.g., [HW08, PW04, HKS04]. Jamkhedkar et al. who present a DRM architecture that separates rights expression from enforcement [JH08, JH09]. Arnab and Hutchison present LiREL which is a formal REL [AH10]. In contrast to our work, these RELs do not allow restrictions on other policies.

---

^{6}http://primelife.ercim.eu/, accessed August 8th 2012

In the privacy community, there exist approaches that check processes for compliance to privacy policies, e.g., [LPB06, CT09]. Such approaches are only applicable if there is a complete view on processes in which information is used.

Basically the discussed approaches to usage control aim at giving access to information only to eligible entities. As argued before, for many applications there is no distinction between entities that are allowed to access information and those that are not allowed, but rather the distinction between allowed and prohibited usages. Thus, the same criticism as for access control also applies to the discussed usage control approaches. Their concept of closed systems is captured in our definition of system-level policies for which our work proposes the alternative approach of data-centric policies, which are suitable for open and decentralised systems.

The **data-purpose algebra** by Hanson et al. allows the modelling of usage restrictions of data and the transformation of the restrictions when data is processed [HBLK⁺07]. In their approach, a data item is associated with its content, the agent who produced it, the set of purposes for which usage is allowed and a set of categories. Depending on the process performed on a data item a function is defined that transforms the allowed usages. Our approach shares the general idea of having a set of allowed usages for data artefacts, which can change depending on the process performed on the artefact. In our approach, transformation functions are not defined directly but restricted by containedIn conditions on policies of produced artefacts. The data-purpose algebra is particularly suitable for expressing transformations which hold for all data items processed by a specific system. In contrast, our approach integrates the transformation functions, i.e., target policy restrictions, into policies of data artefacts, which means that every artefact can define its own transformation functions.

In the following, we briefly discuss specific, relevant **other policy languages**.

P3P is a W3C standard for privacy policies on the web [W3C02]. It is a XML language without formal semantics, which is supplied by various later publications, e.g. [YLA04]. In Section 7.2.3, we discuss how P3P can be translated into our policy approach according to the semantics given by Yu et al. [YLA04].

Ringelstein and Staab present the history-aware PAPEL policy language, which can be used for privacy policies [RS10]. To illustrate the difference between history-awareness and our approach, consider a policy presented in [RS10]: a patient record can only be shared after it is deidentified. PAPEL models the sharing action as compliant, if it was preceded by an deidentification. With our approach, the policy of the health record would specify that a compliant deidentification action can allow a policy for the produced artefact, which permits sharing; the policy engine evaluating the compliance of the sharing actions does not have to know anything about the history of the artefact.

Becker et al. have developed the SecPAL authorisation language [BFG10], which supports rights delegation. SecPAL policies are not attached to data artefacts and do not support obligations. The S4P language for privacy policies by Becker et al. [BMB10] supports obligations, but also evaluates policies on a system level, which requires a certain amount of history-awareness. For example, the compliance of an action, allowed by a rights delegation requires the system to evaluate the rightfulness of the delegation.

Accountability in RDF (AIR) is a policy language based on RDF, extended with formulas using quantified variables that can be used as conditions in nested if-then-else rules [KHW08]. The "else" path is followed if the condition does not hold, which means that the language supports negation on non-atomic conditions. Therefore query containment on AIR policies is not decidable and thus the policy restrictions presented in this work cannot be easily integrated into AIR.

Another semantic policy language is Protune [BDOS10]. It is based on logic programming rules, including negation. Its main focus is not on the classification of situations, but on trust negotiation, which includes the execution of actions. It includes the explanation facility ProtuneX [BOP06], which supports decision justifications and different kind of policy queries, such as how-to queries that tell a user what is needed to fulfill a policy. None of these queries can however be integrated into the conditions of other policies, which is a key feature of our policy language. Bonatti and Mogavero present a restricted version of Protune (e.g. no negation) for which they show decidability of policy comparison, i.e. query containment [BM08]. However, their work does not support integration of the comparisons into policy conditions.

Policies that are attached to their protected artefact are also used in [KSW03, RS10] where they are called sticky policies.

Formalisms for Meta-modelling

Many knowledge representation formalisms have been proposed to accomplish non-classical semantics (e.g. fixed point semantics) and meta-modelling (as present in our expression of containment as an object-level predicate). However, both aspects are usually not integrated, or come with technical restrictions that do not suit our application.

Fixed point operators exist in a number of flavours. Most closely related to our setting are works on fixed point based evaluation of terminological cycles in description logic ontologies [Baa90, Neb91]. Later works have been based on the relationship to the μ-calculus, see [BCM+07, Section 5.6] for an overview of the related literature. As is typical for such constructions, the required monotonicity is ensured on a logical level by restricting negation. This is not possible in our scenario where we focus on the entailment of implications (policy containments). Another approach of defining preferred models where certain predicate extensions have been minimised/maximised is Circumscription [Lif88]. This might provide an alternative way to define a semantics that can capture desired policy containments, but it is not clear if and how entailments could then be computed.

Meta-modelling is possible with first- and higher-order approaches (see, e.g., [Mot07] for an OWL-related discussion) yet we are not aware of any approaches that provide the semantics we intend. Glimm et al. [GRV10], e.g., show how some schema entailments of OWL 2 DL can be represented with ontological individuals and properties, but the classical semantics of OWL would not yield the desired policy containments.

For relational algebra, it has been proposed to store relation names as individuals, and to use an expansion operator to access the extensions of these relations [Ros92]. This allows for queries that check relational containment, but based on a fixed database (closed world) rather than on all possible interpretations (open world) as in our case.

4.9 Discussion

This chapter introduced a language for data-centric usage policies. The language includes a vocabulary for modelling a localised view of the system behaviour relevant to information usages. Furthermore the language consists of a formalism for modelling content-based policy restrictions. The formalism is based on first-order logic extended by a containment relation between policies. We instantiated the formalism using practical knowledge representation languages, namely OWL and Datalog. To further pave the way for practical applications we presented methods to attach policies to artefacts and a number of policy patterns realising commonly found usages restrictions.

Checking the containment of policies is not only possible as part of policy conditions, but naturally can also be considered as an independent function provided by a policy engine, which has proven useful in policy analysis and management, e.g., for searching redundant or obsolete policies [BBC+09, KHP07, AGLL05].

The approach presented in this chapter fulfills the following requirements: R1: *Web Compatibility*, R2: *Formal Semantics*, R3: *Data-centricity of Policies*, R4: *Extendable Vocabulary of Computational Model*, R7: *Expressivity for Common Restrictions*, and partially R8: *Decidable and Practical Classification*.

In the next chapter, we go beyond binary decisions on the compliance of usages to policies and explore further methods for interacting with policies, respectively policy-aware systems.

Chapter 5

Interaction with Policies

Formal policies are good for unambiguous specification of compliant activities, and automated decision-making, that is formal policies are good for computer systems. In applications, where the ultimate users of a policy-aware system are humans, there exists a semantic gap between the formalisation of a policy and its meaning to a human user. The gap shows itself in two particular situations: (i) a user wants to specify a policy formalising his intended activity restrictions, (ii) a user wants to understand why his planned activity is classified as non-compliant. This gap is especially large for applications with non-expert users, consider, e.g., the application of usage policies for creative works: the creator of the work wants to specify a policy, but is an artist, not a computer scientist, the same holds for a user that wants to embed the work into a blog post.

In this chapter, we present a solution for divorcing users from the formalisms underlying policy languages, thus reducing the semantic gap. The solution consists of three components: (i) a structured model, which allows users to compose policies from existing, re-usable policy building blocks (Section 5.1); (ii) an explanation approach, which leverages the structured definition of a policy to provide natural language explanations of non-compliances (Section 5.2); (iii) a method for distinguishing policy violations from obligations that are not yet fulfilled and which can be resolved by corresponding obligation handlers (Section 5.3). The three components were developed with the goal to support our presented data-centric policy language, but are general enough to support other policy languages. We generally base the descriptions of the components on the assumption that a policy has an identifier p and is defined by a first-order logic formula $\varphi_p[x]$ with one free variable. Background knowledge, policy definitions, and descriptions of system behaviours (in our case: information usages) are given in a first-order theory T. We assume that a behaviour described as b is compliant with a policy p if $T \models \varphi_p[b]$. For the structured model and the explanation approach, we can even leave out the requirement for first-order logic and say very generally: T is a description of behaviour b, $\varphi_p[x]$ is a behaviour restriction, and $\models$ is implemented by a decision procedure, which checks whether T describes b in a way compliant to $\varphi_p[x]$. For example the components could be applied to the following two policy languages:

1. WS-Policy [W3C07]: a policy language for describing possible web service interactions. T is represented by an XML document according to the WS-Policy schema, using assertions defined in a number of accompanying standards, e.g. WS-SecurityPolicy [OAS09]. Assertions describe capabilities and requirements for the service interaction. The restriction $\varphi_p[x]$ is given in the same way as T. The decision procedure for

$\models$ determines non-emptiness of the intersection of the normal forms of the interaction description T and the policy definition φ_p. Algorithms for calculating intersections of WS-Policy XML documents are given in the WS-Policy standard, based on syntactic matching of assertion elements.

2. AIR [KHW08]: a general purpose policy language. T is represented by RDF triples using an appropriate vocabulary. $\varphi_p[x]$ is defined as nested production rules, using N3 syntax. The decision procedure is based on a production rules semantics [KBK$^+$10].

We describe in Section 5.4 one special obligation handler that determines a policy which can be assigned to an artefact derived from one or more artefacts whose policies have corresponding restrictions.

Furthermore, we introduce in Section 5.5 a method for requesting data of a specified type for a specified purpose from a data owner. This is useful for partial enforcement of policies, as data access is only granted if the requestor complies to the data owner's policy.

Finally, we discuss related work in Section 5.6 and conclude the chapter in Section 5.7.

Parts of this chapter are based on the following publications: a basic version of the structured model without the explanation component is presented in [SS10a]; our approach for obligation handling is introduced in [Spe12b]; the special obligation handler for policies of derived artefacts is based on [Spe11a]; and the request model is presented in the technical report [Spe12a].

5.1 Structured Model for Policies

The approach to combine re-usable building blocks into activity restrictions, in this case licenses specifying allowed data usages, has proven very successful for Creative Commons[1] and its RDF serialisation [AALY08]. Creative Commons building blocks are *NonDerivs* (forbidding the creation of derivations), *NonCommercial* (forbidding the use for commercial purposes), *Attribution* (requiring the attribution of the original creator, when a protected work is used), and *ShareAlike* (requiring to apply the same license terms to derived works). Creative Commons licenses come in three layers: (a) legal code, (b) human-readable, and (c) machine-readable. The machine-readable layer specifies in RDF, which of the above-mentioned building blocks a license is composed of. The building blocks have a unique identifier, but no formal description of their meaning, i.e., they are not machine-understandable, which means that applications must hardcode the meaning of the limited, fixed set of Creative Commons building blocks. The other major drawback of the Creative Commons models is the composition model which only allows limited possibilities to combine the building blocks.

Our approach is more generic in the sense of supporting a wider range of usage restrictions. Thus, it is not feasible to have a fixed set of building blocks. Instead we propose that the set of building blocks should be open and extendable. In order to enable policy-aware systems to understand previously unknown building blocks, we require that their meaning

---

[1]http://creativecommons.org/

is described in a machine-understandable policy language. A formally and unambiguously defined meaning is also useful for well-known building blocks; e.g., there is confusion about the meaning of the *NonCommercial* in Creative Commons[2].

A human-understandable layer is an integral part of the successful Creative Commons model. We adopt this success factor for our more general policy language and thus require natural language labels and descriptions of building blocks. Such labels are useful in many ways: (i) labels define names of building blocks, and give a first hint to their function, (ii) descriptions can explain the meaning of a block, its intended usage, and give examples, (iii) natural language descriptions can be indexed and used for keyword-based fulltext searching of building blocks, (iv) labels can be used to generate explanations of policy non-compliances, as will be shown in Section 5.2.

A model to compose building blocks should be easily comprehensible by non-expert users, but still provide expressive combinations. A composition model should allow to specify alternatives to reach compliance (e.g., deleting or blocking an artefact after a given time span) and compose an alternative of several building blocks (e.g., requiring both attribution and notification of an artefact's owner). A powerful, yet simple, way to compose policies from basic conditions is the introduction of complex conditions that are conjunctions or disjunctions of both basic and complex conditions. Non-experts can use this model of complex conditions successfully, as filter editors in many email programs demonstrate. The same basic structure model is also underlying WS-Policy [W3C07], a web service standard for expressing policies. The basic conditions in WS-Policy are called assertions, which have a meaning defined in natural language in accompanying standards. In previous work, we have demonstrated how WS-Policy assertions can be linked to ontology concepts, to give them a formal meaning [Spe10]. The main advantage of our previous work is that it kept compatibility to existing WS-Policy tools and engines. In this work, we introduce a new serialisation based on RDF for the following reasons:

- Policies and both basic and complex conditions should be uniquely identifiable and dereferencable, which is supported by the RDF standard through the use of IRIs. In contrast, there is no direct support for global identifiers for individual elements in XML, on which WS-Policy is based.

- Formal definitions of basic conditions should be supported in a wide range of policy languages, including our data-centric usage policy language.

- RDF models are extendable, to support new attributes and descriptions of policies and conditions.

- WS-Policy does not have a standard way to assign natural language descriptions and labels to conditions.

In the following, we describe first the model in abstract terms, and then show its realisation in RDF and how it fits into the web architecture.

---

[2]Creative Commons has commissioned a study about the understanding of commercial vs. non-commercial use [Cre09].

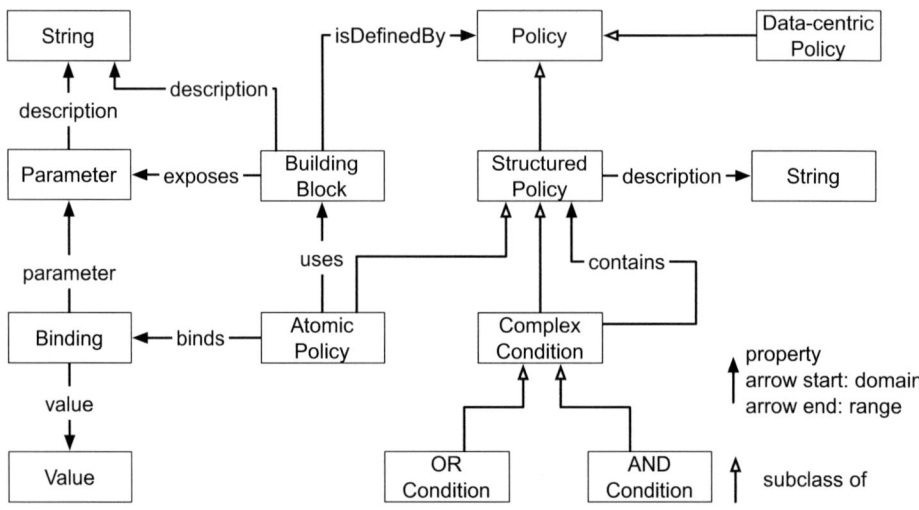

Figure 5.1: Structure model for composing policies

The structure model is visualised in Figure 5.1, where rectangles represent concepts, solid lines with filled arrow heads are properties between instances of the connected concepts, and solid lines with unfilled arrow heads denote a subconcept relationship. The basic concept of policy is subclassed into policies in our previously defined policy language and in the ones given in our structured model. *Structured policies* are either *atomic policies*, or *complex conditions*. Every structured policy has a natural language *description*.

Let $N_S \subset N_P$ be the set of all identifiers of policies in the structured model, then the function description: $N_S \mapsto S$ defines its description, where S is the set of all strings. The type of a structured policy is given by the function type: $N_S \mapsto \{\text{or}, \text{and}, \text{atomic}\}$. A complex condition *contains* a number of child policies, given by the function children: $N_S \mapsto 2^{N_S}$. Complex conditions are either *OR conditions*, i.e. disjunctions, or *AND conditions*, i.e. conjunctions. An *atomic policy* denotes the *use* of a *building block*. A building block *is defined by* a policy, in our case, specified in the data-centric policy language. Building blocks can be parameterised, e.g., a building block restricting usage purposes can take the admissible purposes as a parameter. Atomic policies bind the parameters to concrete *values*. The formal policy of an atomic policy after applying the parameter bindings is given by the function defBy: $N_S \mapsto N_P$.

The defBy function can be implemented easily for policies based on OWL or Datalog. For both cases there exist RDF serialisation, which identify constants by IRIs. In the description of a building block, we can refer to some of those constants as parameters that are exposed by the block. The parameter can be further described in natural language to explain its meaning to users of the block. An atomic policy can define a number of bindings. A binding refers to a parameter of the used building block and assigns a value to it, which can be either a constant (i.e., an IRI), a variable, or a literal value. The defBy function replaces all bound parameters in the specification of the policy defining the building block by the assigned value. The replacement can be reduced to a simple syntactical operation.

Example 9. *For the Creative Commons use case, we define the two exemplary building blocks* B_BY *for allowing usages when attribution is given, and* B_SA *for allowing derivations when a policy equivalent to the parameter* P1 *is set:*

BuildBlock(B_BY)∧isDefinedBy(B_BY, *BY*)∧
        description(B_BY, *"Attribution must be given."*).
BuildBlock(B_SA)∧isDefinedBy(B_SA, *SA*)∧
        description(B_SA, *"Derivations must have equivalent policy."*).
        exposes(B_SA, P1) ∧ Parameter(P1)∧
        description(P1, *"Policy to which equivalence must hold."*),

where the defining policies are given as:

$$BY: \text{Usage}(x) \land \text{wasTriggeredBy}(x, a) \land \text{Attribution}(a).$$
$$SA: \text{Derivation}(x) \land \text{wasGenBy}(z, x) \land \text{hasPolicy}(z, p)\land$$
$$\text{containedIn}(p, \text{P1}) \land \text{containedIn}(\text{P1}, p).$$

A structured policy S_BYSA *modelling the Creative Commons Attribution ShareAlike (CC BY-SA) license can be defined based on the building blocks as follows:*

ORCond(S_BYSA) ∧ contains(S_BYSA, P_BY) ∧ contains(S_BYSA, P_SA)∧
    description(S_BYSA, *"Use with attribution or derive with equivalent policy."*).
AtomicPol(P_BY) ∧ uses(P_BY, B_BY).
AtomicPol(P_SA) ∧ uses(P_SA, B_SA) ∧ binds(P_SA, B1)∧
    description(P_SA, *"Derivation must have policy equivalent to CC BY-SA."*).
Binding(B1) ∧ parameter(B1, P1) ∧ value(B1, S_BYSA).

Example 10. *In this privacy related example, we define a building block, which allows storage (*B_STORE*) and two building blocks, which require deletion (*B_DEL*), respectively blocking (*B_BLOCK*) within a time frame that can be given as parameter:*

BuildBlock(B_STORE) ∧ isDefinedBy(B_STORE, *STORE*)∧
    description(B_STORE, *"Storage is allowed."*).
BuildBlock(B_DEL) ∧ isDefinedBy(B_DEL, *DEL*)∧
    description(B_DEL, *"Deletion must be done within time frame."*).
    exposes(B_DEL, TimeD) ∧ Parameter(TimeD)∧
        description(TimeD, *"Time point by which deletion must be executed."*).
BuildBlock(B_BLOCK) ∧ isDefinedBy(B_BLOCK, *BLOCK*)∧
    description(B_BLOCK, *"Blocking must be done within time frame."*).
    exposes(B_BLOCK, TimeB) ∧ Parameter(TimeB)∧
        description(TimeB, *"Time point by which blocking must be executed."*) ,

where the defining policies are given as:

$STORE$: Storing(x)

DEL: wasTriggeredBy(x, d) ∧ Blocking(d) ∧ performedAt(d, t) ∧ $t ≤$ TimeD

$BLOCK$: wasTriggeredBy(x, b) ∧ Blocking(b) ∧ performedAt(b, t) ∧ $t ≤$ TimeB .

We define a structured policy S_SDB *which allows storage if deletion or blocking occurs by the end of 2012:*

ANDCond(S_SDB) ∧ contains(S_SDB, P_STORE) ∧ contains(S_SDB, S_DB)∧

    description(S_SDB, *"Storage allowed when deleted or blocked by the end of 2012."*).

AtomicPol(P_STORE) ∧ uses(P_STORE, B_STORE).

ORCond(S_DB) ∧ contains(S_DB, P_DEL) ∧ contains(S_DB, P_BLOCK)∧

    description(S_DB, *"Deletion or blocking must be done by the end of 2012."*).

AtomicPol(P_DEL) ∧ uses(P_DEL, B_DEL) ∧ binds(P_DEL, B2)∧

    description(P_DEL, *"Deletion must be done by the end of 2012."*).

Binding(B2) ∧ parameter(B2, TimeD) ∧ value(B2, *"2012-12-31 23:59:59"*).

AtomicPol(P_BLOCK) ∧ uses(P_BLOCK, B_BLOCK) ∧ binds(P_BLOCK, B3)∧

    description(P_BLOCK, *"Blocking must be done by the end of 2012."*).

Binding(B3) ∧ parameter(B3, TimeB) ∧ value(B3, *"2012-12-31 23:59:59"*).

The semantics for a structured policy $p ∈ N_S$ is given by defining the formula $\varphi_p[x]$ in the following way:

$$\varphi_p[x] := \begin{cases} \varphi_{p'}[x], & \text{if type}(p) = \text{atomic} \wedge p' = \text{defBy}(p) \\ \bigwedge_{c \in \text{children}(p)} \varphi_c[x], & \text{if type}(p) = \text{and} \\ \bigvee_{c \in \text{children}(p)} \varphi_c[x], & \text{if type}(p) = \text{or} . \end{cases}$$

Note that the we check compliance to the defining policies of the building blocks independently, i.e., they only share the variable x; other variables of the same name in policies of different building blocks are considered as different. For computing the containedIn relation, we have to create a defining formula for each structured policy, which requires that we rename duplicate variables when merging the formulae of different building blocks.

The RDF representation of this model is straightforward and can be found online[3]. The model being based on RDF has IRIs as identifiers for policies and building blocks; the IRIs should be HTTP URIs, so that dereferencing is possible. Dereferencing the IRI of a building block or policy should return either a machine-understandable or human-readable description, depending on the requesting agent (cf. HTTP content negotiation as used in Linked Data [HB11]). The human-readable descriptions should at least include an HTML page that

---

[3]http://openlids.org/policy/structure/vocab

the user can view in a browser and which displays the natural language description as well as other relevant information about the policy or building block. For structured policies the machine-understandable description should at least include a RDF description in the proposed vocabulary for the structured model. The defining policies of building blocks can have different machine-understandable descriptions, depending on their used formalism, i.e., data-centric policies can be served as either OWL or RIF documents depending on their base formalism (description logics or Datalog).

A question that naturally arises about our proposed structured model: why is it worthwhile to introduce a new formalism (the structured model) in order to hide the existing policy formalisms? Our answers to this question are given in the following:

- The structured model relies on a simple composition technique that is also used in non-expert applications, such as email filter editors.

- Furthermore, the email filter editors show that it is straightforward to build graphical user interfaces for such a model.

- RDF is used only as a serialisation format for the model; the contact with users is done via graphical user interfaces that only use the given natural language labels and descriptions, hiding IRIs and RDF.

- Natural language descriptions enable indexing building blocks and providing keyword-based fulltext search.

Most existing policies are not suitable for re-use as building blocks, as they already cover different aspects. Building blocks should be simple and cover only one aspect of an activity restriction in order to increase re-usability. In the following, we show for the formalisms, underlying the proposed practical data-centric policy languages, how their structure could be lifted to our model and which atomic parts could be used as building blocks:

- Web Ontology Language (OWL): policies are expressed as classes and the instances of the classes are defined to be compliant to the policies. Depending on the used OWL profile, classes can be constructed as conjunctions and disjunctions of other classes. These conjunctions and disjunctions can be lifted to complex AND, respectively OR conditions in our model. Classes using other constructs can be taken as the formal definitions for building blocks.

- Datalog: a rule for a head predicate (e.g., a policy) in Datalog is defined by one or more conjunctions of atoms. If several conjunctions exist, then the head predicate is defined by the disjunction of the conjunctions. Atoms can again use predicates that are defined by further rules, which again are disjunctions of conjunctions. The model of disjunctions and conjunctions can be mapped to our structured model. For creating building blocks it is not necessary to push this to the maximum, e.g., a reasonable building block for requiring communication security could be a disjunction of two conjunctions, both requiring different encryption and signature methods at the same time.

5.2 Explanations for Policy Violations

In case that an information usage is classified as non-compliant, the user is naturally interested in an explanation, so that he can decide whether he can and wants to fix reasons for
non-compliance or whether he has to abstain from the usage. The naive approach to explanations would be to present the user logical justifications for the negative classifications, e.g.,
the proof tree generated by a reasoner. Such justifications are however hard to understand
for humans and especially for non-expert users of a policy-aware system.

In order to be better understandable, the explanation should be given in natural language.
Such natural language explanations are available for many existing policy languages, including approaches that automatically generate the explanations from the policy definitions
(e.g., [BOP06]) and approaches where users can specify the texts for the explanations (e.g.,
[KHW08]).

Explanations can become rather complex in case that there are different alternatives to
reach compliance, each imposing a number of requirements on the activity. Several works
use heuristics to aggregate and structure explanations, e.g., [CR02]. We build upon the idea
introduced by the policy language AIR to structure explanations along the structure given
by the policy specifiers [KHW08]. This decision is based on the assumption, that policy
specifiers compose their policies in a meaningful way (e.g., grouping restrictions on the
policy of a derived artefact together), which is expressed in their structure. The user-given
structure is thus already meaningful and no heuristics have to be employed, which would be
particularly hard to establish in our generic approach, which supports different formalisms
for practical policy languages.

To further address the potential complexity of explanations, we require explanations to
come in different levels of details. Starting with the most abstract explanation on the level
of the whole policy, users can zoom into the details of different parts of the explanations. In
this way, users can fix different issues of their planned activity in isolation.

A further requirement for explanations that we address is that they should be complete in
the sense of being necessary and sufficient explanations. An explanation is necessary, if the
contained alternatives are the only way to reach compliance. An explanation is sufficient, if
compliance is guaranteed when all requirements of an alternative are fulfilled.

In the following, we present our approach for realising complete and zoomable natural-
language explanations, which exploit the user-given structure when specified in our structured model. An explanation starts with an information usage u that is non-compliant to a
policy $p \in N_S$, i.e., $T \not\models \varphi_p[u]$. Based on the policy p's definition, we generate a set of alternatives to reach compliance of u. Each alternative is a set of complex conditions or atomic
policies in the structured model, that have to be fulfilled for compliance. To get more information about the policies in an alternative, there are two possibilities: (i) if it is an atomic
policy, a formalism-specific justification mechanism can be used, and (ii) if it is an complex
condition, the explanation mechanism can be recursively applied to the child policies. We
define a function alts: $\mathcal{A} \times N_S \mapsto 2^{2^{N_S}}$, where $\mathcal{A}$ is the set of all usage descriptions, returning
for an activity and a policy a set of alternatives, where each alternative is a set of policies

required to be fulfilled. The function is given by:

$$\text{alts}(u, p) = \begin{cases} \emptyset, & \text{if } T \models \varphi_p[u] \\ \{\{p\}\}, & \text{if type}(p) = \text{atomic} \\ \{\{c\} \mid c \in \text{children}(p) \wedge T \not\models \neg\varphi_c[u]\}\}, & \text{if type}(p) = \text{or} \\ \{\{c \mid c \in \text{children}(p) \wedge T \not\models \varphi_c[u]\}\}, & \text{if type}(p) = \text{and.} \end{cases}$$

The case where $T \models \varphi_p[u]$ returns the empty set, as u is compliant and so there are no explanations needed for reaching compliance. The case where p is an atomic policy returns the single alternative of fulfilling p, as atomic policies are the finest level of detail that our explanation approach deals with. Policy language specific extensions could of course zoom into the corresponding definition of the atomic block. If u is not compliant to an OR condition p, this means that u is not compliant to any of its children, so we return every satisfiable child as an alternative, because fulfilling one would be sufficient for compliance with p. For an AND condition p to which u is non-compliant there is only a single alternative: fulfil all child conditions to which u is not already compliant.

Having defined the alts function, we now discuss how it can be used to display explanations based on a structured policy. First we define an additional property *explanation* of structured policies (i.e., complex conditions and atomic policies) defining a natural-language explanation what non-compliance to the policy means, respectively how it can be resolved. For the abstract model, we introduce the explanation function: $\text{expl}: N_S \mapsto S$, which returns the value of the explanation property, or if it is missing its RDFS label or its *description* as given in the structure model. The explanation why an activity u is not compliant with a policy p is given as: $\text{expl}(p)$. If the users wishes more details, he is shown a list of alternative solutions, given by $\text{alts}(u, p)$. Each alternative alt is presented as a requirement to fulfil all the policies in alt, where each policy $p' \in$ alt is labelled by $\text{expl}(p')$. Unless a node p' is an atomic policy the user can request more details, which are the list of alternatives given by $\text{alts}(u, p')$ and can again be displayed in the same manner. In this way a recursive zoom into the unfulfilled policy can be given to the user. Note that the alts function can be lazily evaluated just when requested by the user.

Example 11. *Continuing Example 9, we consider a usage action* u1 *that has to be compliant to the policy* S_BYSA *formalising the CC BY-SA license. The plain usage is described as* Usage(u1), *which means that* u1 *is non-compliant to* S_BYSA. *The explanation for the non-compliance is "Use with attribution or derive with equivalent policy."; for further details, we can request the alternatives for making* u1 *compliant, which are given as:*

$$\text{alts(u1, S\_BYSA)} = \{\{P\_BY\}\}.$$

(P_SA is no alternative as usages and derivations are disjoint.) For the alternative P_BY *we get the more specific explanation "Attribution must be given.", which the user can then react on.*

Example 12. *We consider a storage action* s1 *that must be compliant to the policy* S_SDB *from Example 10 that allows storage if deletion or blocking is performed by the end of 2012.*

The plain storage action, described as Storing(s1), *is classified as non-compliant. The only alternative to reach compliance requires compliance to* S_DB, *for which in turn exist two alternatives as given by:*

$$\text{alts}(\text{s1}, \text{S\_DB}) = \{\{\text{P\_DEL}\}, \{\text{P\_BLOCK}\}\}.$$

The alternatives have the explanations "Deletion must be done by the end of 2012.", respectively "Blocking must be done by the end of 2012.".

The explanations can be displayed in an application specific manner, e.g., as HTML with descriptions of failed complex conditions that contain links for zooming into the corresponding details. Furthermore for concrete applications, the displaying process can sort and prune alternative solutions in an appropriate way.

There are applications, in which the policy itself contains sensitive parts that should be hidden from a user, and thus not be part of explanations. Examples include lists of users authorised to access a confidential document, which can be itself confidential information, as it could help an attacker to learn something about the content of the document. In such cases additional metadata about parts of the policy is needed to express their confidentiality. Support for such a feature could easily be integrated in our approach due to the extendability of our RDF-based structure model.

5.3 Obligation Handling

In situations, where a data usage is classified non-compliant to the used artefact's policy, we have to distinguish between policy violations and not yet fulfilled obligations. Obligations are parts of policy conditions that can be temporarily unfulfilled. The non-fulfillment of these conditions will be fixed after a certain amount of time to reach compliance. Consider for example the obligation to attribute the original creator of an artefact when it is used: using the artefact is classified as non-compliant but only temporarily until the attribution is given and thus compliance reached. If usage is restricted to non-commercial purposes and a usage is classified as non-compliant because it has a commercial purpose, the violation is not temporary and thus there is not an obligation required, but the usage should be prevented. In the following, we present an approach to distinguish violations and obligations for usages classified as non-compliant to a policy.

Consider a data usage described by the theory T, where a policy subject u is found non-compliant to a policy P defined by $\varphi_P[x]$. The solution is structured along the following steps:

1. finding out why u is non-compliant;

2. if u can be made compliant by adding new facts, identify the required facts;

3. identify obligations in the facts;

4. checking whether obligation handling makes the usage compliant;

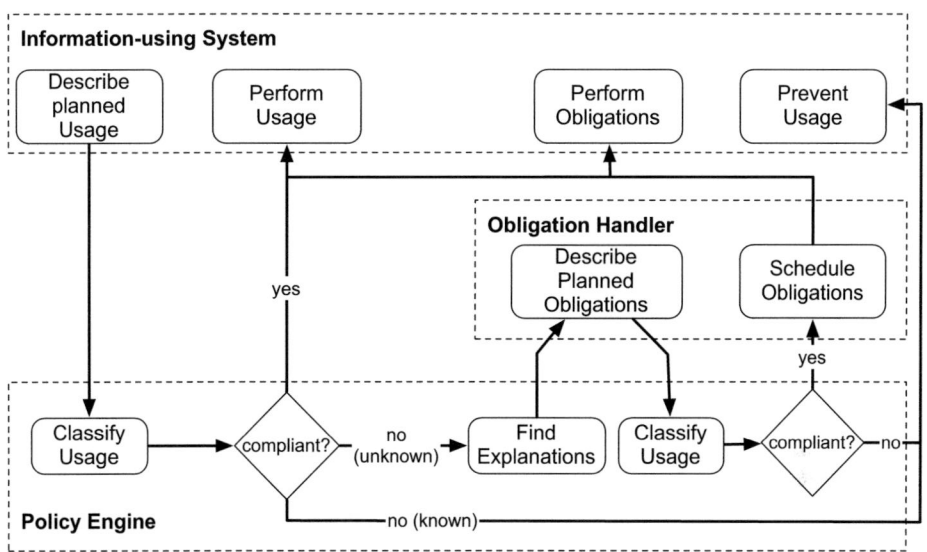

Figure 5.2: Architecture of a Information-using Policy-aware System with Automated Obligation Handling

  5. if compliance is given, schedule the obligations with the corresponding handlers.

A system architecture realising the complete process of Steps 1 to 5 is visualised in Figure 5.2.

Step 1: Finding out why u is non-compliant:
We consider u to be non-compliant with P, if we cannot infer that u makes φ_P true, i.e., $T \not\models \varphi_P[u]$. One reason why we cannot infer $\varphi_P[u]$ can be that it contradicts T, i.e., $T \models \neg\varphi_P[u]$. In case of a contradiction, we cannot establish $\varphi_P[u]$ by adding new facts (e.g., from describing the fulfilment of an obligation), because of the monotonicity of FOL. As such contradictions cannot be fixed by obligation handling, we only proceed if $T \not\models \varphi_P[u]$ and $T \not\models \neg\varphi_P[u]$.

Example 13. *Consider the following theories describing data usages:*

$$T_1: \text{Usage(u1)} \land \text{hasPurpose(u1, r1)} \land \text{NonCommercial(r1)}.$$
$$T_2: \text{Usage(u2)} \land \text{wasTriggeredBy(u2, a2)} \land \text{Attribution(a2)}.$$
$$T_3: \text{Usage(u3)} \land \text{hasPurpose(u3, r3)} \land \text{Commercial(r3)}.$$

All three theories T_1, T_2, T_3 do not *model a usage compliant to the policy BY-NC as defined by:*

$$BY\text{-}NC: \text{Usage}(x) \land \text{wasTriggeredBy}(x, a) \land \text{Attribution}(a) \land$$
$$\text{hasPurpose}(x, r) \land \text{NonCommercial}(r).$$

However, $T_3 \models \neg\varphi_{BY-NC}[u3]$ and thus will be disregarded in further examples.

Step 2: Identify suitable theories to add:

Next, we search for a set $\mathcal{E}$ of theories that make u compliant to P. The search naturally translates into a problem that can be solved by abductive reasoning. The term of abductive reasoning goes back to Peirce [Pei55] and refers to finding an explaining hypothesis for a circumstance. In other words, for a given observation b find an explanation a from which b can be logically inferred. In this sense, abduction is the reverse of deduction, where b is found for a given a. Abductive reasoning was applied to formal logics and several algorithms were given for various logic formalisms (e.g., [Poo89, BN08, KES11, EMS$^+$04]). In the following, we formally define the used notation for abductive reasoning in FOL. Given a theory T and a set F of atomic facts, find an explanation E, such that F can be inferred from T and E, or more formally: $T \cup E \models F$. Additionally, we require that there exists an interpretation for $T \cup E$, i.e., $T \cup E$ is consistent. For sake of simpler notation, we also apply abduction to find an explanation for a sentence $\varphi[c]$, where $\varphi[x]$ is a formula with the only free variable x. This can be realised by introducing a fresh unary predicate p' and the axiom $\forall x.p'(x) \leftrightarrow \varphi[x]$; then abduction can be applied to finding an explanation for the atomic fact $p'(c)$. Applying abduction to our problem of finding suitable theories for making u compliant to P, we search a set $\mathcal{E}$, such that: $\forall E \in \mathcal{E}.T \cup E \models \varphi_P[u]$. We require that every explanation E is minimal in the sense that

1. there is no other explanation E', which entails E:

$$\forall E \in \mathcal{E}.\nexists E' \in \mathcal{E}.E \neq E' \wedge T \cup E' \models T \cup E \text{ ; and}$$

2. there is no subtheory of E, which is also an explanation:

$$\forall E \in \mathcal{E}.\nexists E'.E' \subseteq E \wedge T \cup E' \models \varphi_P[u].$$

The set of explanations can still be of infinite size, e.g., because of transitive predicates, and the minimality conditions might not always be desired [Poo89]. We leave the exact definition of the explanations selected for $\mathcal{E}$ open to be specified for concrete applications. Similarly, there could be a system-specific preference order on the explanations, therefore we describe the following steps for a single explanation $E \in \mathcal{E}$.

Example 14. *Continuing the previous examples, we choose the following explanation E_1, E_2 such that $T_1 \cup E_1 \models \varphi_{BY-NC}[u1]$ and $T_2 \cup E_2 \models \varphi_{BY-NC}[u2]$:*

$$E_1 : \text{wasTriggeredBy}(u1, a1) \wedge \text{Attribution}(a1).$$
$$E_2 : \text{hasPurpose}(u2, r2) \wedge \text{NonCommercial}(r2).$$

Step 3: Identification of obligations:

An explanation E contains facts that would make u compliant to P. Not all of the facts in E however can be fulfilled by adding the description of an obligation, but could only be the result of complying to an unfulfilled condition (see example below). Depending on the specific application, we thus define a set O of obligations, and for every obligation $o \in O$ a query $q_o(p_1, \ldots, p_n)$ and an obligation handler h_o. The query q_o defines, which kind of required facts can be handled by the corresponding obligation handler h_o.

Example 15. *In our example, we define one obligation o1 with a handler h_{o1} that can automatically add attributions to data usages. The corresponding query q_{o1} is defined as:*

$$q_{o1}(x, a) \leftarrow \mathsf{wasTriggeredBy}(x, a) \wedge \mathsf{Attribution}(a).$$

The bindings for the query are passed to the obligation handler h_o, which will return a FOL theory T' that describes the planned fulfilment of the obligations identified by the bindings.

Example 16. *In our example, for E_1 the query q_{o1} gives the binding $\{x \mapsto \mathsf{u1}, a \mapsto \mathsf{a1}\}$, for which the handler h_{o1} plans to create an attribution action, described by the returned theory:*

$$T'_1: \mathsf{wasTriggeredBy}(\mathsf{u1}, \mathsf{a1'}) \wedge \mathsf{Attribution}(\mathsf{a1'}).$$

For the explanation E_2, the query q_{o1} gives no bindings, and thus the obligation handler only returns the empty theory T'_2.

Step 4: Checking if obligation handling leads to compliance:
After getting the descriptions of the planned obligation fulfilments, we want to ensure that fulfilling them is sufficient to make u compliant. For this we check whether $T \cup T' \models \varphi_P[\mathsf{u}]$. If this is the case, we can proceed to the next step and schedule the planned obligation fulfilments (**Step 5: Obligation handling**). Otherwise, we found out that u is not only a temporary violation, but should be prevented completely.

Example 17. *In our example, we see that $T_1 \cup T'_1 \models \varphi_{BY\text{-}NC}[\mathsf{u1}]$, but $T_2 \cup T'_2 \not\models \varphi_{BY\text{-}NC}[\mathsf{u2}]$. Thus, we prevent u2 from execution, but allow u1 and tell the obligation handler h_{o1} to schedule the attribution a1'.*

In order, to ensure that every obligation can be unambiguously assigned to an obligation handler, one can require that the q_o queries define pairwise disjoint sets for different obligations. Another, weaker, requirement would be that no obligation definition is subsumed by an other definition.

5.4 Target Policy Determination

In this section, we present an approach to the problem of finding a policy for an artefact derived from a number of other artefacts. The policy of the derived artefact, the *target policy*, has to be compliant to applicable restrictions in the policies of the used artefacts. We

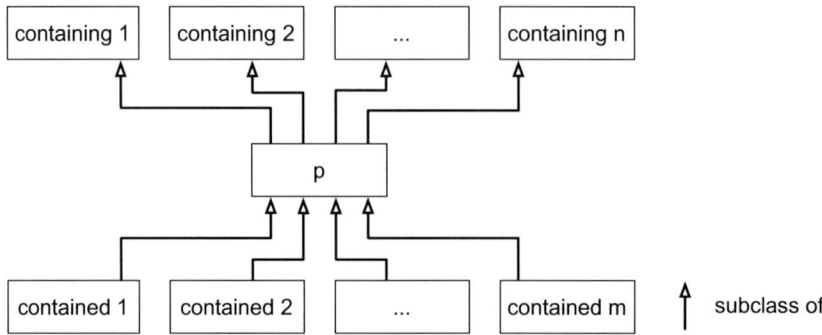

Figure 5.3: Relation between target policy and policy restrictions

treat the determination of the correct target policy as a specific obligation ot, for which we present a handler h_{ot} in the following.

The query for ot is given by:

$$q_{ot}(p_1, p_2) \leftarrow \Big(\text{wasGenBy}(a, x) \wedge \text{hasPolicy}(a, p_1) \wedge \text{containedIn}(p_1, p_2) \vee$$
$$\Big(\text{wasGenBy}(a, x) \wedge \text{hasPolicy}, a, p_2) \wedge \text{containedIn}(p_1, p_2)\Big).$$

For determining the target policy P of an artefact a1, we describe the artefact without further defining P as follows: hasPolicy(a1, P). The obligation handler will then receive a set of bindings for p_1, p_2, where one of them is P and the other is a policy in which P must be contained (in case that p_1 maps to P) or the other is a policy which must be contained by P (in case that p_2 maps to P). Let B be the set of bindings passed to h_{ot}, we define two sets:

$$\text{containing} = \{p_c \mid \{p_1 \mapsto P, p_2 \mapsto p_c\} \in B\}$$
$$\text{contained} = \{p_c \mid \{p_1 \mapsto p_c, p_2 \mapsto P\} \in B\}.$$

Figure 5.3 visualises the relation between P and the policies in containing (denoted as containing 1, . . . , containing n) and the relation between P and the policies in contained (denoted as contained 1, . . . , contained m). Formally we define the problem as: find a definition φ_P for policy P, such that:

$$\text{containedIn}(P, c), \qquad \forall c \in \text{containing}$$
$$\text{containedIn}(c, P), \qquad \forall c \in \text{contained}.$$

Our approach for finding such a P is as follows: (i) we determine the most general policy contained in all $c \in$ containing (see below); (ii) we check, whether the most general policy contains all $c \in$ contained, if it does, we have found the target policy, otherwise it does not exist, i.e., there is no legal way to combine the used artefacts. The most general policy contained in a set S of policies denotes the policy requiring only conditions, which are necessary to ensure containment in the S policies, and pose no further restrictions.

Example 18. *Consider the following Datalog-based definitions for the policies PA, PB, PC, and PD:*

$$PA: A(x).$$
$$PB: B(x).$$
$$PC: A(x) \land B(x) \land C(x).$$
$$PD: A(x) \land B(x).$$

We assume that there is no background knowledge, which relates the predicates A, B, and C. While PC is contained both in PA and PB it is not as general as PD, which is also contained in PA and PB, but does require the C(x) restriction found in PC. In fact, PD only contains two conditions, one required for containment in PA and one required for containment in PB. Thus, PD is the most general policy contained in both PA and PB.

The most general policy contained in a set of policies can be simply constructed by taking the conjunction of all policies in the set, which is directly supported by all three presented policy formalisms, i.e., the structured model, OWL-based policies, and Datalog-based policies. Such a conjunction may however contain redundant restrictions, e.g., when one policy or a part of one policy is contained in another policy. A conjunction in the structured model could be reduced to a normal form, where the redundant parts can be eliminated. However, an integral feature of the structured model would be lost, namely the user-given grouping of restrictions, which are exploited by our explanation approach. For OWL, respectively description logics, there exist several works for computing most general subconcepts of a concept, which could be exploited for optimising the definition of the most general contained policy, e.g., [San03]. In the following, we present a method for Datalog-based policies to create a reduced most general policy P' contained in each policy in the set containing.

Example 19. *As an example for illustrating the computation of the most general contained policy, we consider an derivation that has to be compliant to the two policies BY and BY-SA, defined as follows:*

$$BY: (\mathsf{Usage}(x) \land \mathsf{wasTriggeredBy}(x, y) \land \mathsf{Attribution}(y)) \lor$$
$$(\mathsf{Derivation}(x) \land \mathsf{wasGenBy}(z, x) \land \mathsf{hasPolicy}(z, v) \land \mathsf{containedIn}(v, BY)) .$$

$$BY\text{-}SA: (\mathsf{Usage}(x) \land \mathsf{wasTriggeredBy}(x, a) \land \mathsf{Attribution}(a)) \lor$$
$$(\mathsf{Derivation}(x) \land \mathsf{wasGenBy}(b, x) \land \mathsf{hasPolicy}(b, c) \land$$
$$\mathsf{containedIn}(c, BY\text{-}SA) \land \mathsf{containedIn}(BY\text{-}SA, c)) .$$

We model a derivation d1 *of two artefacts and assign a generic policy P to it:*

$$\mathsf{Derivation}(\mathsf{d1}) \land \mathsf{wasGenBy}(\mathsf{a1}, \mathsf{d1}) \land \mathsf{hasPolicy}(\mathsf{a1}, P) \land$$
$$\mathsf{used}(\mathsf{d1}, \mathsf{a2}) \land \mathsf{hasPolicy}(\mathsf{a2}, BY) \land$$
$$\mathsf{used}(\mathsf{d1}, \mathsf{a3}) \land \mathsf{hasPolicy}(\mathsf{a3}, BY\text{-}SA).$$

The target policy obligation handler will compute the sets

$$containing = \{BY, BY\text{-}SA\}$$
$$contained = \{BY\text{-}SA\}$$

For finding P' we assume that the formula φ_p for each policy $p \in$ containing is in disjunctive normal form (DNF) consisting of $n(p)$ conjunctions, i.e., of the form $\varphi_p[x] \leftrightarrow \varphi_p^1[x] \vee \ldots \vee \varphi_p^{n(p)}[x]$. The DNF is the standard way to express unions of conjunctive queries (UCQs) in Datalog and is also a natural way to model policies, as every conjunction models one compliant type of information use (e.g., a sharing or storage). We define P' as the conjunction of all UCQs of the containing policies:

$$\text{P'}: \quad \bigwedge_{p \in \text{containing}} \varphi_p[x].$$

We transform this conjunction again into a disjunction of the form:

$$\text{P'}: (\varphi_{p1}^1[x] \wedge \ldots \wedge \varphi_{pm}^1) \vee$$
$$\ldots \vee$$
$$(\varphi_{p1}^1[x] \wedge \ldots \wedge \varphi_{pm}^{n(pm)}[x]) \vee$$
$$\ldots \vee$$
$$(\varphi_{p1}^{n(p1)}[x] \wedge \ldots \wedge \varphi_{pm}^{n(pm)}[x]),$$

assuming that containing $= \{p1, \ldots, pm\}$. We reduce this disjunction of conjunctions in three steps:

1. Remove unsatisfiable conjunctions.

2. Remove every redundant conjunction $c_1(x) \leftrightarrow \varphi_{p1}^{i1}[x] \wedge \ldots \wedge \varphi_{pm}^{im}[x]$, i.e., such $c_1(x)$ for which there exists a conjunction $c_2(x) \leftrightarrow \varphi_{p1}^{j1}[x] \wedge \ldots \wedge \varphi pm^{jm}[x]$, such that $\exists k.ik \neq jk$ and $\forall x.c_1(x) \rightarrow c_2(x)$ (if $\forall x.c_1(x) \leftrightarrow c_2(x)$ holds then keep only one of the conjunctions). The conjunction $c_1(x)$ is redundant because every usage allowed by c_1 is also allowed by c_2.

3. Reduce each remaining conjunction $c(x) \leftrightarrow \varphi_{p1}^{i1}[x] \wedge \ldots \wedge \varphi_{pm}^{im}[x]$ by removing each condition $\varphi_{pk}^{ik}[x]$ which contains another condition $\varphi_{pl}^{il}[x]$ for $k \neq l$ (if the conditions are equivalent then keep only one). Such a condition $\varphi_{pk}^{ik}[x]$ is redundant and can be removed because all its requirements are fulfilled whenever the condition $\varphi_{pl}^{il}[x]$ is fulfilled.

Example 20. *Continuing the last example, we create the disjunction for P' as follows:*

$$\text{P'}: (\varphi_{BY}^1[x] \wedge \varphi_{BY\text{-}SA}^1[x]) \vee \tag{5.1}$$
$$(\varphi_{BY}^1[x] \wedge \varphi_{BY\text{-}SA}^2[x]) \vee \tag{5.2}$$
$$(\varphi_{BY}^2[x] \wedge \varphi_{BY\text{-}SA}^1[x]) \vee \tag{5.3}$$
$$(\varphi_{BY}^2[x] \wedge \varphi_{BY\text{-}SA}^2[x]), \tag{5.4}$$

where

$$\varphi^1_{BY}[x] \leftrightarrow \text{Usage}(x) \wedge \text{wasTriggeredBy}(x, y) \wedge \text{Attribution}(y)$$

$$\varphi^2_{BY}[x] \leftrightarrow \text{Derivation}(x) \wedge \text{wasGenBy}(z, x) \wedge \text{hasPolicy}(z, v) \wedge \text{containedIn}(v, BY)$$

$$\varphi^1_{BY\text{-}SA}[x] \leftrightarrow \text{Usage}(x) \wedge \text{wasTriggeredBy}(x, a) \wedge \text{Attribution}(a)$$

$$\varphi^2_{BY\text{-}SA}[x] \leftrightarrow \text{Derivation}(x) \wedge \text{wasGenBy}(b, x) \wedge \text{hasPolicy}(b, c) \wedge$$
$$\text{containedIn}(c, BY\text{-}SA) \wedge \text{containedIn}(BY\text{-}SA, c)$$

We see that $\varphi^1_{BY}[x]$ is disjoint with $\varphi^2_{BY\text{-}SA}[x]$ and that $\varphi^2_{BY}[x]$ is disjoint with $\varphi^1_{BY\text{-}SA}[x]$ (because usages and derivations are disjoint), thus we can remove the disjunctions with numbers 5.2 and 5.3 from the definition of P'. There are no redundant conjunctions to remove, so we continue to the reduction of the conjunctions. The conjunction in Equation 5.1 consists of the two equivalent conditions $\varphi^1_{BY}[x]$ and $\varphi^1_{BY\text{-}SA}[x]$, so it is enough to keep $\varphi^1_{BY\text{-}SA}[x]$. In the conjunction in Equation 5.4, we can remove $\varphi^2_{BY}[x]$ as it contains $\varphi^2_{BY\text{-}SA}[x]$, so it is enough to keep $\varphi^2_{BY\text{-}SA}[x]$. The final result for P' is thus:

$$P': \varphi^1_{BY\text{-}SA}[x] \wedge \varphi^2_{BY\text{-}SA}[x],$$

which is equivalent to the CC BY-SA license. This finding is confirmed by the Creative Commons compatibility chart[4], which states that derivations of data licensed by CC BY or CC BY-SA can be assigned the CC BY-SA license.

5.5 Requesting Information

A data processor that wants to collect data from a data owner, cannot always simply model his intended collection action and check its compliance with the owner's policies, for the following reasons:

- The data owner does not want to publish his full policy, as this could reveal confidential information, about which data exists, and about its access rights.

- The data owner gives access to data, only when collection is allowed, thus the data requestor cannot refer to data artefacts in his collection action, as he does not know their identifier.

As a solution, we introduce a request model, which is visualised in Figure 5.4. A data request either refers to a data element or directly to a data artefact, and a policy under which the requestor intends to use the data. The term data element is adopted from P3P [W3C02] and denotes a subclass of artefact, to which a data owner can assign his artefacts. E.g., a user can state that the artefact containing his street address realises the data element user address. If a data requestor asks to collect the user address, the data owner's system knows that granting the request, involves the collection of the street address artefact, and thus can check the

---

[4]see Point 2.16 in http://wiki.creativecommons.org/FAQ, accessed 15th June 2011

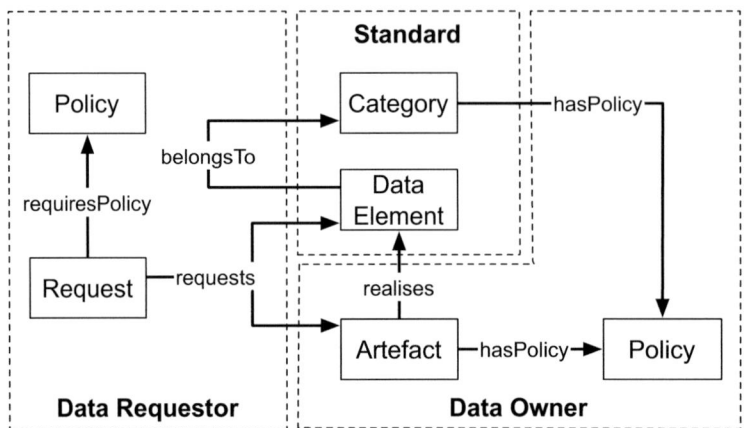

Figure 5.4: Model of requests, data elements and categories. Dashed boxes denote by their bold labelling where the corresponding knowledge is specified.

applicable policies accordingly. Furthermore, the requestor can state to which categories a data element belongs. This is stated by the requestor, as the same data elements can be used in different ways, by different requestors, e.g., an IP address can be classified in the categories personal identifier or geographical information. The data owner can assign policies to categories, e.g., his IP address may be accessible under different conditions, depending on the category under which it is requested.

Checking compliance of a data request is done with the following procedure:

1. The requestor sends a request for data either by referring directly to artefacts or indirectly to data elements. Attached to the request is a policy specifying the intended usage of the data and optionally a specification in which category he classifies the requested data elements.

2. The data owner selects the applicable artefacts, i.e., the directly addressed artefacts and the ones belonging to the requested data elements.

3. Data artefacts with no attached policy but belonging to a data element with an assigned category inherit the policy of the category.

4. The data owner checks, whether the request policy is containedIn the attached policies of all selected data artefacts.

5. If all containments hold, the data artefacts with their corresponding policies can be shared with the requestor.

6. If one containment does not hold, the request is denied.

Depending on the concrete application, the request process can be varied in the following ways:

- Instead sharing all or none requested artefacts, it is also possible to share the subset of artefacts for which the request policy is compliant. This is especially useful if a data element is requested, for which a number of artefacts exist, that are in a hierarchical relation, e.g. differing in detail level. An example would be a request for the birthdate of a person, which can be represented by two different artefacts with different policies, one only containing the year of birth, whereas the other contains the exact day, month and year of birth. In this case depending on the request policy, either no information, the year of birth, or the day of birth can be given out in return to a request for the birthdate.

- Instead of attaching the user's policy for an artefact or a category to copies of the artefact that are shared with a requestor, it is also possible to attach the policy of the requestor. For a successful request, the requestor's policy is always equal or more strict than the policy of the owner, so it might be desirable to grant only the rights to the requestor, that he needs. This is especially useful, if the data owner's policy contains sensitive information, e.g., about which entities can have access to an artefact.

5.6 Related Work

We split the discussion of related work into three parts corresponding to the different contributions of this chapter: (i) structured policy model and explanations, (ii) obligation handling, and (iii) target policy determination.

Structured Policy Model and Explanations

Most similar to our approach is the policy language AIR by Kagal et al. [KHW08]. It comes both with a structured model, where rules have identifiers and can be re-used [KJK11], and an explanation facility that leverages the user-given structure. There are two main advantages of our solutions:

- More flexible structure model. The AIR structure is based on if-then-else rules with a production rule semantics [KBK$^+$10]. In comparison, our model is based on conjunctions and disjunctions for which we have shown compatibility to different formalisms (e.g. Datalog and OWL). Furthermore, our structure model supports the use of different policy languages (AIR could be one of them).

- Complete explanations. AIR explanations are not complete, because they only point to the last failed rule leading to non-compliance. The last failed rule is not always necessary as there can be other rules leading to compliance. The last failed rule is neither always sufficient as there can be another following rule imposing further requirements for compliance.

The structured model in the Creative Commons RDF serialization [AALY08] is not as expressive as our model, because it cannot express disjunctions, e.g., it is not possible to express that either derivations or commercial usage are allowed, but not both.

Our structured model can use different kinds of policy languages, as long as they express policies that define sets of compliant activities. This corresponds to the notion of goal-based policies in [KW04]. The structure of some existing goal-based policy languages can be lifted to our proposed model. We have shown possibilities for the lifting of Datalog-based languages (e.g., Protune [BDOS10], SecPAL [BFG10], PAPEL [RS10]) and OWL-based languages (e.g., KAoS [UBJ⁺03]). SecPAL hides its logical grounding by presenting the policy specifier a syntax resembling natural language [BFG10].

Generating human-understandable explanations for formal policies has been treated in several previous works. The works by Chalupsky and Russ [CR02] and by Bonatti et al. [BOP06] employ heuristics to structure and reduce the size of explanations. Kapadia et al. consider meta-policies in their explanations in order to hide parts of the explanation for security reasons [KSC04]. In their approach atomic policy blocks are represented as propositional variables, which have no inter-dependencies. The policy language-specific explanation facilities could be used in our approach to give further explanation details beyond the level of atomic policies.

Croitoru et al. propose explanations for norms specified as conceptual graphs [COML10]. Some results of their visual presentation of explanations could possibly be used by our approach, which focuses on the generation of explanations.

Obligation Handling

As noted before, the term of abductive reasoning goes back to Peirce [Pei55] and many technical solutions for different logic formalisms were developed, e.g., [Poo89, BN08, EMS⁺04, KES11]. Related to our task to find out the reasons for a policy non-compliance are so-called *why not*, respectively *how to* questions [BOP06]. Becker and Nanz explicitly mention the use of abductive reasoning in policy systems to determine what is missing to reach compliance [BN08], however do not apply abduction to obligation handling. Their algorithms for abductive reasoning for Datalog-based policies can be adapted for our formalisms. Not targeted at policies but at formal knowledge systems in general is the work of Chalupsky and Ross for answering *why not* queries, i.e., giving reasons why some desired inference does not hold [CR02]. The applications of explanations and abduction to policies have in common that they aim at helping the user to reach compliance. Our goal is to automatically identify obligations and pass them to an obligation handler. Not all missing pieces described by an explanation can just be regarded as obligations, but could also be violations of the policy. Finding out, which pieces are obligations and whether they cover the full explanation is a non-trivial task for a policy-based system, for which we presented to the best of our knowledge, the first solution.

Xu and Fong present a policy language with obligations [XF11], for which they list a set of requirements taken from surveying obligation policy languages in the literature, including [ML85, DDLS01, GF05, IYW06, HPB⁺07]. In contrast to the languages analysed by Xu and Fong and the language they propose, there are no special logic operators for representing obligations in our approach. Instead, domain- and application-specific types of obligations can be defined. We model only desired goal states, i.e., the states compliant to a policy, and leave computation of what has to be done to reach compliance (including the fulfilment of obligations) to the policy system. This is in contrast to the other approaches, which specify the actions that have to be performed directly using the obligation operators. In the following, we describe how the requirements identified by Xu and Fong [XF11] are handled by our approach:

- *Trigger* and *obligation*: define under which conditions the obligation is applicable, and what the obligation is. In our approach, both are described in one logical formula specifying the desired and compliant goal states.

- *Temporal constraint*: specifies the time span in which an obligation should be fulfilled. In our approach, this can be modelled, if needed, as part of the domain ontology. Depending on the application, different models of time spans can be employed, e.g., (i) attribution must be given at the same time as usage, or (ii) deletion of artefact must take place latest one year after it was stored.

- *Penalty* or *reward*: what happens if the obligation is violated (*penalty*), respectively fulfilled (*reward*). A penalty can just be modelled as another possibility to reach compliance, namely by executing the protected actions and fulfilling the penalty instead of the obligation. A reward is simply a more relaxed policy, i.e., allowing more actions if the obligation is also fulfilled.

Target Policy Determination

Existing work in the area of policy composition deals with conflict resolution between possibly contradicting policies. Rei is a policy language, which enables users to specify meta-policies that prioritise certain policies in case of conflicts [KFJ03]. Furthermore, there are several approaches for specifying formally how policy classifications should be generated based on the component policies. Bonatti et al. [BDS02], and Ni et al. [NBL09] propose algebras for composing policies. Bruns and Huth present an approach based on four-valued logic to represent not only positive and negative policy decisions, but also undefined and conflicting decisions [BH08]. All these approaches have in common that they directly compose policies, which is only part of the problem that we discussed in this work. We only support policy intersection to compose policies. The key challenges of our approach are: (i) to find the relevant policies, which have to be composed, and (ii) to aggregate the composed policy in order to be non-redundant, as in our case the composed policy is not only used for evaluation, but is again an artefact that is presented to and modifiable by the owner of the composition.

5.7 Discussion

This chapter presented methods for interacting with policies and policy-aware systems that go beyond the binary classification of usages into compliant or non-compliant to a policy For enabling policy specifiers to formalise their intended activity restrictions without having to use the policy formalism directly, we proposed a structured model for re-using policy building blocks. Policies can be composed as basic building blocks or as complex conditions, which are conjunctions and disjunctions of basic building blocks or other complex conditions. Dereferencing the identifier of a building block allows to retrieve the formal representation of the defined policy, which enables machines to consume previously unknown building blocks.

In case of a planned activity that is non-compliant to a policy given in the structured model, we showed how explanations can be generated to help the user modifying the activity in order to reach compliance. By re-using labels and descriptions of building blocks and complex policy conditions, we ensure that explanations are given in natural language. Explanations can become complex and thus our approach defines a recursively applicable function to show alternative ways to compliance, which is used to provide different levels of details. The structure along which the alternatives are aggregated is not determined by heuristics but instead leverages the user-given policy structure, under the assumption that policy specifiers compose their policies in a meaningful way. The alternatives that our explanation approach presents are: (i) necessary, meaning that they are the only way to reach compliance, and (ii) sufficient, meaning that fulfilling the requirements of one alternative guarantees compliance.

Furthermore, we presented a novel approach to formalise obligations and other compliance conditions in a uniform way. The approach enables goal-based policies on a high conceptual level without the need for users to learn special operators in the policy language. Instead, definitions of obligations can be specified using domain- and application-specific vocabularies that are defined and understood by the users. Explanations about what a policy subject lacks to compliance are found by abductive reasoning. We presented a method to check whether an explanation is fully covered by obligations and to identify the obligations.

A special obligation handler was defined for determining an admissible policy for an artefact that is derived from a number of original artefacts. We showed an approach for reducing derived Datalog-based policies in order to remove redundancies.

Finally, we presented a request model that allows data processors to express their information and policy needs to data owners, which can then check whether to serve the request or not depending on their own privacy policies.

The methods presented in this chapter fulfill the requirements R6: *Support for Obligations* and R9: *User Interactions with Hidden Formal Logic.*

Chapter 6

Extensions to the Linked Data Architecture

The Linked Data principles for decentralised and interlinked information systems already cover to a large extent the requirements derived from our scenarios. In this chapter, we present extensions for the missing parts: support for information services and completeness notions for queries. We illustrate the need for these parts and their solutions using the example of Alice who wants to gather a list of the descendants of Queen Elizabeth II and for each of them a picture with information about where it was taken (see Section 2.1.1).

Alice can find information about the royal family as Linked Data via DBpedia, which includes the names of the family members and also some links to photos. The photos however are missing geographical information, so she needs an alternative source of pictures. Flickr supports geographical information for photos, but does not allow arbitrary access to their database, but only via predefined service interfaces. Thus, to cover her information needs, we have to integrate the Flickr services with the Linked Data from DBpedia. Furthermore, to check which geographical feature with a human-understandable name is near to the location of a photo, given as latitude and longitude, she needs to invoke another service. She chooses the GeoNames service, which relates geographical points to nearby points of interests (e.g., the Buckingham Palace). This relation cannot be fully materialised but must be provided as a service, as there is an infinite number of geographical points, which can be given with arbitrary precision.

Another concern for Alice is that she gets all descendants of the queen. She specifies that she trusts DBpedia to have complete information about the royal family and thus algorithms can give a complete answer under this assumption. A further advantage of this restriction is that she does not have to consider arbitrary other sources on the web which brings two major benefits: (i) she does not have to crawl the whole Linked Data web connected to DBpedia, but only the relevant parts for the query; and (ii) statements about the royal family can be restricted to DBpedia, which Alice trusts, thus avoiding that arbitrary user profiles on the web can claim that they are children of the queen.

To give Alice access to all the data and services in a convenient way, she needs a query engine that supports query answering by following links between the distributed information sources, and automatically integrates information from services. Furthermore the engine has to have basic support for automatic inferences, e.g., to support the transitivity of the *has descendant* relation, and to connect different identifiers of the same entities, which frequently occur in different information sources.

In Section 6.1, we define our notion of information services and present the LInked Data Services (LIDS) approach to integrate such services with Linked Data. We define a number of completeness notions for Linked Data query processing and define their relations in Section 6.2. In Section 6.3, we present an engine for answering queries over Linked Data and services according to our completeness notions. Finally, we discuss related work in Section 6.4 and conclude the chapter in Section 6.5.

Parts of this chapter are presented in previous publications: Linked Data Services in [SH10, SH11], and the completeness notions for Linked Data queries in [HS12].

6.1 Linked Data Services (LIDS)

Information services are commonly provided via web APIs based on Representational State Transfer (REST) principles [Fie00, RR07] or via web services based on the WS-* technology stack [Erl04, Pap07]. Currently deployed information services use HTTP as transport protocol, but return data as JSON or XML, which requires glue code to combine data from different APIs with information provided as Linked Data. Linked Data interfaces for services have been created, e.g., in form of the book mashup [BCG07] which provides RDF about books based on Amazon's API, or twitter2foaf, which encodes a Twitter follower network of a given user based on Twitter's API. However, the interfaces are not formally described and thus the link between services and data has to be established manually or by service-specific algorithms. For example, to establish a link between person instances (e.g., described using the FOAF vocabulary[1]) and their Twitter account, one has to hard-code which property relates people to their Twitter username and the fact that the URI of the person's Twitter representation is created by appending the username to `http://twitter2foaf.appspot.com/id/`.

In this section, we present the LInked Data Services (LIDS) approach for creating Linked Data interfaces to information services as defined in Section 6.1.1. The approach incorporates formal service descriptions that enable (semi-)automatic service discovery and integration. Specifically, we present the following components: an access mechanism for LIDS interfaces based on generic web architecture principles (URIs and HTTP) (Section 6.1.2); a generic lightweight data service description formalism, instantiated for RDF and SPARQL graph patterns (Section 6.1.3); and an algorithm for interlinking existing data sets with LIDS (Section 6.1.4)

6.1.1 Information Services

Our notion of information services is as follows:

Information services return data dynamically derived (i.e., during service call time) from supplied input parameters. Information services neither alter the state of some

---

[1] `http://www.foaf-project.org/`

entity nor modify data. In other words, information services are free of any side effects. They can be seen as data sources providing information about some entity, when given input in the form of a set of name/value pairs. The notion of data services include Web APIs and REST-based services providing output data in XML or JSON.

Information services are related to web forms or the "Deep Web" [RGM01], but take and provide data rather than free text or documents.

Example 21. *The Flickr API provides besides other functionality a fulltext search for photos. In order to search for photos of Prince Charles, which are tagged as portraits and have geographic information we can access the following URI (after adding an application-specific API key to the URI):*

```
http://api.flickr.com/services/rest/?method=flickr.photos.search&
text=charles,+prince+of+wales&format=json&sort=relevance
```

with the following (abbreviated) result:

```
...
{"photos":{"page":1, "pages":12, "perpage":100, "total":"1122",
  "photo":[{"id":"5375098012", "owner":"50667294@N08", "secret":"c8583acbbe",
           "server":"5285", "farm":6,
           "title":"The Prince of Wales at
                    Queen Elizabeth Hospital Birmingham"},
          {"id":"2614868465", "owner":"15462799@N00", "secret":"50af5f09c9",
           "server":"3149", "farm":4,
           "title":"Prince Charles" ...},
          {"id":"4472414639", "owner":"48399297@N04", "secret":"cb8533c199",
           "server":"4025", "farm":5,
           "title":"HRH Prince Charles Visits Troops in Afghanistan" ...}
          ... ] } }
```

The returned information is given in JSON in a service-specific vocabulary. To retrieve further information about the first photo with the id 5375098012, we have to know service-specific rules to build the links to those information sources, e.g., we can construct the URI `http://farm6.staticflickr.com/5285/5375098012_c8583acbbe.jpg` *according to the Flickr URI construction rules[2] to access the JPEG of the actual photo; or we can access the following URI to get further information on the photo:*

```
http://api.flickr.com/services/rest/?method=flickr.photos.getInfo&
photo_id=5375098012&format=json
```

Retrieving the URI (again with appended API key) gives the following result:

---
[2]`http://www.flickr.com/services/api/misc.urls.html`

```
{"photo":{"id":"5375098012", "secret":"c8583acbbe", "server":"5285",
        "farm":6, "license":"6", ...
        "location":{ "latitude":52.453616, "longitude":-1.938303, ...},
        ... }}
```

Using the retrieved geographical coordinates, we can build the URI for calling GeoNames's findNearbyWikipedia *service, which relates given latitude/longitude pairs to Wikipedia articles describing geographical features that are nearby. This requires first Flickr-specific knowledge how to extract the latitude and longitude of the image and GeoNames-specific knowledge how to construct the URI for service call, which is:*

```
http://api.geonames.org/findNearbyWikipedia?lat=52.453616&lng=-1.938303
```

The (abbreviated) result is the following:

```
<?xml version="1.0" encoding="UTF-8" standalone="no"?>
<geonames>
<entry>
 <lang>en</lang>
 <title>Birmingham Women's Fertility Centre</title>
 ...
 <lat>52.4531</lat>
 <lng>-1.9389</lng>
 <wikipediaUrl>
  http://en.wikipedia.org/wiki/Birmingham_Women%27s_Fertility_Centre
 </wikipediaUrl>
 ...
 <distance>0.0702</distance>
</entry>
...
<entry>
 <lang>en</lang>
 <title>University (Birmingham) railway station</title>
 ...
 <lat>52.451</lat>
 <lng>-1.936</lng>
 <wikipediaUrl>
  http://en.wikipedia.org/wiki/University_%28Birmingham%29_railway_station
 </wikipediaUrl>
 <distance>0.3301</distance>
</entry>
...
</geonames>
```

This simple example shows that integrating data from several (in this case only two) services is difficult for the following reasons:

- *different serialisation formats are used (e.g., JSON, XML);*

- *entities are not represented explicitly, and are thus difficult to identify between different services. For example, the geographical point returned by the Flickr API does not occur in the output of the GeoNames service. Therefore it is not possible to link the results based on the service outputs alone, but only with service-specific gluing code.*

6.1.2 LInked Data Services (LIDS)

Linked Data Services provide a Linked Data interface for information services. To make these services adhere to Linked Data principles a number of requirements have to be fulfilled:

- the input for a service invocation with given parameter bindings must be identified by a URI;

- resolving that URI must return a description of the input entity, relating it to the service output data;

- the description must be returned in RDF format.

We call such services *Linked Data Services (LIDS)*.

Example 22. *Inputs for the LIDS version of the* findNearbyWikipedia *service are entities representing geographical points given by latitude and longitude, which are encoded in the URI of an input entity. Resolving such an input URI returns a description of the corresponding point, which relates it to Wikipedia articles about geographical features which are nearby.*

Defining that the URI of a LIDS call identifies an input entity is an important design decision. Compared to the alternative – directly identifying output entities with service call URIs – identifying input entities has the following advantages:

- the link between input and output data is made explicit;

- one input entity (e.g., a geographical point) can be related to several results (e.g., Wikipedia articles);

- the absence of results can be easily represented by a description without further links;

- the input entity has a constant meaning although data can be dynamic (e.g., the input entity still represents the same point, even though a subsequent service call may relate the input entity to new or updated Wikipedia articles).

More formally we characterise a LIDS by:

- Linked Data Service endpoint: *ep*, an HTTP URI.

- Local identifier *i* for the input entity of the service.

- Inputs X_i: names of parameters.

The URI of a service call for a parameter assignment μ (mapping X_i to corresponding values) is constructed in the following way (where addition is understood as string concatenation and subtraction removes the corresponding suffix if it matches):

$$uri(ep, X_i, \mu) = ep + "?" + \sum_{x \in X_i}(x + "=" + \mu(x) + "\&") - "\&".$$

Additionally we introduce an abbreviated URI schema that can be used if there is only one required parameter (i.e. $|X_i| = 1, X_i = \{x\}$):

$$uri(ep, X_i, \mu) = ep + "/" + \mu(x).$$

Please note that the above definition coincides with typical Linked Data URIs. We define the input entity that is described by the output of a service call as

$$inp(ep, X_i, \mu, i) = uri(ep, X_i, \mu) + "\#" + i.$$

Example 23. *We illustrate the principle using the openlids.org wrapper for GeoNames[3]* `findNearbyWikipedia`. *The wrapper is a LIDS, defined by:*

- *endpoint ep =* `gw:findNearbyWikipedia`*;*

- *local identifier i =* `point`*;*

- *inputs X_i =* {`lat, lng`}.

For a binding μ = {`lat` $\mapsto$ 52.4536, `lng` $\mapsto$ −1.9383} *the URI for the service call is* `gw:findNearbyWikipedia?lat=52.4536&lng=-1.9383` *and returns the following description:*

```
@prefix dbpedia: <http://dbpedia.org/resource/> .
@prefix geo: <http://www.w3.org/2003/01/geo/wgs84_pos#> .

gw:findNearbyWikipedia?lat=52.4536&lng=-1.9383#point
  foaf:based_near dbpedia:Centre_for_Human_Reproductive_Science;
  ...
  foaf:based_near dbpedia:University_Birmingham_railway_station.

dbpedia:Centre_for_Human_Reproductive_Science
    geo:lat "52.453";
    geo:long "-1.9388".

dbpedia:University_%28Birmingham%29_railway_station
    geo:lat "52.451";
    geo:long "-1.936".
...
```

---

[3] `http://km.aifb.kit.edu/services/geonameswrap/`, abbreviated as `gw`.

6.1.3 Describing Linked Data Services

In this section, we define an abstract model of LIDS descriptions.

Definition 13. *A LIDS description consists of a tuple* (ep, CQ_i, T_o, i) *where ep denotes the LIDS endpoint,* $CQ_i = (X_i, T_i)$ *a conjunctive query, with* X_i *the input parameters and* T_i *the basic graph pattern specifying the input to the service,* T_o *a basic graph pattern describing the output data of the service, and i the local identifier for the input entity.*

The meaning of ep and X_i were already explained in the previous section. We define X_i to be the selected variables of a conjunctive query, whose body specifies the required relation between the input parameters. T_o specifies the minimum output that is returned by the service for valid input parameters. More formally:

- $\mu \in \mathcal{M}^4$ is a valid input, if $\mathsf{dom}(\mu) = X_i$;

- for a valid μ, resolving $uri(ep, X_i, \mu)$ returns a graph

$$D_o \supseteq \{T' \subseteq D_{impl} \mid \exists \mu \in \mathcal{M}.\mu(T_o) = T'\},$$

where D_{impl} is the potentially infinite virtual data set representing the information provided by the LIDS.

Example 24. *We describe the* findNearbyWikipedia *openlids.org wrapper service as* (ep, CQ_i, T_o, i) *with:*

$$ep = \texttt{gw : findNearbyWikipedia}$$
$$CQ_i = (\{\texttt{lat}, \texttt{lng}\}, \{\texttt{?point geo : lat ?lat . ?point geo : long ?lng}\})$$
$$T_o = \{\texttt{?point foaf : based\_near ?feature}\}$$
$$i = \texttt{point}$$

Relation to Source Descriptions in Information Integration Systems

Note that the LIDS descriptions can be transformed to source descriptions with limited access patterns, in a Local-as-View (LaV) data integration approach [Hal01]. With LaV, the data accessible through a service is described as a view in terms of a global schema. The variables of a view's head predicate that have to be bound in order to retrieve tuples from the view are prefixed with a \$. For a LIDS description (ep, CQ_i, T_o, i), we can construct the LaV description:

$$ep(\$I_1, \dots, \$I_k, O_1 \dots, O_m) \; :- \; p_1^i(\dots), \dots, p_n^i(\dots), p_1^o(\dots), \dots, p_l^o(\dots).$$

Where $CQ_i = (X_i, T_i)$, with $X_i = \{I_1, \dots, I_k\}$ and $T_i = \{(s_1^i, p_1^i, o_1^i), \dots, (s_n^i, p_n^i, o_n^i)\}$, $T_o = \{(s_1^o, p_1^o, o_1^o), \dots, (s_l^o, p_l^o, o_l^o)\}$, and $\mathsf{vars}(T_o) \setminus \mathsf{vars}(T_i) = \{O_1, \dots, O_m\}$.

We propose for LIDS descriptions the separation of input and output conditions for three reasons: (i) the output of a LIDS corresponds to an RDF graph as described by the output pattern, not to tuples as it is common in LaV approaches, (ii) it is easier to understand for users, and (iii) it is better suited for the interlinking algorithm as shown in Section 6.1.4.

---

[4] $\mathcal{M}$ is the set of all variables bindings. See Definition 5 on page 31.

Describing LIDS using RDF and SPARQL Graph Patterns

In the following we present how LIDS descriptions can be represented in RDF, thus enabling that LIDS descriptions can be published as Linked Data. The basic format is as follows (unqualified strings consisting only of capital letters are placeholders and explained below):

```
@prefix lids: <http://openlids.org/vocab#>

LIDS a lids:LIDS;
    lids:lids_description [
        lids:endpoint ENDPOINT ;
        lids:service_entity ENTITY ;
        lids:input_bgp INPUT ;
        lids:output_bgp OUTPUT ;
        lids:required_vars VARS ] .
```

The RDF description is related to our abstract description formalism in the following way:

- LIDS is a resource representing the described Linked Data service;

- ENDPOINT is a URI corresponding to ep;

- ENTITY is the name of the entity i;

- INPUT and OUTPUT are basic graph patterns encoded as a string using SPARQL syntax. INPUT is mapped to T_i and OUTPUT is mapped to T_o.

- VARS is a string of required variables separated by blanks, which is mapped to X_i.

From this mapping, we can construct an abstract LIDS description $(ep, (X_i, T_i), T_o, i)$ for the service identified by LIDS.

Example 25. *In the following we show the RDF representation of the formal LIDS description from Example 24:*

```
:GeowrapNearbyWikipedia a lids:LIDS;
  lids:lids_description [
    lids:endpoint
      <http://km.aifb.kit.edu/services/geonameswrap/findNearbyWikipedia>;
    lids:service_entity "point" ;
    lids:input_bgp "?point a Point . ?point geo:lat ?lat .
                                    ?point geo:long ?long" ;
    lids:output_bgp "?point foaf:based_near ?feature" ;
    lids:required_vars "lat long" ] .
```

In future, we expect a standardised RDF representation of SPARQL, which does not rely on string encoding of basic graph patterns. One such candidate is the SPIN SPARQL Syntax[5], which is part of the SPARQL Inferencing Notation (SPIN)[6]. We are planning to re-use such a standardised RDF representation of basic graph patterns and variables in future versions of the LIDS description model.

---

[5]http://spinrdf.org/sp.html
[6]http://spinrdf.org/

6.1.4 Algorithm for Interlinking Data with LIDS

In the following, we describe how existing data sets can be automatically enriched with links to LIDS, which can happen in different settings. Consider for example:

- processing of a static data set, inserting links to LIDS and storing the new data;

- an Linked Data server that that dynamically adds links to LIDS;

- a data browser that augments retrieved data with data retrieved from LIDS.

We present an algorithm that, based on a fixed local dataset, determines and invokes the appropriate LIDS and adds the output to the local dataset.

Given an RDF graph G and a LIDS description $l = (ep, CQ_i = (X_i, T_i), T_o, i)$ the following formula defines a set of entities in G and equivalent entities that are inputs for the LIDS (+ is again string concatenation):

$$equivs_{G,l} = \left\{(\mu(i), uri(ep, X_i, \mu) + \text{"\#"} + i) \mid \mu \in \mathsf{bindings}(T_i, G)\right\}.$$

The obtained equivalences can be either used to immediately resolve the LIDS URIs and add the data to G, or to make the equivalences explicit in G, for example, by adding the following triples to G:

$$\{x_1 \ \mathtt{owl:sameAs} \ x_2 \mid (x_1, x_2) \in equivs_{G,l}\}.$$

We illustrate the algorithm using LIDS versions of the Flickr API and the GeoNames services. The example and the algorithm are visualised in Figure 6.1. Consider a photo #photo537 for which the Flickr returns an RDF graph with latitude and longitude properties:

```
#photo537 rdfs:label "The Prince of Wales ...";
          geo:lat  "52.453616";
          geo:long "-1.938303".
```

In the first step, the data is matched against the available LIDS descriptions (for brevity we assume a static set of LIDS descriptions) and a set of bindings are derived. Further processing uses the GeoNames LIDS which accepts latitude/longitude as input. After constructing a URI which represents the service entity, an equivalence (owl:sameAs) link is created between the original entity #photo537 and the service entity:

```
#photo537 owl:sameAs
          gw:findWikipediaNearby?lat=52.453616&long=-1.938303#point.
```

Next, the data from the service entity URI can be retrieved, to obtain the following data:

```
@prefix dbpedia: <http://dbpedia.org/resource/> .
gw:findWikipediaNearby?lat=52.453616&lng=-1.938303#point
          foaf:based_near foaf:based_near dbpedia:FertCentre
          foaf:based_near dbpedia:UniStation.
...
```

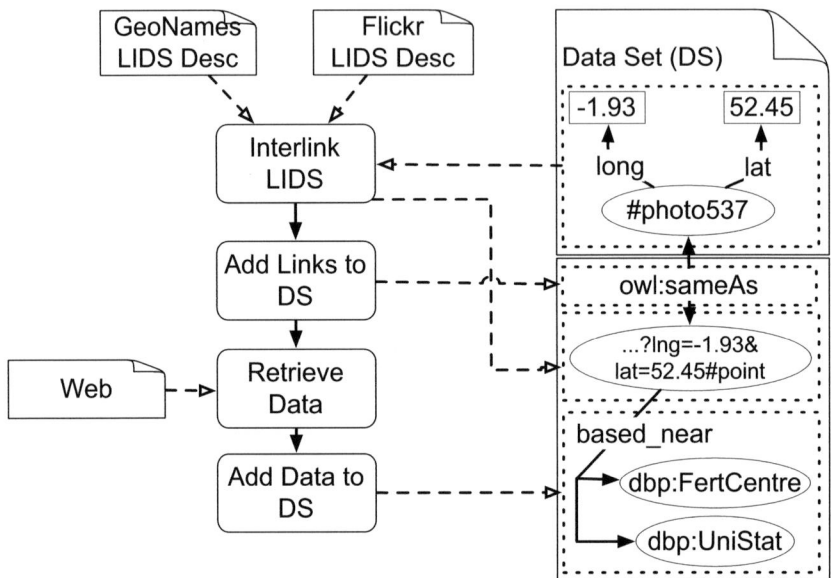

Figure 6.1: Interlinking example for GeoNames LIDS

Please observe that by equating the URI from the input data with the LIDS entity URI, we essentially add the returned foaf:based_near statements to #photo537. Should the database underlying the service change, a lookup on the LIDS entity URI returns the updated data which can then be integrated. As such, entity URIs can be linked in the same manner as plain Linked Data URIs.

6.2 Completeness Notions for Linked Data Query Processing

We present several completeness classes that rigorously define which sources may contribute to an answer to Linked Data queries. We explain our approach with the help of an example, which is described in Section 6.2.1. In Section 6.2.2, we extend and generalise the idea of authoritative sources from [HHP08], which we use to define completeness for single triple patterns in Section 6.2.3. We consider entire queries in Section 6.2.4 and define three completeness classes for triple patterns and conjunctive queries: one that considers the entire web, one that considers documents in the surrounding of sources derived from the

Table 6.1: Example RDF graph about eight persons distributed over six documents.

No	Triple			Document	Triples
1	ezII:i	p:hasChild	charles:i .	ezII	1, 2, 3
2	ezII:i	p:hasChild	ezII:Ed .	charles	4,5
3	ezII:Ed	p:hasChild	ezII:Louise .	harry	-
4	charles:i	p:hasChild	william:i .	william	-
5	charles:i	p:hasChild	harry:i .	jack	6, 7, 8
6	jack:i	p:hasChild	jack:John .	p	-
7	ezII:i	p:hasChild	jack:i .		
8	ezII:Ed	p:hasChild	harry:i .		

query and one that considers documents based on the query execution. Finally, we show in Section 6.2.5 how the completeness classes are related to each other.

Please note that our results apply to both web and intranet environments, as long as data providers follow Linked Data principles. Our results also apply to Dataspaces [FHM05] without central registries.

6.2.1 Example

We begin with an example of an RDF graph and a query over that graph. We chose simplified identifiers and graphs restricted to representing the "has child" relationship for brevity. The example is structured along the royal family but only a subset of the existing relations are represented.

Example 26. *Figure 6.2 shows an example RDF graph with triples and the documents in which they are contained are listed in Table 6.1. Note that in our simplified example some documents (e.g.,* harry*) are empty, but in a real dataset the documents would contain further triples specifying e.g. the name and spouse of* harry:i*. We represent the "has child" relationship as* p:hasChild*. We use the labels* ezII:i, charles:i, harry:i, william:i, ezII:Ed, ezII:Louise, jack:i, *and* jack:John *to denote the person resources, and numbers* $1 \ldots 8$ *to denote triples. Now, assume the query* Q_{ex} *depicted in Figure 6.3 consisting of the triple patterns listed in Table 6.2. The overall goal is to find bindings μ to the variables in the query.*

A system with access to the entire graph in Figure 6.2 could evaluate the query using standard query processing techniques. However, on the Linked Data web, the graph is distributed across multiple sources in form of web-accessible RDF files (henceforth called documents).

The identifiers ezII, charles, harry, william, jack, p represent documents; the right part of Table 6.1 lists the six documents and the triples they contain. Please note that the assignment is rather arbitrary and can differ, as maintainers of documents are free to decide which triples they host. One thing we can assume, though, is that identifiers are associated

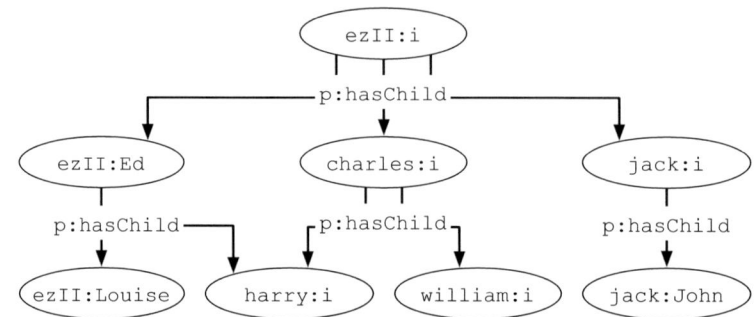

Figure 6.2: Visualisation of example RDF graph.

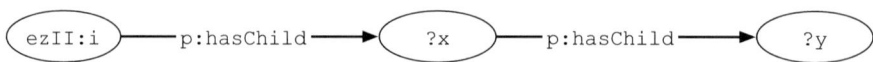

Figure 6.3: Visualisation of example query for grandchildren of Elizabeth II

with documents (as mandated by the Linked Data principles [BL06]). Thus, we can assume that we get some triples with identifier ezII:i when looking up the corresponding document ezII (and similarly, ezII:Ed for ezII and charles:i for charles, jack:i for jack).

Now, to answer the query, we perform a lookup on ezII, which results in triples 1 - 3 from which we can derive bindings ezII:Ed and charles:i for ?x, and ezII:Louise for ?y. Next, we perform a lookup on charles which returns triples 4 and 5, from which we can derive william:i and harry:i for ?y. As a result, we arrive at the bindings as depicted in Table 6.3. Please note that the bindings {?x ↦ jack:i, ?y ↦ jack:John} (via source jack) and {?x ↦ ezII:Ed, ?y ↦ harry:i} (via source jack) cannot be reached via link traversal.

The example illustrates a couple of issues: first, a link-traversal algorithm cannot discover documents which are not referenced in any already known document. Second, assuming a larger graph, the link traversal process could actually go on for a long time, as more and more new documents are discovered and accessed. In the rest of this section we show how to decide which subset of documents should be accessed to derive answers to queries.

Table 6.2: Example query for grandchildren of Elizabeth II

No	Triple pattern
1	ezII:i p:hasChild ?x .
2	?x p:hasChild ?y .

Table 6.3: Bindings for variables in Q_{ex} with contributing triples and documents.

μ	$\mu(?x)$	$\mu(?y)$	Triples	Documents
μ_1	ezII:Ed	ezII:Louise	2, 3	ezII
μ_2	charles:i	william:i	1, 4	ezII, charles
μ_3	charles:i	harry:i	1, 5	ezII, charles

6.2.2 Authoritative Documents

We introduce the notion of authoritative document for an identifier, that is, we define which information resource can talk authoritatively about a specific identifier. In other words, we restrict the documents which can make statements containing certain identifiers. Our notion is an extension and generalisation of the idea of authoritative source from [HHP08].

The notion of authoritativeness is important on the web, which consists of a motley selection of data sources, some of which may provide questionable information. Also, we use authoritativeness to specify which information resources are necessary to have complete information about an identifier.

Definition 14 (Authoritative Document). *Document u talks with authority about a triple t if there is a correspondence between u and any identifier from t, i.e., $co(s(t)) = u$, $co(p(t)) = u$ or $co(o(t)) = u$. We call a document u to be subject-authoritative for t if $co(s(t)) = u$ (s-auth in short). Analogously, p-auth and o-auth relate a document to the identifier of a predicate or object.*

Example 27. *Consider the triples and documents from Figure 6.2. Document* ezII *talks with authority about triples 1-3, namely s-auth for 1-3 and o-auth for triples 2 and 3. Document* jack *contains triple 8 using identifiers* ezII:Ed*,* p:hasChild*, and* ezII:Louise *without authority, as there is no connection in* co *between any of the identifiers and* jack*.*

Definition 15 (Authority Types). *We can have atomic authority types s, p, or o denoting whether a triple has been stated with authority regarding its subject, predicate or object. We can combine atomic authority types using conjunction and disjunction to arrive at the set of possible authority types $\mathcal{A} = \{\perp, s, p, o, s \vee p, s \vee o, p \vee o, s \vee p \vee o, s \wedge p, s \wedge o, p \wedge o, s \wedge p \wedge o\}$. Note that $\perp$ denotes no authority.*

Example 28. *In the following, we explain two exemplary authority types[7]:*

- *A triple t is stated $s \wedge o$-auth, if both $t \in \text{deref}(co(s(t)))$ and $t \in \text{deref}(co(o(t)))$.*

- *A triple t is stated $s \vee p \vee o$-auth, if $t \in \text{deref}(co(s(t)))$ or $t \in \text{deref}(co(p(t)))$ or $t \in \text{deref}(co(o(t)))$.*

Note that it would be possible to mix the conjunctive and disjunctive authority types: E.g. a triple t stated with $p \vee (s \wedge o)$ authority must be contained either in $\text{deref}(co(p(t)))$ or in

---

[7]deref denotes a IRI lookup and returns the corresponding RDF graph. See Definition 2 on page 30.

both deref(co($s(t)$)) *and* deref(co($o(t)$)). We disregard mixed authority types because: (i) the consequences of mixing conjunctive and disjunctive authorities create much confusion, and (ii) we found no practical examples requiring them.

Based on the notion of authority types we introduce a modified deref function, the derefa function, which only selects triples that satisfy specified authority types.

Definition 16 (Authoritative Lookup). *The function* derefa: $I_I \times \mathcal{A} \mapsto \mathcal{G}$ *models a Linked Data lookup and returns the graph represented in an information resource while applying the specified authority types, i.e., filtering the triples which do not adhere to the authority criteria. Please note that* derefa *might perform additional lookups if those are required for clarifying the authoritativeness of a triple.*

Example 29. *The function* derefa(charles, $s \wedge o$) *involves* deref(charles), *yielding the triples* charles:i p:hasChild william:i *and* charles:i p:hasChild harry:i *, and subsequently requiring also* deref(co(william:i)), *respectively* deref(co(harry:i)) *to verify that the triples also occur in* william, *respectively in* harry *(which is not the case in our example graph).*

In case $a = \perp$ the results for deref and derefa coincide.

We now give examples in which some of the authoritativeness types are useful:

- $a = s$: useful if attributes of entities and their links to other entities should only be described by one authoritative source. E.g., a document authoritative for a given foaf:Person should be the only one who can state the person's foaf:name and foaf:knows properties.

- $a = o$: useful to restrict membership in protected classes. E.g., only the document co(ex:TrustedPerson) may specify members of ex:TrustedPerson.

- $a = p$: useful to restrict the usage of protected properties. E.g., only the document co(ex:trust_rating) may specify triples with a ex:trust_rating property.

- $a = s \vee o$, respectively $a = s \vee p \vee o$: a triple can be stated by the corresponding document of the triple's subject or object (or predicate, respectively). Gives certain trust guarantees as only triples from corresponding documents are considered.

- $a = s \wedge o$, respectively $a = s \wedge p \wedge o$: a triple must be stated by all corresponding information resources of the triple's subject and object (and predicate, respectively), which is stronger than the disjunctive variant. Can be useful as assumption in closed data webs, when mandating every document contains complete information about the identifiers used in the document, allowing to get complete description for any IRI by dereferencing that IRI, independent of the position in a triple.

The different authority types specify the documents that can contribute certain triples to query results, thus paving the way towards defining completeness.

6.2.3 Authoritative Documents for Triple Patterns

We now show which documents are relevant to a triple pattern p under a specified authority type a. If we assure that these documents are dereferenced, we can state that p has been completely answered under a. Based on complete answers to single triple patterns, we define complete answers to Basic Graph Pattern queries in Section 6.2.4.

Consider a triple pattern p for which we want to get bindings. In Linked Data query evaluation, the query processor has to dereference (lookup) IRIs which yields data, which in turn is matched with the triple pattern to ultimately yield bindings.

Thus, to get all possible bindings on the web, we would need to get all information sources $\mathcal{I}_I$ on the web and match the resulting graphs to the triple pattern p. However, based on the notion of authoritative source, we can answer a triple pattern p completely, given a defined authority type.

Example 30. *Consider the triple pattern p_1 = `ezII:i p:hasChild ?x`. If we restrict the answers to be derived from s-auth triples, we are sure to get all those triple if we perform a lookup on `ezII:i`, that is, $\mathsf{derefa}(\mathsf{co}(\texttt{ezII:i})), s)$. Thus, we have answered p_1 completely under s-auth assumption.*

We now use the definition of $\mathcal{A}$ to derive, given a triple pattern and authority specification, the subset of $\mathcal{I}$ we have to dereference to find the complete set of bindings for the pattern.

Definition 17 (Completely Sufficient Documents). *We define $\mathsf{csuff}\colon \mathcal{P} \times \mathcal{A} \mapsto 2^{2^{I \times V}}$, which, given a pattern and an authority type, returns a set of alternative documents sets, each of which is sufficient to completely answer the triple pattern.*

$$
\mathsf{csuff}(t, a) = \begin{cases}
\{\mathcal{I}_I\}, & \text{if } a = \bot \\
\{\{\mathsf{s}(t)\}\}, & \text{if } a = s \\
\{\{\mathsf{p}(t)\}\}, & \text{if } a = p \\
\{\{\mathsf{o}(t)\}\}, & \text{if } a = o \\
\{\{\mathsf{s}(t)\}, \{\mathsf{p}(t)\}\}, & \text{if } a = s \wedge p \\
\{\{\mathsf{s}(t)\}, \{\mathsf{o}(t)\}\}, & \text{if } a = s \wedge o \\
\{\{\mathsf{p}(t)\}, \{\mathsf{o}(t)\}\}, & \text{if } a = p \wedge o \\
\{\{\mathsf{s}(t)\}, \{\mathsf{p}(t)\}, \{p(o)\}\}, & \text{if } a = s \wedge p \wedge o \\
\{\{\mathsf{s}(t), \mathsf{p}(t)\}\}, & \text{if } a = s \vee p \\
\{\{\mathsf{s}(t), \mathsf{o}(t)\}\}, & \text{if } a = s \vee o \\
\{\{\mathsf{p}(t), \mathsf{o}(t)\}\}, & \text{if } a = p \vee o \\
\{\{\mathsf{s}(t), \mathsf{p}(t), \mathsf{o}(t)\}\}, & \text{if } a = s \vee p \vee o
\end{cases}
$$

Note that when no authority type is given ($a = \bot$), we would need to retrieve the set of all documents to arrive at complete answers. There can be several alternatives that are sufficient for completely answering a pattern (see $s \wedge o$ authority), and each alternative can require more than one position (see $s \vee o$ authority).

Example 31. *A triple t stated with $s \wedge o$ authority must be contained in the two graphs* deref(co($s(t)$)) *and* deref(co($o(t)$)). *If we require that triples matching a pattern must be stated with $s \wedge o$ authority, it is sufficient to know the subject or the object position of the pattern, because dereferencing one of them will contain all relevant triples. To check that the found triples are indeed given with $s \wedge o$ authority, one has to check whether dereferencing the other position will also contain the triple, but this is a trivial implementation issue. A triple t stated with $s \vee o$ authority must be contained in either of the two graphs* deref(co($s(t)$)) *or* deref(co($o(t)$)). *If we require that triples matching a pattern must be stated with $s \vee o$ authority, we have to know the subject and object position, because both of them could provide relevant triples when dereferenced.*

If we know that a triple t exists in the documents $\mathcal{I}_I$ under an authority type a, we can infer that t exists in the corresponding document of one IRI of each alternatively sufficient IRI set (denoted as L for aLternative):

$$t \in \mathsf{derefa}(\mathcal{I}_I, a) \rightarrow \forall L \in \mathsf{csuff}(t, a).\exists l \in L.t \in \mathsf{derefa}(\mathsf{co}(l), a).$$

The fact that the triple must be contained in all alternatives may not sound intuitive at first, but every alternative is sufficient to determine whether the triple exists.

Example 32. *Consider the triple pattern p_1 =* ezII:i p:hasChild ?x. *We illustrate the complete answers for p_1 under different authority types:*

- *s-auth:* csuff(p_1, s) = {{ezII:i}}, *so there is only one alternative for completely answering p_1: retrieve the graph* derefa(ezII:i, s), *which results in the following bindings: μ_1 = {?x $\mapsto$* ezII:Ed}, *and μ_2 = {?x $\mapsto$* charles:i}.

- *s $\wedge$ p-auth:* csuff($p_1, s \wedge p$) = {{ezII:i}, {p:hasChild}}, *so to find all bindings for p_1 it is sufficient to retrieve either the graph* derefa(ezII:i, $s \wedge p$) *or the graph* derefa(p:hasChild, $s \wedge p$). *However, both graphs are empty, as there is no triple in* co(p:hasChild) = p *and thus none of the triples in* co(ezII:i) = ezII *is "confirmed", as required by $s \wedge p$ authority. Please note that the invocation of* derefa *may involve additional lookups to ensure that triples adhere to a given authority type. These additional lookups only invalidate existing results but never contribute new ones.*

- *s $\vee$ o-auth:* csuff($p_1, s \vee o$) = {{ezII:i, ?x}}, *so we cannot answer p_1 completely, because there is only one alternative, which would require a binding for ?x.*

One complication arises when all alternatives returned by csuff contain variables instead of IRIs. In this case, the pattern cannot be completely answered under the authority scheme. However, if we have conjunctions of several triple patterns, another pattern may be used to find complete bindings for the variables in a sufficient alternative, thus making the conjunction completely answerable. We define completeness for such conjunctions in the next section.

6.2.4 Completeness of Basic Graph Patterns

In the following, we address the problem of answering queries consisting of several patterns (so-called Basic Graph Patterns). A query Q consisting of several patterns $tp_0, tp_1, \ldots tp_n$ can be completely answered if the corresponding required positions of a triple pattern are bound either by a constant or by a variable in another completely answerable pattern in the query. As discussed before, different authority types are suitable for different triples, thus we define a mapping for assigning a required authority to every pattern in a query.

Definition 18 (Authority Mapping). *We define a mapping* $\alpha\colon Q \mapsto \mathcal{A}$ *that assigns triple patterns in Q to different authority types. The set of all such mappings is denoted as $\mathcal{AU}$.*

Definition 19 (Authoritative Query Bindings). *We extend the* bindings$\colon Q \times 2^I \mapsto 2^M$ *function to return only bindings satisfying an authority mapping* α: bindings$^\alpha(Q, I) = \{\mu \in M \mid \mathrm{dom}(\mu) = \mathrm{vars}(Q) \wedge \forall p \in Q . \mu(p) \in \cup_{u \in I}\mathrm{derefa}(u, \alpha(p))\}$.

We define completeness via a set s of documents that have to be retrieved to completely answer a query Q, i.e., a set s is complete for an authority mapping α, if bindings$^\alpha(Q, s)$ contains all desired query results. A natural requirement for such a set s of documents is that it holds the same results for Q as the entire Linked Data web, i.e. bindings$^\alpha(Q, s) = $ bindings$^\alpha(Q, \mathcal{I}_I)$. This is however in general not possible to check without complete knowledge of deref($\mathcal{I}_I$), due to the open world assumption.

As it is infeasible to materialise the entire Linked Data web, i.e., deref($\mathcal{I}_I$), and thus instead we are searching for a subset $s \subset \mathcal{I}_I$, where $|s| \ll |\mathcal{I}_I|$, which can be accessed at query time and so that deref(s) contains sufficient information to answer the query Q.

Thus, we define that a set s of documents is complete for query Q given an authority mapping α, if complete(Q, α) $\subseteq s$, where complete is one of the different completeness classes introduced in the following:

- web-complete wc$\colon Q \times \mathcal{AU} \mapsto 2^{\mathcal{I}_I}$ which is mainly of theoretical interest when considering the web, but possibly applicable to controlled environments such as intranets;

- seed-complete sc$\colon Q \times \mathcal{AU} \mapsto 2^{\mathcal{I}_I}$ which is practical and a pragmatic solution, if no authority restrictions are given;

- query-reachable-complete qrc$\colon Q \times \mathcal{AU} \mapsto 2^{\mathcal{I}_I}$ which defines complete results under given authority types for a certain class of queries.

We now formally define the three different completeness classes and then discuss the relationships between the different notions in Section 6.2.5.

Web-complete Set (WC)

The web-complete set gives the results of the query, when it is evaluated over the whole Linked Data web, i.e. $\mathcal{I}_I$. However it is sufficient to evaluate over every document that helps to produce a result binding, (could also be a duplicate of a binding that can be produced without it). Without authority restrictions, every document can contain arbitrary triples, thus there is no other way of determining the set than accessing every $u \in \mathcal{I}_I$ or having some form of index structure, which has accessed every such u before.

Definition 20. *With authority restriction, we define web-complete (WC) as the set of documents that contain a triple, which is part of a result when evaluating Q over $\mathcal{I}_I$.*

$$\mathsf{wc}(Q, \alpha) = \{u \in \mathcal{I}_I \mid \exists \mu \in \mathsf{bindings}^{\alpha}(Q, \mathcal{I}_I).$$
$$\exists p \in Q.\, \mu(p) \in \mathsf{derefa}(u, \alpha(p))\}.$$

Example 33. *Considering our running example of query Q_{ex}, we get depending on the two authority mappings α_1 and α_2:*

- *Let $\alpha_1(p) = \bot$, for $p \in Q_{ex}$:* $\mathsf{wc}(Q_{ex}, \alpha_1) = \{\mathtt{ezII}, \mathtt{charles}, \mathtt{jack}\}$.

- *Let $\alpha_2(p) = s$, for $p \in Q_{ex}$:* $\mathsf{wc}(Q_{ex}, \alpha_2) = \{\mathtt{ezII}, \mathtt{charles}\}$.

Seed-complete Set (SC)

The seed-complete set consists of all documents that can be reached via following triple paths of maximum length of the query beginning from triples in the documents identified by the IRIs in the query. The intuition is a traversal of $\mathcal{I}_I$ to get the documents that are up to n hops away.

In the size-restricted seed-complete set, we fix n to $|Q|$, i.e., the number of patterns in the query Q. In an alternative, length-restricted seed-complete set (which we leave open for future work), we can fix n to the depth of the query, i.e., the length of longest path in the query, starting from a constant.

As there can be several different IRIs in the query and from each IRI there can start several paths of triples, we possibly end up with forests, consisting of several trees starting in different triples.

Definition 21 (Forest). *A triple forest grounded in a set of seed IRIs is a list of triples, where each triple is either in the seed IRIs, or in the corresponding document of a resource occurring in a previous triple in the list. The function* $\mathsf{forests}\colon 2^{\mathcal{I}_I} \times \mathbb{N} \mapsto 2^{\mathcal{T}^*}$ *returns all forests of triples of size up to n, starting with the triples in the seed IRIs s:*

$$\mathsf{forests}(s, n) = \bigcup_{j \in [1..n]} \{(t_1, \ldots, t_j) \in \mathcal{T}^j \mid \forall i \in [1..j].\quad t_i \in \bigcup_{u \in s} \mathsf{deref}(u) \vee$$
$$\exists k \in [1..i\text{-}1].t_i \in \bigcup_{u \in \mathsf{iris}(t_k)} \mathsf{deref}(u)\}.$$

Definition 22. *We define the seed completeness set (SC) to contain all documents corresponding to IRIs in the forests grounded in the query's IRIs:*

$$\mathsf{sc}(Q, \alpha) = \mathsf{co}(\mathsf{iris}(\mathsf{forests}(\mathsf{iris}(Q), |Q|))).$$

Example 34. *Considering our running example of query* Q_{ex}:

$$\text{iris}(Q_{ex}) = \{ezII:i, p:hasChild\}$$
$$|Q_{ex}| = 2$$
$$\text{forests}(\text{iris}(Q_{ex}), |Q_{ex}|) = \{(t_1), (t_1, t_1), (t_1, t_2), (t_1, t_3), (t_1, t_4), (t_1, t_5),$$
$$(t_2), (t_2, t_1), (t_2, t_2), (t_2, t_3),$$
$$(t_3), (t_3, t_1), (t_3, t_2), (t_3, t_3)\}.$$
$$\text{sc}(Q_{ex}, \alpha) = \{ezII, \texttt{charles}, \texttt{harry}, \texttt{william}\},$$

where t_i *stands for triple number i from the running example (see Section 6.2.1).*

Instead of iris(Q) we might provide user-specified additional seed IRIs, and instead of the size of the query $|Q|$ we might provide a user-specified length.

Query-reachable-complete Set (QRC)

We first define the notion of completely answerable queries for a given authority mapping α. Based on this notion, we specify the set of documents required to answer such a query completely in the sense of obtaining the same results, as when the query would be evaluated over the web-complete set. The equivalence of the result sets is shown in Section 6.2.5.

Definition 23 (Completely-answerable Query). *A query is completely answerable if the triple patterns can be brought into an order, such that for each triple pattern p, there exists a set of RDF terms sufficient to completely answer p, where each term is either an IRI or a variable occurring in a previous pattern. The predicate* caq^{α} *defines the completely answerable property of a query under an authority mapping* α:

$$\text{caq}^{\alpha}(Q) \leftrightarrow (|Q| = 1 \wedge Q = \{p\} \wedge \exists L \in \text{csuff}(p, \alpha(p)).\forall l \in L.l \in \mathcal{I}_N) \vee$$
$$(|Q| > 1 \wedge \exists Q_n, Q_1.Q_n \cup Q_1 = Q \wedge Q_n \cap Q_1 = \emptyset \wedge \text{caq}^{\alpha}(Q_n) \wedge Q_1 = \{p\} \wedge$$
$$\exists L \in \text{csuff}(p, \alpha(p)).\forall l \in L.l \in \mathcal{I} \vee l \in \text{vars}(Q_n)).$$

In other (recursive) words: a query Q is completely answerable if either Q is of size 1 and there exists a set of sufficient terms which are all IRIs in Q, or one can remove a pattern p from the query, such that the resulting query Q_n *is completely answerable, and p has a set of required terms which are either IRIs or variables bound by query* Q_n.

An IRI must be in the query-reachable-complete set if it occurs in a forest, starting in the IRIs of the query, which is a result for a completely answerable subquery of the original query.

Definition 24 (Completely Answerable Subqueries). *The function* $\text{csq}^{\alpha}: Q \mapsto 2^Q$ *returns all completely-answerable subqueries of a query:*

$$\text{csq}^{\alpha}(Q) = \{Q' \subseteq Q \mid \text{caq}^{\alpha}(Q')\}.$$

The forests, which are results for a completely answerable subquery of Q are defined by the function qforests$^\alpha$ as a subset of all forests starting in the IRIs contained in the query:

$$\text{qforests}^\alpha(Q) = \{F \in \text{forests}(\text{co}(\text{iris}(Q)), |Q|) \mid \exists Q' \in \text{csq}^\alpha(Q) \wedge \exists \mu \in \mathcal{M}.\mu(Q') = F\}.$$

Definition 25. *We define the query-reachable-complete (QRC) set, to contain all documents corresponding to IRIs in the forests that produce bindings for a completely answerable subquery of Q:*

$$\text{qrc}(Q, \alpha) = \text{co}(\text{iris}(\text{qforests}^\alpha(Q))).$$

Example 35. *Considering our running example of query Q_{ex}, we get for α, where $\alpha(p) = s$, for all $p \in Q_{ex}$:*

$$\text{csq}^\alpha(Q_{ex}) = \{Q_{ex}, \{(ezII\!:\!i, p\!:\!hasChild, ?x)\}\}$$
$$\text{qforests}^\alpha(Q_{ex}) = \{(t_1), (t_1, t_4), (t_1, t_5), (t_2), (t_2, t_3)\}$$
$$\text{qrc}(Q_{ex}, \alpha) = \{ezII, charles, harry, william\},$$

where t_i stands for triple number i from the running example (see Section 6.2.1). We can see that $\text{wc}(Q_{ex}, \alpha) \subset \text{qrc}(Q_{ex}, \alpha)$, meaning that the query reachable set produces all bindings available in the web under the authority mapping α. In Section 6.2.5 we show this in general for all completely answerable queries.

6.2.5 Relations Between Completeness Classes

In the following, we show the relation between the different completeness classes.

Theorem 2. *QRC results are a subset of SC results:* $\text{qrc}(Q, \alpha) \subseteq \text{sc}(Q, \alpha)$.

Proof. Theorem 2 is obvious from the definitions of qrc and sc, as $\text{qforests}^\alpha(Q) \subseteq \text{forests}(\text{co}(\text{iris}(Q)), |Q|))$. □

Theorem 3. *SC query results are a subset of WC results:* $\text{bindings}^\alpha(Q, \text{sc}(Q, \alpha)) \subseteq \text{bindings}^\alpha(Q, \text{wc}(Q, \alpha))$.

Proof. Theorem 3 is obvious from the definition, as web complete is defined to contain all bindings, and thus seed complete cannot contain more bindings. □

Theorem 4. *For a query Q that is completely answerable under an authority mapping α, the bindings for query reachable complete and web complete coincide:* $\text{bindings}^\alpha(Q, \text{qrc}(Q, \alpha)) = \text{bindings}^\alpha(Q, \text{wc}(Q, \alpha))$.

Proof. We proof the equivalence of the sets, by showing their mutual containment:
(1) $\text{bindings}^\alpha(Q, \text{qrc}(Q, \alpha)) \subseteq \text{bindings}^\alpha(Q, \text{wc}(Q, \alpha))$
follows from the definition: web completeness means that every (in this case α-authoritative) result is found.
(2) $\text{bindings}^\alpha(Q, \text{wc}(Q, \alpha)) \subseteq \text{bindings}^\alpha(Q, \text{qrc}(Q, \alpha))$

is shown by induction on the query size. As bindings is monotonic over the set of documents, we reduce this case to showing that $\mathsf{wc}(Q, \alpha) \subseteq \mathsf{qrc}(Q, \alpha)$, if $\mathsf{caq}^\alpha(Q)$.

Induction start for a query Q of size 1:

from $\mathsf{caq}^\alpha(Q) \wedge |Q| = 1 \wedge u \in \mathsf{wc}(Q, \alpha)$ follows that there exists a binding μ for Q over $\mathcal{I}_I$, which maps the single triple pattern $p \in Q$ to a triple from u: $\exists \mu \in \mathsf{bindings}^\alpha(Q, \mathcal{I}_I).\mu(p) \in \mathsf{derefa}(u, \alpha(p))$. This implies that $u \in \mathsf{co}(\mathsf{iris}(\mu(p)))$, for $\alpha(p) \neq \bot$, which is ruled out by the definition of caq. Furthermore, we know that $(\mu(p)) \in \mathsf{forests}(\mathsf{co}(\mathsf{iris}(Q)), 1)$, as $\mu(p)$ is a query answer to $Q = \{p\}$, and p must be completely answerable, given that $\mathsf{caq}^\alpha(Q)$. It follows, that $(\mu(p)) \in \mathsf{qforests}^\alpha(Q)$ and thus: $u \in \mathsf{qrc}(Q, \alpha)$.

We form the induction hypothesis:

$$\mathsf{caq}^\alpha(Q) \wedge u \in \mathsf{wc}(Q, \alpha) \wedge |Q| = n \to u \in \mathsf{qrc}(Q, \alpha).$$

The inductive step: given $\mathsf{caq}^\alpha(Q) \wedge u \in \mathsf{wc}(Q, \alpha) \wedge |Q| = n + 1$, we can split Q into Q_n and Q_1, such that $Q = Q_n \cup Q_n \wedge Q_n \cap Q_1 = \emptyset \wedge |Q_1| = 1 \wedge \mathsf{caq}^\alpha(Q_n)$ (follows from $\mathsf{caq}^\alpha(Q)$). Accordingly our argument can be split into two cases:

Case (2.1): u is also in the web complete set of Q_n: $\mathsf{caq}^\alpha(Q_n) \wedge |Q_n| = n \wedge u \in \mathsf{wc}(Q_n, \alpha)$. We can use the induction hypothesis and conclude $u \in \mathsf{qrc}(Q_n, \alpha)$ and because the reachable completeness set is monotonic (a larger query still has the smaller query as a subquery), we conclude: $u \in \mathsf{qrc}(Q, \alpha)$.

Case (2.2): u is not in the web complete set of Q_n, thus it must be contributed by a variable binding or a constant in Q_1. Evaluating Q_1 has to be done only for the bindings of Q_n, other results that do not join with the results for Q_n cannot contribute an result for Q. As $\mathsf{caq}^\alpha(Q)$, we know that there exists a set of terms sufficient for completely answering Q_1, in which all terms are either constants or variables already occurring in Q_n. Therefore, we can reduce the case to considering only those $\mu(Q_1)$, where μ is a result binding for Q_n. Thus, $\mu(Q_1)$ is completely answerable, and we can use the induction start:

$\mathsf{caq}^\alpha(\mu(Q_1)) \wedge |Q_1| = 1 \to u \in \mathsf{qrc}(Q_1, \alpha) \to u \in \mathsf{qrc}(Q, \alpha).$ 	□

6.2.6 A Note on owl:sameAs and Query Reachable Completeness

Linked Data builds upon RDF, which lacks data modelling features except for `rdf:type` that relates instances to classes. Additionally some modelling constructs from RDFS and OWL are used, mainly the subclass and subproperty relationships from RDFS, and the `owl:sameAs` relation is popular to interlink different vocabularies and datasets. The property `owl:sameAs` is also used for stating equivalence of entities in datasets and entities provided by LIDS. The implication of a u_1 `owl : sameAs` u_2 statement is that every triple using u_1 (u_2) implies the same triple with u_1 (u_2) replaced by u_2 (u_1). In the following, we briefly discuss the effects on query reachable completeness.

Instead of directly evaluating patterns on the graph consisting of the triples of the dereferenced IRIs, we take the fixed point of applying the following three rules to the graph:

```
?s2 ?p  ?o  :- ?s ?p ?o  ,  ?s owl:sameAs ?s2 .
?s  ?p2 ?o  :- ?s ?p ?o  ,  ?p owl:sameAs ?p2 .
?s  ?p  ?o2 :- ?s ?p ?o  ,  ?o owl:sameAs ?o2 .
```

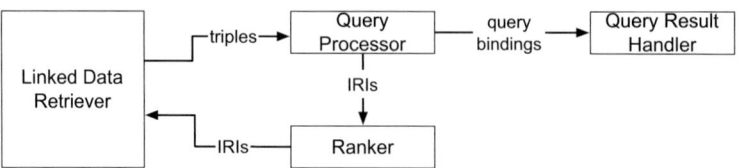

Figure 6.4: General architecture for Linked Data query engines.

The derived triples inherit the authority types of the original triple binding to ?s ?p ?o. It is also possible to restrict the valid authority types for the owl:sameAs pattern.

From the rules above follows that if an IRI u_1 is part of qforests$^{\alpha}(Q)$ and it holds that u_1 owl : sameAs u_2 then also $u_2 \in$ qforests$^{\alpha}(Q)$. Thus, both co(u_1) and co(u_2) are dereferenced for query reachable completeness and all query bindings constituted by triples originally stated using u_1 and triples originally stated using u_2 are found.

6.3 Query Processing over Linked Data and Services

Query processing over Linked Data via following links found in the query and in retrieved data is treated by several works [HBF09, LT10, HHK$^+$10, LT11]. We extend such query engines to support answering several queries at the same time. We show how we can add support for completeness notions, rule-based reasoning, and service integration via appropriate queries and query result handling procedures.

Existing work can be abstracted to a general architecture for Linked Data query engines as visualised in Figure 6.4. The core of the architecture is a query processor, which continuously consumes RDF triples and emits query bindings. Additionally the query processor passes IRIs found in the processed triples to a ranking component. Whether all found IRIs or only a subset are passed to the ranker is system-specific. The ranker decides which of the IRIs should be dereferenced and in which order. The retriever component does the dereferencing by performing the corresponding HTTP lookups or using locally cached data and passes the retrieved triples to the query processor. Query processing is started by dereferencing a set of seed IRIs, usually the IRIs found in the original query, and stopped when the ranker decides that all relevant IRIs have been retrieved, respectively a maximum number of IRIs were retrieved.

Instead of building special mechanisms into the query processor to extract IRIs that should be retrieved, we define queries identifying the relevant IRIs. Our approach has two main advantages: (i) the queries provide a precise definition of the relevant IRIs; and (ii) the query processor can be regarded as a black box that consumes triples and produces query bindings without the need to modify it for passing IRIs to a ranking component.

In the following, we describe the extended architecture for our proposed Linked Data query engine. Figure 6.5 illustrates the architecture.

The queries to identify relevant IRIs are derived from the completeness notion that should be fulfilled. Seed completeness can be reached by selecting all IRIs that bind to the query

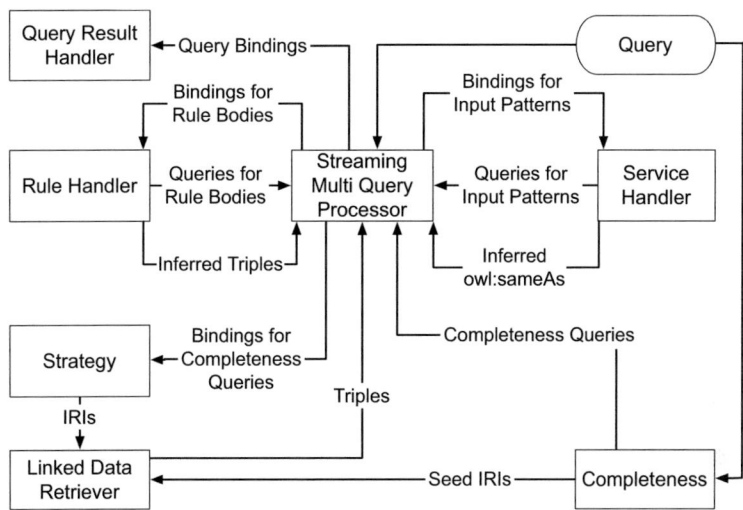

Figure 6.5: Architecture for Linked Data query evaluation with support for completeness, rules, and services.

consisting of the single pattern ?s ?p ?o matching all triples. The seed IRIs are simply the IRIs in the query. The depth restriction that limits the hops from the seed IRIs is enforced by the lookup strategy, which we explain below. For query reachable completeness we define as relevant the IRIs that bind to a variable in one of the completely answerable subqueries of the original query. The seed IRIs are again the IRIs in the query. For (theoretical) web completeness we do not need any query for identifying relevant IRIs, as the seed is already the complete set of information resources on the web ($\mathcal{I}_I$).

In previous approaches the query processor passes found IRIs to the ranking component, which decides which subset of the IRIs should be retrieved. In our approach, the queries derived from the completeness specify a set of IRIs, which all should be retrieved, at least up to a certain depth. To emphasise this difference, we use the term lookup strategy instead of ranker to denote the component in our system that determines the order in which IRIs should be retrieved. Bindings produced by our query processor have provenance information, i.e., for every bound variable we track which information source contained the binding value. Using the source information, we can construct a link graph in the strategy component and implement the strategy as classical graph traversal algorithm, e.g., breadth first search or limited depth first search.

The query processor handles multiple queries at the same time to support the queries identifying the relevant IRIs for a completeness notion. Furthermore, we exploit the multi query capability to implement rule-based reasoning and Linked Data Service (LIDS) integration: both the body of rules and the input patterns of LIDS are basic graph patterns, i.e., queries. Each rule gets a query result handler that instantiates the head of the rule, i.e., replacing the variables in the head pattern using the binding received for the body, and passes the inferred triples as input to the query processor. For services the query result handler builds the IRI of the service call based on the binding for the input pattern and produces a `owl:sameAs` triple between the input entities in the original data and in the result of the service call.

In Section 6.3.1, we describe how we realise the query processor handling multiple queries at the same time. Section 6.3.2 discusses how we can create provenance graphs of query results and thus check the query processing for policy compliance.

6.3.1 Multi Query Streaming Processor

We realise the multi query streaming processor (MQSP) as a multi threaded component with threads for the single pattern dispatcher, each join operator, and each binding consumer of a query. The single pattern dispatcher evaluates all single triple patterns by receiving triples and generating corresponding bindings for the matching patterns. The bindings are pushed to the relevant joins and query binding consumers. The joins are implemented as symmetric hash join operators [WA91].

The query plan is optimised by reusing not only single triple patterns, but also joins across different queries. Especially, when considering query reachable completeness, the lookup queries are always subqueries and thus can be evaluated entirely by listening to join operators, which are needed anyway for the evaluation of the original query.

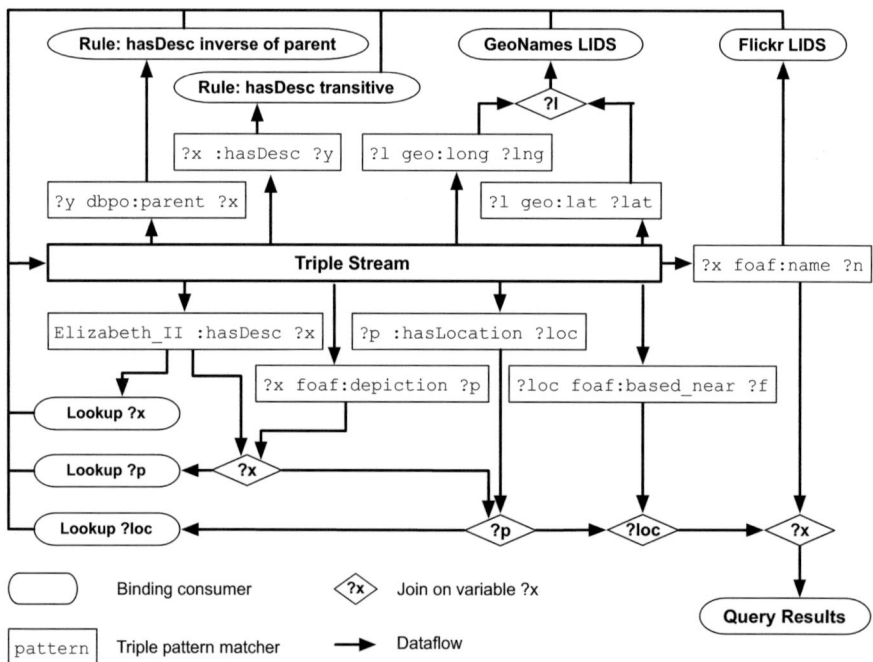

Figure 6.6: Partial Query Plan for Evaluating a User Query with Services and Rules

The dataflow network shown in Figure 6.6 evaluates the query plan generated for Alice's query. We can see that both triple patterns (e.g., `Elizabeth_II :hasDesc ?x`) and joins (e.g., the first join on `?x`) are re-used, i.e., have multiple outgoing edges to binding consumers. The triple stream is initialised by retrieving the Linked Data representation of Queen Elizabeth II from DBpedia, which will yield bindings for the `?y dbpo:parent ?x` triple pattern. The bindings will be consumed by the rule expressing that `hasDesc` is the inverse of `dbpo:parent`. The inferred `hasDesc` triples will be added to the triple stream and now the `Elizabeth_II :hasDesc ?x` pattern will match leading to Linked Data retrievals for the IRIs binding to `?x`. The newly retrieved sources will produce further matches for

- `?y dbpo:parent ?x`: leading to more inferred `hasDesc` triples, which in turn will match for the rule expressing that `hasDesc` is transitive and thus produce more bindings for descendants of Elizabeth II.

- `?x foaf:name ?n`: leading to invocations of the Flickr service, which will return pictures for the Queen's descendants with geographical information that will match as input for the GeoNames service and so forth.

The network will continuously produce new rule-based inferences (the part of the network visualised in the top left corner), new potential service invocations (the part visualised in the top right corner), and most importantly results for Alice's query (the bottom part of the network). Processing will stop when all initial data sources (in this case the DBpedia source about Elizabeth II) and the bindings for the lookup queries (bottom left part of the network) are processed and no new sources to lookup were identified.

6.3.2 Policy-awareness by Tracking Provenance of Query Results

We consider a query result as a derivation of the information sources that were used to produce the result [Spe11b]. A triple (s, p, o) that is retrieved via a Linked Data lookup from information source u is extended to a quad (s, p, o, u) recording the origin of the triple. Whenever a binding for a triple pattern or a set of triple patterns is generated, we not only store the variable and the value to which it is bound, but also the origin of the bound value. A triple produced by a rule is assigned a special information source that is regarded as a derivation of the sources that contributed to the binding fulfilling the rule's condition. For each query result, we can generate a provenance graph, describing the result as an artefact that is generated by a derivation that uses all information sources recorded as origins for the values in the query result. Information sources can have assigned policies as described in Section 4.6. Please note, that results can contain IRIs, e.g., the address of an picture, which can have policies not recorded in the provenance graph of the result; we consider such an IRI and the content obtainable by dereferencing the IRI as different artefacts.

6.4 Related Work

We structure the discussion of related work along the three parts of this chapter: (i) integrating Linked Data and Services, (ii) completeness notions for Linked Data queries, (iii) query processing over Linked Data and services.

Integrating Linked Data and Services

Our work provides an approach to open up data silos for the Web of Data. Previous efforts in this direction are confined to specialised wrappers, for example the book mashup [BCG07]. Other state-of-the-art data integration systems [TFHS10] use wrappers to generate RDF and then publish that RDF online rather than providing access to the services that generate RDF directly. In contrast to these ad-hoc interfaces, we provide a uniform way to construct such interfaces, and thus our work is applicable not only to specific examples but generally to all kinds of data silos. Furthermore, we present a method for formal service description that enables the automatic service integration into existing data sets.

SILK [VBGK09] enables the discovery of links between Linked Data from different sources. Using a declarative language, a developer specifies conditions that data from different sources has to fulfill to be merged, optionally using heuristics in case merging rules can lead to ambiguous results. In contrast, we use Linked Data principles for exposing content of data-providing services, and specify the relationship between existing data and data provided by the service using basic graph patterns. Alternatively, the LIDS approach could also be adapted to use the SILK language for input conditions.

There exists extensive literature about semantic descriptions of web services. We distinguish between two kinds of works: (i) general semantic web service (SWS) frameworks, and (ii) stateless service descriptions.

General SWS approaches include OWL-S [W3C04a] and WSMO [RKL+05] and aim at providing extensive expressivity in order to formalise every kind of web service, including complex business services with state changes and non-trivial choreographies. The expressivity comes at a price: SWS require complex modelling even for simple data services using formalisms that are not familiar to all Semantic Web developers. In contrast, our approach focuses on simple information services and their lightweight integration with Linked Data.

Closely related to our service description formalism are works on semantic descriptions of stateless services (e.g., [ISPG08, HZB+06, ZC06]). Similar to our approach these solutions define service functionality in terms of input and output conditions. Most of them, except [ISPG08], employ proprietary description formalisms. In contrast, our approach relies on standard basic graph patterns. Moreover, our work provides a methodology to provide a Linked Data interface to services.

Norton and Krummenacher propose an alternative approach to integrate Linked Data and services, so-called Linked Open Services (LOS) [NK10]. LOS descriptions also use basic graph patterns for defining service inputs and outputs. One difference is that our work uses name-value pairs for parameters whereas LOS consume RDF. Thus, in contrast to LOS, the LIDS approach allows that service calls are directly linkable from within Linked Data, as service inputs are encoded in the query string of a URI. The RESTdesc approach semantically describes REST services using N3 [VSD⁺11]. While RESTdesc also uses BGPs as part of N3 for input and output description, the described services are not confined to communicate RDF. Thus, RESTdesc services require additional measures to integrate with Linked Data.

Completeness Notions for Linked Data queries

Early work on queries over the web graph include [MM97] and [AV00]. [HBF09] introduced Linked Data query processing via link traversal. Subsequent work [Har11, HHK⁺10, LT10, HMZ10, UHPD12] lack a rigorous specification of termination criteria (some use heuristics). [FGP12] introduces a navigation language, which can be used to specify fragments of the Linked Data graph. However, the navigation language has different characteristics than our query language based on BGPs and thus the fragment specifications are not directly comparable to our completeness notions. Hartig analyses the computability of SPARQL queries over Linked Data under different semantics [Har12a, Har12b]. The notion of semantics in [Har12a] roughly corresponds to our notion of completeness: the full-web semantics is similar to our web-completeness, whereas the reachability-based semantics can be considered as an abstract concept, while we provide two actual completeness classes. While [Har12a] shows that in the general case the full-web semantics is not computable, we show that under certain authority constraints it is possible to achieve results equivalent to web-completeness.

Query Processing over Linked Data and Services

Stream-based reasoning addresses the problem of evaluating queries over continuously updated data sets under the incorporation of background knowledge [CCG10, BBC⁺10]. In our work, we use information obtained from query evaluation to dynamically add new data sources to the input stream. Additionally, we incorporate data from service invocations identified and performed during the run time of the query engine.

Creating dataflow networks (e.g., [AK07, PSK⁺09, LK09]) and their optimised execution (e.g., [BK08]) enable information access via constructing execution plans that can involve reasoning, service calls and retrieval of information from the web. The drawback of previous approaches is the requirement to have upfront knowledge of the schemas for the used services and data sources, which is not given with Linked Data which embraces the hypermedia principle of links between sources.

Mediator systems (e.g. Information Manifold [LRO96]) are able to answer queries over heterogeneous data sources, including services on the web. Information-providing data services are explicitly treated, e.g. in [TAK04, BCB07]. For an extensive overview of query answering in information integration systems, we refer the interested reader to [Hal01]. All these works have in common that they generate top-down query plans, which is possible because of the completely known schema of the targeted relational databases. In contrast, our proposed approach employs a data-driven query plan, where heterogeneous schemas can be aligned with rules, service calls are constructed when enough input data is found, and services are invoked if they are relevant for the data at hand.

Several systems support decentralised query evaluation over Linked Data [HBF09, LT10, HHK+10, LT11]. Our approach extends such systems by supporting a clear notion of completeness, rule-based reasoning and the integration of services and streaming sources.

ETALIS is a system for intelligent Complex Event Processing (iCEP) featuring processing of RDF streams, stream reasoning, and the parallel evaluation of multiple queries (respectively events) [AFRS11, ARFS12]. The domain knowledge is restricted to RDFS ontologies, but SPARQL CONSTRUCT queries are supported that can be used to implement further Datalog rules, which corresponds to the expressiveness of our system. The supported event descriptions are more expressive than our conjunctive queries by allowing aggregations, negation, and conditions on time stamps of triples. While ETALIS could potentially be used as an implementation of the multi query streaming processor in our approach, it has no direct support for the main features of our system, namely: (i) automated invocation and integration of Linked Data Services; (ii) dynamic discovery of new information sources during query execution; and (iii) query answering according to the proposed completeness notions.

6.5 Discussion

In this chapter, we presented the Linked Data Service (LIDS) approach for integrating information services in a uniform way into Linked Data. Besides providing a methodology for providing a Linked Data interface to services, the LIDS approach also includes a formal description model of the service functionality. We defined both an abstract description model and a concrete grounding in RDF.

Based on the concept of authority that information sources can have for certain kinds of statements, we defined three notions of completeness for queries over Linked Data: web complete, seed complete, and query reachable complete. In general, web completeness is only of theoretical interest, as it requires complete knowledge of the whole Linked Data web. Seed completeness is a pragmatic approach to limit the information sources that have to be accessed to those that are reachable from the IRIs given in a query. Query reachable completeness further minimises the set of required sources to those that bind to variables of subqueries of the original query. We defined a class of completely answerable queries for which the results obtained by evaluating a query over the query reachable set coincides with the results over the whole Linked Data web.

Furthermore, we discussed the implementation of a system for answering queries over Linked Data, which incorporates our introduced extensions for information services and completeness notions. The integration is facilitated by support for rule-based reasoning, which enables the alignment of different vocabularies.

In this chapter we extended Linked Data technologies, which already fulfill requirement R10: *Decentralised Architecture for Interlinked Information*, by methods for fulfilling the requirements R11: *Support for Information Services* and R12: *Completeness Notions for Queries*.

Chapter 7

Implementation and Evaluation

In this chapter, we show how practical decentralised policy-aware systems can be realised based on the technologies presented in this thesis. We achieve this by introducing in Section 7.1 concrete syntaxes for the policy languages and prototypical implementations of the policy engine. In Section 7.2, we apply the implementations in proof-of-concept solutions for the scenarios presented in Section 2.1 to show the feasibility of our proposed methods. The scenarios also evaluate the semantics of the policy language by showing that it is aligned with the intuitions behind the Creative Commons licenses and the W3C standard P3P.

Besides the feasibility studies, we conducted experiments to measure the performance of policy classifications (Section 7.3), interlinking of LIDS with existing datasets (Section 7.4), and query answering over Linked Data and services (Section 7.5).

We argue for the practical applicability of our completeness notions by analysing Linked Data available on the web with respect to its authority relations between documents and contained information (Section 7.6).

We discuss how our approach addresses the identified requirements in Section 7.7. We summarise the evaluation results in Section 7.8. Parts of this chapter are based on the evaluations of the following publications [SH11, KS11b, Spe12a].

7.1 Syntax and Implementation

We based the semantics of our policy language on abstract first-order logic, but also showed two concrete fragments that can be used for practical languages: OWL DL and Datalog. We argued that there exist web standards for serialising both languages: OWL/XML and OWL/RDF for OWL DL; and RIF for Datalog. All serialisations used IRIs as identifiers, so we can define syntaxes for our policy language in a simple way by (i) defining IRIs for the special containedIn and compliantTo predicates, and (ii) defining the language construct to express policies.

For the IRIs, we choose `http://openlids.org/policy/vocab#containedIn` for the containedIn predicate and `http://openlids.org/policy/vocab#compliantTo` for the compliantTo predicate. All other concepts introduced for the policy language are part of our provenance vocabulary with the base IRI `http://openlids.org/provenance/vocab#`, e.g., the IRI `http://openlids.org/provenance/vocab#Artefact` identifies the concept of an artefact.

We model OWL-based policies as OWL concepts with the same identifier as the policy. Using the same identifier both as an individual (e.g., in containedIn conditions) and as concept (i.e., in the policy definition) is referred to as punning [W3C09c, Section 2.4.1]. The semantics of OWL DL treat individuals and classes as disjoint even when they have the same identifier. Policies expressed in our language are thus valid OWL, but the desired inferences about policy compliance are only reached by a standard OWL reasoner if the correct containedIn relations between all used policies are materialised in the knowledge base. Our implementation of an OWL-based policy engine is using repeated calls to a standard OWL reasoner through the OWL API [HB09, API]. The knowledge base containing the policy definitions and background knowledge is loaded into the reasoner together with statements that containedIn holds between all defined policies. We then query the reasoner for subsumption between each pair of classes defining policies. In the next step, we load the original knowledge base into the reasoner together with statements that containedIn holds between all pairs of policies where the subsumption held in the previous step. Again we query the reasoner for subsumption between policy classes and repeat the last step until we reach a fixed point, i.e., until exactly the subsumptions between those policy classes hold that were specified to be contained in each other in the input. The fixed point knowledge base can then be used to check compliance of individuals describing artefact using processes by checking their class membership in the corresponding policy-defining classes. We tested the policy engine with the OWL reasoner Hermit [Her].

RIF is an official W3C standard for expressing rules, but there is a lack of tools and programming libraries supporting RIF. Thus, we additionally support expressing rules in the form of SPARQL construct queries, where the rule body is specified in the where clause of the query and the rule head is specified in the construct clause of the query.

Example 36. *The following SPARQL construct queries formalise rules expressing that* has descendant *is the inverse of the DBpedia predicate* parent *and is transitive:*

```
prefix owl: <http://www.w3.org/2002/07/owl#>
prefix vocab: <http://openlids.org/examples/ezII/vocab#>
prefix dbpo: <http://dbpedia.org/ontology/>

CONSTRUCT { ?x vocab:hasDescendant ?y } WHERE {
    ?y dbpo:parent ?x
}

CONSTRUCT { ?x vocab:hasDescendant ?z } WHERE {
    ?x vocab:hasDescendant ?y .
    ?y vocab:hasDescendant ?z
}
```

We express policies as rules defining the conditions that a process must fulfill so that it is compliantTo the policy.

Example 37. *A simple policy PD allowing every process is modelled as:*

```
prefix policy: <http://openlids.org/policy/vocab#>
prefix prov: <http://openlids.org/provenance/vocab#>

CONSTRUCT { ?x policy:compliantTo PD } WHERE {
    ?x rdf:type prov:Process
}
```

Formula 4.2 ($\forall x, y.\text{containedIn}(x, y) \leftrightarrow \forall z.(\text{compliantTo}(z, x) \rightarrow \text{compliantTo}(z, y))$) that defines the relation between compliantTo and containedIn is outside of Datalog and thus cannot be computed by standard Datalog reasoners. Instead, we apply a similar approach to the one for OWL-based policies by layering the policy engine on top of a Datalog reasoner, which is repeatedly called to derive the containedIn relation by checking query containment of the policy-defining queries. We implemented the Datalog policy engine based on the Datalog engine DLV [DLV].

We developed a prototypical implementation of the obligation handling approach for Datalog-based policy languages. The implementation translates the Datalog policies into Prolog in order to use the abductive reasoning engine HYPROLOG [HYP] running on SWI-Prolog [SP]. The prototype is not optimised, but is able to find and handle obligations for simple examples based on our use cases in less than 1 second on a 2.4 GHz standard laptop computer.

7.2 Realisation of Scenarios

In this section, we outline how the scenarios introduced in Section 2.1 can be realised using the methods presented in this thesis. For space and readability reasons we only showcase interesting exemplary aspects of the solutions.

7.2.1 Open Licenses for Copyright-protected Information

Alice wants to get a list of the descendants of Queen Elizabeth II and for each descendant a picture together with geographical information where it was taken. To gather the information she uses the Linked Data query engine with support for LIDS and rules. The query she formulates is:

```
prefix vocab: <http://openlids.org/examples/ezII/vocab#>
prefix dbpo: <http://dbpedia.org/ontology/>
prefix dbp: <http://dbpedia.org/resource/>
prefix foaf: <http://xmlns.com/foaf/0.1/>
prefix flickrlids: <http://openlids.org/flickrlids/vocab#>

SELECT ?n ?p ?f WHERE {
  dbp:Elizabeth_II vocab:hasDescendant ?x .
    ?x foaf:name ?n .
    ?x foaf:depiction ?p . ?p flickrlids:hasLocation ?loc .
```

```
        ?loc foaf:based_near ?f
}
```

Alice specifies that all patterns should be matched only with subject authoritative stated triples. The relevant triples that the Linked Data query engine can obtain when dereferencing `http://dbpedia.org/resource/Elizabeth_II` are as follows:

```
dbp:Anne,_Princess_Royal              dbpo:parent  dbp:Elizabeth_II .
dbp:Charles,_Prince_of_Wales          dbpo:parent  dbp:Elizabeth_II .
dbp:Prince_Andrew,_Duke_of_York       dbpo:parent  dbp:Elizabeth_II .
dbp:Prince_Edward,_Earl_of_Wessex     dbpo:parent  dbp:Elizabeth_II .
```

We notice that the data uses dbpo:parent instead of the vocab:hasDescendant property used in the query. We formalise that vocab:hasDescendant is the transitive closure of the inverse of dbpo:parent, with the following rules:

```
prefix vocab: <http://openlids.org/examples/ezII/vocab#>
prefix dbpo: <http://dbpedia.org/ontology/>

CONSTRUCT { ?x vocab:hasDescendant ?y } WHERE {
    ?y dbpo:parent ?x
}

CONSTRUCT { ?x vocab:hasDescendant ?z } WHERE {
    ?x vocab:hasDescendant ?y .
    ?y vocab:hasDescendant ?z
}
```

Together with this background knowledge the query processor can derive a list of descendants (bindings for ?x) and their names (bindings for ?n). In the following, we list an excerpt of the bindings:

```
?x => dbp:Charles,_Prince_of_Wales          ?n => "Charles, Prince of Wales"
?x => dbp:Anne,_Princess_Royal              ?n => "Princess Anne"
?x => dbp:Prince_Andrew,_Duke_of_York       ?n => "Prince Andrew"
?x => dbp:Prince_Edward,_Earl_of_Wessex     ?n => "Prince Edward"
?x => dbp:Peter_Phillips                    ?n => "Peter Phillips"
?x => dbp:Zara_Phillips                     ?n => "Zara Phillips"
?x => dbp:Prince_William,_Duke_of_Cambridge ?n => "Prince William"
?x => dbp:Prince_Harry_of_Wales             ?n => "Prince Harry of Wales"
?x => dbp:Princess_Beatrice_of_York         ?n => "Princess Beatrice"
?x => dbp:Princess_Eugenie_of_York          ?n => "Princess Eugenie of York"
?x => dbp:Lady_Louise_Windsor               ?n => "Lady Louise Windsor"
?x => dbp:James,_Viscount_Severn            ?n => "Viscount Severn"
?x => dbp:Laura_Lopes                       ?n => "Laura Lopes"
```

Note that Laura Lopes is returned as a result as her relation to her stepfather Prince Charles is modelled in DBpedia using the `dbpo:parent` property. Further note that the children Savannah Phillips and Isla Elizabeth Phillips of Peter Phillips were not yet represented in the accessed DBpedia version and are thus missing.

While some of the descendants binding to `?x` have associated pictures linked via the `foaf:depiction` property, none of them has geographic information. So the query engine has to invoke the LIDS version of the Flickr service to retrieve additional photos with geographical information. We wrapped the Flickr API so that it takes the name of a person and returns a list of photos of the person together with their locations. The LIDS description is given as follows:

```
:FlickrLIDS a lids:LIDS;
  lids:lids_description [
    lids:endpoint
      <http://km.aifb.kit.edu/services/flickrlids/depictions>;
    lids:service_entity "person" ;
    lids:input_bgp "?person foaf:name ?name";
    lids:output_bgp "?person foaf:depiction ?p .
                     ?p :hasLocation ?loc .
                     ?loc geo:lat ?lat . ?loc geo:long ?long" ;
    lids:required_vars "name" ] .
```

Furthermore the query engine has to invoke the LIDS version of the GeoNames service (as described in Section 6.1.2) to find nearby located geographical features given the latitude and longitude of a picture. Finally in our experiments we obtained 358 results from which Alice can select one result per descendant. For example the result for Prince Charles is:

```
?n => "Charles, Prince of Wales"
?p => <http://farm6.staticflickr.com/5285/5375098012_c8583acbbe.jpg>
?f => dbp:Centre_for_Human_Reproductive_Science
```

As the query engine tracks the information sources which contributed to a query result, we can create the provenance graph of the query result r1 as follows:

$$\text{Derivation(d1)} \wedge \text{wasGenBy(r1,d1)} \wedge$$
$$\text{used(d1,dbp:Charles,\_Prince\_of\_Wales)} \wedge$$
$$\qquad \text{hasPolicy(dbp:Charles,\_Prince\_of\_Wales,BY-SA)} \wedge$$
$$\text{used(d1,depictions:Charles,+Prince+of+Wales)} \wedge$$
$$\qquad \text{hasPolicy(depictions:Charles,+Prince+of+Wales,PD)} \wedge$$
$$\text{used(d1,geowrap:lat=52.453616\&long=-1.938303)} \wedge$$
$$\qquad \text{hasPolicy(geowrap:lat=52.453616\&long=-1.938303,BY)}.$$

The DBpedia resource inherits the license of Wikipedia (CC BY-SA), whereas the data from GeoNames LIDS inherits the license of the GeoNames data, which is CC BY. The target policy determination algorithm derives a policy for r1 that is contained in BY-SA and BY and contains BY-SA, i.e., a policy equivalent to BY-SA, which the query engine thus assigns to the query result r1. Note that the derived policy only holds for the query result, but no to the linked photo, which has a license that the owner of the photo can specify on Flickr (in our case the photo has a CC BY-ND license). When Alice uses the result and the picture linked in the result in her blog post the following provenance graph describes this usage:

$$\text{Usage}(\text{u1}) \wedge \text{used}(\text{u1}, \text{r1}) \wedge \text{hasPolicy}(\text{r1}, \text{BY-SA}) \wedge$$
$$\text{used}(\text{u1}, \texttt{http://farm6.staticflickr.com/...jpg}) \wedge$$
$$\text{hasPolicy}(\texttt{http://farm6.staticflickr.com/...jpg}, \text{BY-ND}).$$

The usage u1 is classified as non-compliant because the picture is used without giving attribution. In Section 5.3, we presented an obligation handler for identifying missing attributions, which we assume is used by the policy-aware blogging software that Alice uses. The obligation handler adds attributions for the data in the query result, i.e., attributions to DBpedia and GeoNames, and for the image, i.e., attribution to the Flickr user owning the photo. Automatic construction of attributions for Creative Commons-licensed content is discussed in [SKBL09]. After adding the attributions, the usage is classified as compliant, and Alice can publish her blog post.

Creative Commons Compatibility Matrix

In this section, we show how to model Creative Commons licenses using our policy language, and perform several experiments to confirm that the semantics of the formal policies corresponds to the meaning of the original licenses. We already modelled the PD, BY, BY-ND, and BY-SA licenses in Section 4.5.2, thus here we present the missing policies for the licenses Attribution NonCommercial (CC BY-NC), Attribution NonCommercial ShareAlike (CC BY-NC-SA), and Attribution NonCommercial NoDerivs (CC BY-NC-ND):

$$\text{BY-NC}: (\text{Usage}(x) \wedge \text{wasTriggeredBy}(x, y) \wedge \text{Attribution}(y) \wedge$$
$$\text{hasPurpose}(x, u) \wedge \text{NonCommercial}(u)) \vee$$
$$(\text{Derivation}(x) \wedge \text{wasGenBy}(z, x) \wedge \text{hasPolicy}(z, v) \wedge$$
$$\text{containedIn}(v, \text{BY-NC}))$$
$$\text{BY-NC-SA}: (\text{Usage}(x) \wedge \text{wasTriggeredBy}(x, y) \wedge \text{Attribution}(y) \wedge$$
$$\text{hasPurpose}(x, u) \wedge \text{NonCommercial}(u)) \vee$$
$$(\text{Derivation}(x) \wedge \text{wasGenBy}(z, x) \wedge \text{hasPolicy}(z, v) \wedge$$
$$\text{containedIn}(v, \text{BY-NC-SA}) \wedge \text{containedIn}(\text{BY-NC-SA}, v))$$
$$\text{BY-NC-ND}: \text{Usage}(x) \wedge \text{wasTriggeredBy}(x, y) \wedge \text{Attribution}(y) \wedge$$
$$\text{hasPurpose}(x, u) \wedge \text{NonCommercial}(u).$$

For showing that our approach overcomes the incompatibility problem introduced by name-based restrictions, as stated by Lessig [Les05], we modelled equivalent policies for every license, but with a different name. E.g., for Attribution, ShareAlike we created the BY-SA-SYN policy in the following way:

$$\text{BY-SA-SYN}: (\text{Usage}(x) \wedge \text{wasTriggeredBy}(x, y) \wedge \text{Attribution}(y)) \vee$$
$$(\text{Derivation}(x) \wedge \text{wasGenBy}(z, x) \wedge \text{hasPolicy}(z, v) \wedge$$
$$\text{containedIn}(v, \text{BY-SA-SYN}) \wedge \text{containedIn}(\text{BY-SA-SYN}, v))$$

For every pair of original policy P and renamed policy P-SYN, our policy engine infers that both are equivalent, i.e., both containedIn(P, P-SYN) and containedIn(P-SYN, P) hold.

We modelled for every combination $(p_{\text{orig}}, p_{\text{deriv}})$ of Creative Commons licenses a derivation, which uses an artefact with policy p_{deriv} and generates a new artefact with policy p_{deriv}. If such a derivation is compliant to p_{orig}, we know that p_{deriv} is a valid license for derivations of p_{orig} licensed artefacts. For example we model a derivation of a CC BY licensed artefact, which generates a CC BY-SA licensed new artefact:

$$\text{Derivation}(u1) \wedge \text{used}(u1, r1) \wedge \text{hasPolicy}(r1, \text{BY}) \wedge$$
$$\text{wasGenBy}(r2, u1) \wedge \text{hasPolicy}(r2, \text{BY-SA}).$$

As policy BY-SA is contained in policy BY, the derivation u1 is compliant, meaning that a derivative of a Creative Commons attribution licensed artefact can be published under a CC attribution, share-alike license. With this experiment we constructed a table of valid policy combinations, which is shown in Table 7.1 and corresponds (as expected) to the official compatibility chart[1] of Creative Commons.

Furthermore, we modelled a policy representing the GNU Free Documentation License (GFDL)[2]. The GFDL is a license for texts, which allows copying, modification and redistribution and requires derivatives to have the same license. There are some differences to the Creative Commons attribution, share-alike license; for example, that the GFDL requires logging of all changes. GFDL licensed content cannot be published under a Creative Commons license (except for special cases such as used by Wikipedia, which are allowed by corresponding relicensing clauses), whereas content with a CC attribution license can be published with the GFDL license[3]. The (in)compatibilities can also be inferred from our formalisation.

We note that, besides its use for conformance checking, the computation of containedIn can also assist in modelling policies. For example, one can readily infer that any ShareAlike (SA) requirement is redundant when a NoDerivs (ND) requirement is present as well: adding SA to any ND license results in an equivalent license, i.e. one finds that the licenses are mutually contained in each other.

Table 7.1: Allowed policies for derivations of artefacts with Creative Commons license

		Policy of derived artefact						
		pd	by	by-nc	by-nc-nd	by-nc-sa	by-nd	by-sa
Policy of original artefact	pd	✓	✓	✓	✓	✓	✓	✓
	by		✓	✓	✓	✓	✓	✓
	by-nc			✓	✓	✓		
	by-nc-nd							
	by-nc-sa					✓		
	by-nd							
	by-sa							✓

```
PA           MPol           AUPol          SWPol          SPol
type: AND -contains-> type: Atomic -> type: Atomic -> type: Atomic -> type: Atomic
             isDefBy: M     isDefBy: AU    isDefBy: PSW   isDefBy: S

             B1             DSPol          DOSPol         DPol
             type: OR -contains-> type: AND -contains-> type: OR -contains-> type: Atomic
                                                                      isDefBy: PDER
```

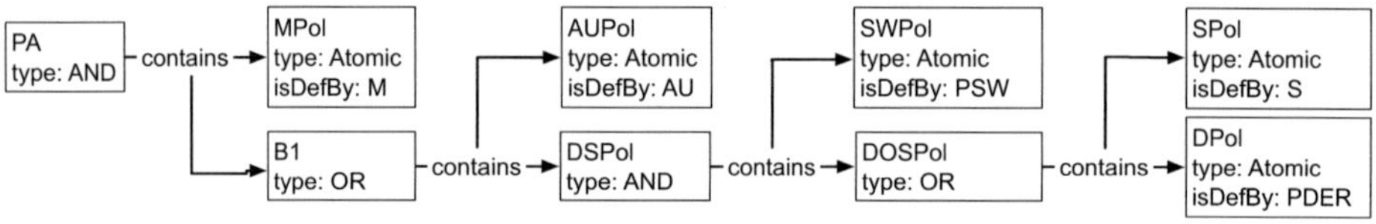

Figure 7.1: Visualisation of the structured policy PA for Acme's sales data.

7.2.2 Information Mashups for Decision Support

Bob, a manager of the Acme corporation, integrates relevant data sources for analysis in an OLAP software. He uses the technologies presented in [FKO+12] to create a data warehouse from the relevant Linked Data sources while producing a provenance graph of the contained data. The resulting data warehouse uses the RDF Data Cube vocabulary [W3C12a], which Bob can then expose to OLAP clients via the methods shown in [KOH12]. The relevant used data sources that Bob integrates and their corresponding policies are given as follows:

- Company internal data source r1 about sales data. Managers can use r1 for analytical purposes, make derivations and share the data with other managers. We formalise the usage restrictions as policy PA using the structured model as follows (visualised in

---

[1]see Point 2.16 in http://wiki.creativecommons.org/FAQ, accessed 15th June 2011
[2]http://www.gnu.org/licenses/fdl.html
[3]see   http://wiki.creativecommons.org/Interoperability_between_Creative_Commons_
licenses_and_GFDL, accessed 15th June 2011

Figure 7.1):

ANDCond(PA) ∧ contains(PA, MPol) ∧ contains(PA, B1)∧

    description(PA, "Managers can use for analytics, derive, and

                              share under same conditions.")∧

AtomicPol(MPol) ∧ uses(MPol, MBlock) ∧ isDefinedBy(MBlock, M)∧

ORCond(B1) ∧ contains(B1, AUPol) ∧ contains(B1, DSPol)∧

AtomicPol(AUPol) ∧ uses(AUPol, AUBlock) ∧ isDefinedBy(AUBlock, AU)∧

ANDCond(DSPol) ∧ contains(DSPol, SWPol) ∧ contains(DSPol, DOSPol)∧

AtomicPol(SWPol) ∧ uses(SWPol, SWBlock) ∧ isDefinedBy(SWBlock, PSW)∧

    description(SWPol, "Sharing is only allowed under same conditions.")∧

ORCond(DOSPol) ∧ contains(DOSPol, DPol) ∧ contains(DOSPol, SPol)∧

AtomicPol(DPol) ∧ uses(DPol, DBlock) ∧ isDefinedBy(DBlock, PDER)∧

AtomicPol(SPol) ∧ uses(SPol, SBlock) ∧ isDefinedBy(SBlock, S)∧

    description(SPol, "Sharing is only allowed when the recipient is a manager.") ,

where the defining policies are given as:

$$M: \mathrm{Process}(x) \wedge \mathrm{performedBy}(x, m) \wedge \mathrm{Manager}(m)$$

$$AU: \mathrm{Usage}(x) \wedge \mathrm{hasPurpose}(x, u) \wedge \mathrm{Analytical}(u)$$
$$PSW: \mathrm{Process}(x) \wedge \mathrm{wasGenBy}(a, x) \wedge \mathrm{hasPolicy}(a, p) \wedge \mathrm{containedIn}(p, PA))$$
$$S: \mathrm{Sharing}(x) \wedge \mathrm{recipient}(x, r) \wedge \mathrm{Manager}(x)$$
$$PDER: \mathrm{Derivation}(x) .$$

- Data source r2 containing information about geographic regions and their demographics as obtained from Eurostat. The policy PB formalises the usage restrictions, which allow free usage and redistribution under the condition that Eurostat is acknowledged.

$$PB: (\mathrm{Usage}(x) \wedge \mathrm{wasTriggeredBy}(x, y) \wedge \mathrm{Attribution}(y) \wedge \mathrm{recipient}(y, \mathrm{Eurostat}))\vee$$
$$(\mathrm{Sharing}(x) \wedge \mathrm{wasGenBy}(a, x) \wedge \mathrm{hasPolicy}(x, p) \wedge \mathrm{containedIn}(p, PB))\vee$$
$$(\mathrm{Derivation}(x) \wedge \mathrm{wasGenBy}(a, x) \wedge \mathrm{hasPolicy}(x, p) \wedge \mathrm{containedIn}(p, PB)) .$$

- Historical stock prices of Acme available in the data source r3, for which Acme has purchased a licensed that allows it to be used internal of the company, formalised as policy PC:

$$PC: (\mathrm{Usage}(x) \wedge \mathrm{performedBy}(x, e) \wedge \mathrm{employedBy}(e, \mathrm{Acme}))\vee$$
$$(\mathrm{Sharing}(x) \wedge \mathrm{wasGenBy}(a, x) \wedge \mathrm{hasPolicy}(x, p) \wedge \mathrm{containedIn}(p, PC)\wedge$$
$$\mathrm{recipient}(e, x) \wedge \mathrm{employedBy}(e, \mathrm{Acme}))\vee$$
$$(\mathrm{Derivation}(x) \wedge \mathrm{wasGenBy}(a, x) \wedge \mathrm{hasPolicy}(x, p) \wedge \mathrm{containedIn}(p, PC)) .$$

In the following, we show the provenance graph of the integrated data warehouse r4 to which Bob assigns a policy PD that allows him to share the data for use by all employees when acknowledgment of Eurostat is given:

$$\text{Derivation(d1)} \land \text{wasGenBy(r4, d1)} \land \text{hasPolicy(r4, PD)} \land$$
$$\text{performedBy(d1, Bob)} \land \text{Manager(Bob)} \land$$
$$\text{used(d1, r1)} \land \text{hasPolicy(r1, PA)} \land$$
$$\text{used(d1, r2)} \land \text{hasPolicy(r2, PB)} \land$$
$$\text{used(d1, r3)} \land \text{hasPolicy(r3, PC)}\,.$$

$$\text{PD}: \text{Sharing}(x) \land \text{performedBy}(x, m) \land \text{Manager}(m) \land$$
$$\text{recipient}(x, e) \land \text{employedBy}(e, \text{Acme}) \land$$
$$\text{wasGenBy}(a, x) \land \text{hasPolicy}(a, p) \land \text{containedIn}(p, \text{PD}')$$
$$\text{PD}': \text{Usage}(x) \land \text{performedBy}(x, e) \land \text{employedBy}(e, \text{Acme}) \land$$
$$\text{wasTriggeredBy}(x, y) \land \text{Attribution}(y) \land \text{recipient}(y, \text{Eurostat})\,.$$

The derivation action d1 is classified as non-compliant with policy PA. The reason for the non-compliance is that the assigned policy PD is not contained in PA. Remember that containedIn is implemented by instantiating the policy which should be contained and then checking compliance to the policy that should contain. Thus, we can apply the explanation component to determine why PD is not contained in PA. After zooming to the relevant atomic policies (SPol and SWPol)[4], Bob gets the explanations "Sharing is only allowed when the recipient is a manager." and "Sharing is only allowed under same conditions.", so he fixes the policies PD and PD' to restrict recipients and users to managers and in turn the derivation action d1 for creating the data ware house is classified as compliant.

7.2.3 Data Privacy in the Smart Energy Grid

We assume the energy provider stores his relations using the hasCustomer property linking to their representations as maintained by the customers' smart meters, which use the properties hasDevice and consumed to specify the customer's electric devices and their energy consumption event. Thus the energy provider can retrieve all relevant consumption events of his customer with the following query:

```
SELCT ?cust ?device ?consumption WHERE {
    :EnergyProvider hasCustomer ?cust .
    ?cust hasDevice ?device .
```

---

[4]Let rd be the action modelled by instantiating PD. Making rd compliant to PA requires being compliant to B1 as rd is already compliant to MPol. Compliance to B1 is only possible via being compliant to DSPol because rd already violates AUPol. DSPol requires fulfillment of SWPol and SPol (because DOSPol is required and DPol is violated).

```
        ?device consumed ?consumption
}
```

The provider can specify that he expects subject authority for all three patterns and will get the complete set of data under the notion of query reachable completeness.

Depending on the requestor and the requested data, Carol defines different policies that should be attached to the released data. Carol's smart meter assigns the policy PM to energy consumption data that is given to her energy provider. Assuming the date of the data access is 01.05.2012, the policy is defined as

$$\text{PM}: (\mathsf{Usage}(x) \wedge \mathsf{hasPurpose}(x, u) \wedge \mathsf{Billing}(u)) \vee$$
$$(\mathsf{Storing}(x) \wedge \mathsf{wasGenBy}(a, x) \wedge \mathsf{hasPolicy}(x, p) \wedge \mathsf{containedIn}(p, \text{PM}) \wedge$$
$$\mathsf{wasTriggeredBy}(x, d) \wedge \mathsf{Deletion}(d) \wedge \mathsf{performedAt}(d, t) \wedge t < 01.05.2013).$$

The consumption data that is given to the energy optimiser service has assigned policy EO, restricting the use to consulting purposes until the data is anonymised and then can be used and shared for statistical purposes:

$$\text{EO}: (\mathsf{Usage}(x) \wedge \mathsf{hasPurpose}(x, u) \wedge \mathsf{Consulting}(u)) \vee$$
$$(\mathsf{Anonymisation}(x) \wedge \mathsf{wasGenBy}(a, x) \wedge \mathsf{hasPolicy}(a, p) \wedge \mathsf{containedIn}(p, \text{STAT}))$$
$$\text{STAT}: (\mathsf{Usage}(x) \wedge \mathsf{hasPurpose}(x, u) \wedge \mathsf{Statistical}(u)) \vee$$
$$(\mathsf{Sharing}(x) \wedge \mathsf{wasGenBy}(a, x) \wedge \mathsf{hasPolicy}(a, p) \wedge \mathsf{containedIn}(p, \text{STAT})).$$

The policy for the washing machine is a straightforward adaption of the PM policy, which allows usage for consulting instead of billing purposes.

When Carol TV's posts the information about which movies she watched to her social network, Carol specified that the following policy should be attached:

$$\text{TV}: (Sharing(x) \wedge \mathsf{recipient}(x, f) \wedge \mathsf{hasFriend}(\text{Carol}, f) \wedge$$
$$\mathsf{wasGenBy}(a, x) \wedge \mathsf{hasPolicy}(a, p) \wedge \mathsf{containedIn}(p, \text{FR}))$$
$$\text{FR}: Usage(x).$$

Translation of P3P

P3P is a W3C standard for expressing privacy policies of web sites [W3C02]. Real world usage of P3P is limited [BRDM07], but nonetheless, we think that it is beneficial to show that our approach is able to formalise P3P policies. One of the drawbacks of P3P is the lack of a formally defined semantics, which can be mitigated by the translation to our policy language. Our translation restricts to the requested data usages expressed in P3P; leaving out information about the requesting entity and remedies, which are modelled in P3P, but which we consider orthogonal to our usage model and policy language. The notion of a P3P policy refers to a declaration which data is collected by a web provider and in which ways it will be used, processed and shared. Thus, in our terminology, a P3P policy corresponds to a data request. For our request model, we adapted the P3P notions of data elements and categories, such that a P3P policy can be naturally transformed into a request for the corresponding data artefacts in our approach. However, P3P allows to specify that certain data elements, usage purposes and other aspects of the policy are optional (either opt-in or opt-out), which results in a set of requests in our formalism: one request for every combination of required and optional elements (see opt-in and opt-out pattern).

We base our translation on the formal semantics given to P3P by Yu et al. [YLA04]. The semantics interprets a P3P policy as a set of tuples for three different relations:

```
d-purpose(data,purpose,required)
d-recipient(data,recipient,required)
d-retention(data,retention)
```

The d-purpose relation describes for which purposes some data element (identified by its IRI) is used. The required field is either opt-in, opt-out, or always. The d-recipient relation describes with whom (recipients as defined in P3P) the data element is shared. The d-retention relation describes for how long a data element is stored, in terms of the P3P-defined retention periods. Furthermore Yu et al. define two more relations:

```
d-collection(data,optional)
d-category(data,category)
```

The d-collection relation describes whether it is optional or required to provide the data element. The d-category relation assigns data elements to P3P categories, which can be used to match user policies.

The optionalities given by the required and optional fields, as well as the specification, which data elements and categories are requested are translated into sets of different requests, as discussed above. What remains is the translation of the desired policy assigned to a request, which is the disjunction of the translation for every desired purpose into a usage action, every desired recipient into a sharing action, and every desired retention into a storage action.

P3P defines a number of purposes, each can be translated into a subclass of Purpose in our approach. Optionally the purposes can be put into a class hierarchy; Lämmel and Pek specify a partial order of purposes in terms of the amount of privacy preserved, which could be used for modelling a hierarchy [LP12, LP10]. For a purpose value U, we define the purpose concept PurposeU and model the following policy condition:

$$\mathsf{Usage}(x) \wedge \mathsf{hasPurpose}(x, u) \wedge \mathsf{PurposeU}(u) \, .$$

Notable are the P3P defined purposes pseudo-decision and pseudo-analysis, when compared to individual-decision and individual-analysis: the meaning is that the data is pseudonymised before it is used for decisions or analysis, i.e. the same purposes meant by the individual-... purposes. As it is possible with our approach to model extended rights after pseudonymising data, we consider only the two purposes decision and analysis, and in the pseudo case model that data is first pseudonymised before used for these purposes.

A value r for a requested `recipient` is modelled as a sharing action. The `recipient` in P3P, however, does not refer to instances or classes of specific recipients, but uses some pre-defined constants: public, delivery, other-recipient, unrelated, ours, and same. As Lämmel and Pek state, nothing is known about the privacy policies of recipients other than ours and same [LP12]. We thus model sharing with one of these recipients as a sharing action with a resulting artefact that has a policy allowing every action. In our model, we do not differentiate between sharing with some unrelated entity that makes no statement about its privacy and the public. The recipient ours is not translated at all, as there is no sharing action to model. The same recipient is translated into a sharing action, where the resulting artefact has a policy, which is contained in the requested policy. This translation shows a strong point of our approach, because the meaning of "same" can be given explicitly to refer to the employed privacy policies.

Values for `retention` are translated into storing actions. Retention in P3P includes values for stating that data is deleted after being used for the stated purpose or after the legal requirement for storing is passed. For such values, it is not possible in a general approach without further background knowledge to specify absolute time spans, after which a deletion should be triggered. Therefore, such retention values are modelled as subclasses of storing. There are also P3P extensions, which allow the specification of concrete time spans, such as e.g. one year, which are translated into obligations to delete the data before the absolute time value to which the retention value evaluates.

7.3 Efficiency of Policy Reasoning

We approach the discussion of efficiency for reasoning with our proposed policy formalism in two ways: (i) theoretical considerations about the number of iterations needed to reach the greatest fixed point; and (ii) performance experiments that show the scalability barriers and simple methods to overcome them for realistic problems.

7.3.1 Static Complexity Analysis

For each iteration of the P_T operator[5], a reasoner for the underlying formalism must check query containments. We abstract from this reasoning process and consider its complexity as a parameter RC. The overall complexity of the policy engine is given by RC multiplied by the number of iterations of P_T needed to reach a fixed point. As an upper bound on the number of iterations, we can give $|N_P|^2$ (where N_P is the set of all policy names), as in every application of P_T at least one containedIn assumption is removed or the greatest fixed point is reached. This is however only a worst case upper bound that is not expected to occur for the following two reasons:

- typically not all policies will be interconnected in such a way, that containment of two policies depends on containment between all other policies; thus, several containments

---

[5]The P_T operator computes for a set of assumed containedIn statements, the actual containedIn statements that hold based on the policy definitions. See Definition 11 on page 46.

can be removed in the same iteration. In general, one may presume that even big numbers of policies do rarely expose a linear dependency that would lead to long iterations for reaching a fixed point.

- as the containment relation as given by the underlying formalism is transitive, the transitivity is also found for the containedIn predicate after each application of T_P. This implies that the removal of one containment assumption will in many cases necessarily result in additional removal of assumptions. As an example, we consider three policies p_1, p_2, p_3: the removal of containedIn(p_1, p_3) from N_P^2 also implies the removal of either containedIn(p_1, p_2) or containedIn(p_2, p_3) as otherwise the transitivity property would be violated. Determining the number of steps maximally needed to reach the smallest possible set of containments, i.e., the empty set $\emptyset$, is related to counting the number of partial orders on the set N_P[6]. For counting this number, there is currently no explicit, general formula that can be used, but values up to $|N_P| = 18$ were calculated explicitly [Pfe04][7].

As an example, take the Creative Commons use case, where we modelled the 7 licenses as 14 policies (for each license we modelled two policies with the same meaning but different names). The greatest fixed point is reached after $n = 2$ iterations, showing that in this case $n = 2 \ll |N_P|^2 = 196$.

In fact, for all aspects of practical examples except one, we found that only a small constant number (≤ 5) of dependencies between policy containments exist, and the fixed point is reached after less than three iterations. The exception to a constant number of dependencies are delegations with a limited depth, where both the number of policies and the interdependencies grow linear with the allowed depth of delegations. However, limited delegation has in all practical cases very low depths, e.g., a possible restriction on sharing of data in a social network may be limited to friends of friends, but not much further as otherwise the depth limit becomes quickly obsolete (cf. the small world phenomenon [Mil67, TM69]).

Thus, we can conclude that for practical applications our extended semantics for the containment relation introduces only a constant increase in complexity.

7.3.2 Performance Experiments

In this section, we describe experiments using our OWL-based and Datalog-based implementations of the policy engines. The experiments in this section were performed on a 2.4 GHz Intel Core2Duo laptop with 4 GB of main memory.

We first measured the absolute amount of time needed to classify the seven Creative Commons licenses and their equivalent but renamed counterparts as described in the previous section. While the OWL-based engine needs 4.10 seconds for the classification, the Datalog-based engine finishes after 0.52 seconds. We can see that the increased expressivity of OWL-

---

[6]After each step the containedIn relation defines a partial order on all policies and after each step either a previously unseen partial order or a fixed point is reached.

[7]See following sequence: http://oeis.org/A001035

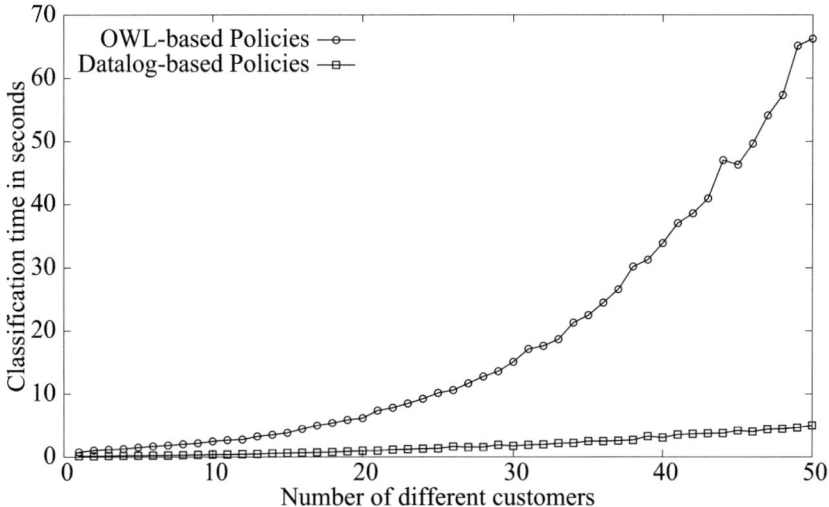

Figure 7.2: Time for classification of anonymisation example for varying number of customers without partitioning of the problem.

based policies comes with a price in terms of increased runtime. Below, we show that the
performance disadvantage of OWL worsens for larger problems.

One big advantage of our data-centric approach to policies is that individual artefact usages can be checked for compliance in isolation. Thus, policy reasoning can usually be
restricted to very small numbers of policies, e.g., for checking the compatibility of two Creative Commons licenses, it is sufficient to include only two policies in the reasoning. An
example for an exception where we have to reason over large number of policies is given
in the following. Consider an energy provider that wants to create an anonymised dataset
containing information from all of his customers. Each customer has a similar yet different
policy, which allows the anonymisation if the specific customer is notified and the policy
of the anonymised artefact is contained in a policy that he specifies. All customers specify
content-wise the same policy, namely that every usage but no derivations are allowed, but all
assign a different name to the policy. The derivation action can now be modelled as using all
the artefacts with their different policies to produce the dataset.

We ran a performance experiment with very small numbers (between one and 50) of customers and recorded the time needed for classification by OWL-based and Datalog-based
policy engines in Figure 7.2. The steep increase of classification time demonstrates that we
cannot scale this to realistic, larger customer numbers in the range of 10,000s. However, we
can split the reasoning task into smaller subtasks which check compliance only considering
a subset of the applicable policies. We can easily do this as there are only dependencies
between the policy of the generated artefact (the anonymised dataset) and each customer
policy, but no dependencies between policies of different customers.

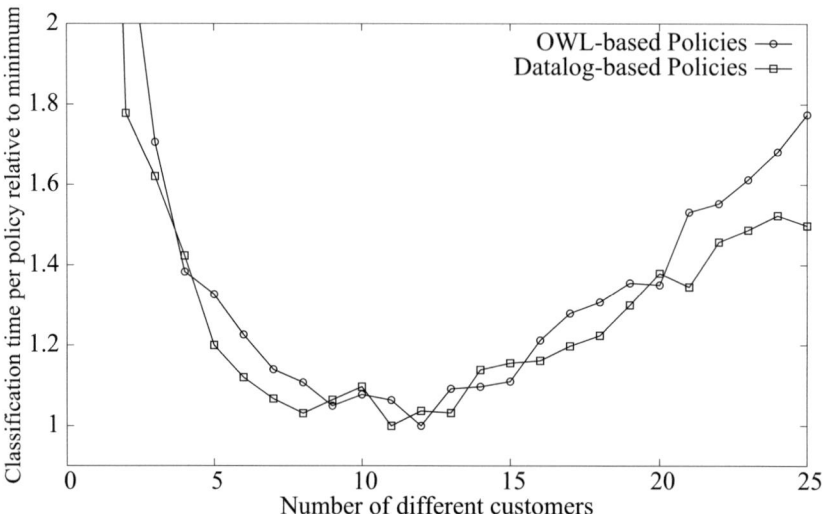

Figure 7.3: Relative classification time per policy for varying sizes of the input problem.

In order to determine the optimal size of subtasks, we analysed the time needed on average per policy for the anonymisation example. We show the time needed relative to the time in the optimal case[8] in Figure 7.3. From the experiment, we conclude that the sweet spot for subtask size is around 25, as every customer specifies two policies and the lowest time per policy is achieved with 12 customers and there is one additional policy: the one of the energy provider.

We evaluated two possibilities for splitting the reasoning into subtasks: (i) on the policy-aware application level, i.e., the application sequentially submits subproblems to the policy engine; and (ii) on the policy engine level, i.e., the policy engine automatically divides the problem and solves them sequentially. The performance of both approaches for a Datalog-based policy engine is shown in Figure 7.4. The automatic division on the policy engine level performs considerable worse than the application level partitioning, which grows linearly with the problem size. The reason is that the policy engine cannot efficiently determine which parts of the overall problem are relevant for each subtask and includes also parts where it is in doubt in order to avoid wrong inferences. For a total of 102,592 customers the application-level partitioning approach takes 6214 seconds to classify the usage. While still improvable, e.g., through parallelisation, we consider the run time acceptable for such a large task.

---

[8]For each run we measured the total time and divided it by the number of policies in the run. Then we divided the time per policy by the minimum time per policy achieved for the corresponding policy formalism (OWL-based or Datalog-based).

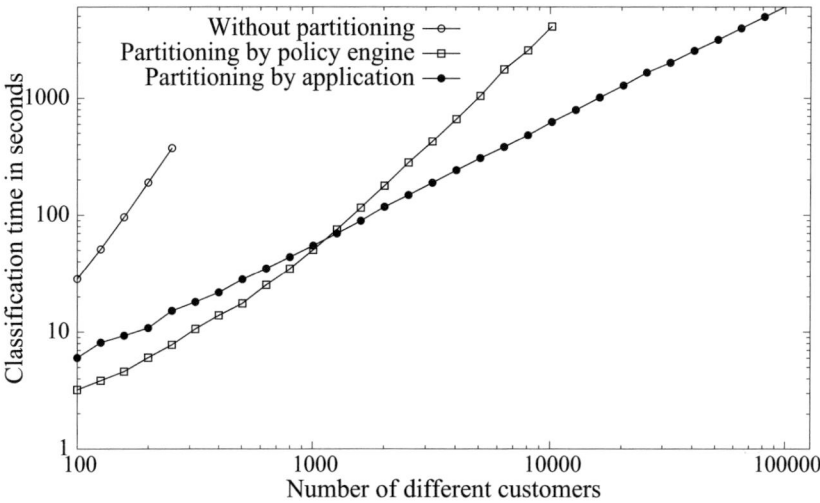

Figure 7.4: Time for classifiying large numbers of policies with problem partitioning.

7.4 Implementing and Interlinking Linked Data Services

We first present several LIDS services which we have made available, and then cover the evaluation of performance and effectiveness of the presented algorithm for interlinking Linked Data with LIDS. Source code and test data for the implementation of the interlinking algorithm, as well as other general code for handling LIDS and their descriptions can be found online[9]. All experiments were conducted on a 2.4 GHz Intel Core2Duo laptop with 4 GB of main memory.

7.4.1 Implementing LIDS Services

In this section, we show how we applied the LIDS approach to construct publicly available Linked Data interfaces for selected existing services.

The following services are hosted on Google's App Engine cloud environment. The services are also linked on `http://openlids.org/` together with their formal LIDS descriptions and further information, such as IRIs of example entities.

- GeoNames Wrapper[10] provides three functions:
    - finding the nearest GeoNames feature to a given point,
    - finding the nearest GeoNames populated place to a given point,
    - linking a geographic point to resources from DBpedia that are nearby.

---

[9]`http://code.google.com/p/openlids/`
[10]`http://km.aifb.kit.edu/services/geowrap/`

- GeoCoding Wrapper, returning the geographic coordinates of a street address.

- Twitter Wrapper[11] links Twitter account holders to the messages they post.

The effort to produce a LIDS wrapper is typically low. The interface code that handles the service IRIs and extracts parameters can be realised by standardised code or even generated automatically from a LIDS description. The main effort lies in accessing the service and generating a mapping from the service's native output to a Linked Data representation. For some services it is sufficient to write XSLTs that transform XML to RDF, or simple pieces of procedural code that transform JSON to RDF. Effort is higher for services that map web page sources, as this often requires session and cookie handling and parsing of faulty HTML code. However, the underlying data conversion has to be carried out whether or not LIDS are used. Following the LIDS principles is only a minor overhead in implementation; adding a LIDS descriptions requires a SPARQL query to describe the service.

7.4.2 Interlinking Existing Data Sets with LIDS

We implemented a streaming version of the interlinking algorithm shown in Section 6.1.4 based on NxParser[12]. For evaluation of the algorithm's performance and effectiveness we interlinked the Billion Triple Challenge (BTC) 2010 data set[13] with the `findNearby` geowrapper. In total the data set consisted of 3,162,149,151 triples and was annotated in 40,746 seconds (< 12 hours) plus about 12 hours for uncompressing the data set, result cleaning, and statistics gathering. In the cleaning phase we filtered out links to the geowrapper that were redundant, i.e., entities that were already linked to GeoNames, including the GeoNames data set itself. The original BTC data contained 74 different domains that referenced GeoNames IRIs. Our interlinking process added 891 new domains that are now linked to GeoNames via the geowrap service. In total 2,448,160 new links were added[14]. Many links referred to the same locations, all in all there were links to ca. 160,000 different geowrap service calls. These results show that even with a very large data set, interlinking based on LIDS descriptions is feasible on commodity hardware. Furthermore, the experiment showed that there is much idle potential for links between data sets, which can be uncovered with our approach.

7.5 Efficiency of Query Processing over Linked Data, Rules, and Services

We have shown the feasibility of performing a query over Linked Data and services including rule-based reasoning in Section 7.2.1. In this section, we describe performance experiments made with LODR, our implementation of the query engine as presented in Section 6.3.

---

[11]http://km.aifb.kit.edu/services/twitterwrap/
[12]http://sw.deri.org/2006/08/nxparser/
[13]http://km.aifb.kit.edu/projects/btc-2010/
[14]Linking data is available online: http://people.aifb.kit.edu/ssp/geolink.tgz

Table 7.2: Performance characteristics of Alice's query

Measurements	live mode	proxy mode
Number of results	2,402	2,402
Number of retrieved IRIs	1,411	1,411
Run time	265.66 s	11.59 s

All experiments were run on a virtual machine with 4 CPU cores of the Intel x64 architecture, each running with 2.26 GHz and total RAM of 8 GB. The virtual machine was hosted in KIT's Open Nebula cloud.

We compared LODR with the following query engines:

- SQUIN: a query engine for Linked Data queries [SQU, HBF09, Har11]. In contrast to LODR, SQUIN is implemented with pull-based operators and has no direct support of query reachable completeness.

- Jena TDB: a centralised RDF store, which stores RDF in an optimised way on the hard disk together with indices [Jen].

Experiments for LODR and SQUIN were either run *live* accessing the actual Linked Data on the web, or in *proxy* mode, where data is cached in a local instance of the Cumulus RDF store [LH11]. Cumulus RDF is an HTTP proxy that serves Linked Data stored in a Cassandra backend. All queries were repeated six times and the measurements collected as follows:

- For Jena and proxy mode queries: the measurements of the first repetition are discarded as it is regarded as a warm up. The measurements of repetitions two to six are averaged.

- For live mode queries: measurements were averaged over the runs with the most retrieved information sources. Runs with fewer information sources are discarded as this means that sources were unavailable which has an effect on performance and query results.

7.5.1 Linked Data, Rules, and Services

In this section, we present performance characteristics of executing Alice's query about Queen Elizabeth II's descendants and pictures of them with geographical information (see Section 7.2.1). The Flickr LIDS and GeoNames LIDS were hosted locally on the machine performing the query in live mode, but the LIDS had to access the wrapped services (i.e., the Flickr API and the GeoNames services) on the web. The retrieved quads were loaded into a Cumulus RDF instance and we repeated the query in proxy mode. The measurements of both runs are shown in Table 7.2.

Not surprisingly, both live and proxy mode retrieved the same number of information sources and yielded the same results, as the proxy mode uses exactly the data that was retrieved by the live run. The run time of proxy mode is naturally much lower than that of

Table 7.3: Performance characteristics of Alice's query for other Persons

Persons	Number of results	Number of IRIs	Run time
Bill Clinton	204	114	31.15 s
Mohamed Al-Fayed	135	115	36.72 s
Cher	55	75	25.33 s
Nigel Lawson	180	101	26.17 s
Queen Silvia of Sweden	398	351	69.52 s
Barbara Bush	159	137	26.00 s
Princess Irene of the Netherlands	50	77	25.11 s
Prince Edward	116	124	39.06 s
Nancy Pelosi	35	73	27.64 s
Constantine II of Greece	74	122	30.09 s
Diana Quick	5	39	25.06 s
Dick Cheney	265	194	46.97 s

live mode and shows that the query execution with services and rules using our query engine poses only a little overhead compared to the time for accessing data and services on the web, which makes up 95.6 % of total execution time.

Queen Elizabeth II has a large number of descendants with many Flickr photos. We thus performed the query for further persons to show that the approach can be applied in other situations without any customisation. We selected twelve random persons from DBpedia who fulfill three requirements: (i) born on or after January 1st, 1925 (ancient persons rarely have photos on Flickr); (ii) have at least one child recorded on DBpedia; (iii) are still alive (according to DBpedia). The queries were performed in live mode and the results are recorded in Table 7.3. The results show that our approach facilitates an easy adaption of a query to different information needs.

7.5.2 Linked Data and Rules

For evaluating the ability of LODR to perform rule-based reasoning during the evaluation of Linked Data queries we performed experiments using the LUBM benchmark [GPH04, GPH05]. We created a Linked Data version of LUBM datasets of different sizes by loading the data into Cumulus RDF. Cumulus RDF is configured to return for an IRI all triples having the IRI in either subject or object position, thus we can assume subject-and-object authority for all triples and triple patterns. We use LUBM with the scale factors 1, 5, 10, 20; ranging from 100,577 triples (LUBM 1) to 2,688,080 triples (LUBM 20). LUBM datasets describe universities including students studying at the universities and faculty working for the universities. The scale factor determines the number of universities described in a dataset. The queries are the example queries provided by the LUBM project [LUB], which we list in Table 7.4. The domain knowledge of LUBM is specified as an OWL ontology but can be easily converted into rules, which we can use in LODR. Most of the rules are simple subclass

Table 7.4: LUBM Queries (IRI prefixes omitted)

Query Name	Query Text
LQ1	SELECT ?x WHERE { ?X a GradStudent . ?X takesCourse <http://Dept0.Uni0.edu/GradCourse0>}
LQ2	SELECT ?X ?Y ?Z WHERE { ?X a GradStudent . ?Y a University . ?Z a Department . ?X memberOf ?Z . ?Z subOrganizationOf ?Y . ?X undergraduateDegreeFrom ?Y }
LQ3	SELECT ?X WHERE { ?X a Publication . ?X author <http://Dept0.Uni0.edu/AssistantProf0> }
LQ4	SELECT ?X ?Y1 ?Y2 ?Y3 WHERE { ?X a Professor . ?X worksFor <http://Dept0.Uni0.edu/> . ?X name ?Y1 . ?X emailAddress ?Y2 . ?X telephone ?Y3 }
LQ5	SELECT ?X WHERE { ?X a Person . ?X memberOf <http://Dept0.Uni0.edu/> }
LQ6	SELECT ?X WHERE { ?X a Student }
LQ7	SELECT ?X ?Y WHERE { ?X a Student. ?Y a Course. <http://Dept0.Uni0.edu/AssocProf0> teacherOf ?Y . ?X takesCourse ?Y }
LQ8	SELECT ?X ?Y ?Z WHERE { ?X a Student . ?Y a Department . ?X memberOf ?Y . ?Y subOrganizationOf <http://Uni0.edu/>. ?X emailAddress ?Z }
LQ9	SELECT ?X ?Y ?Z WHERE { ?X a Student. ?Y a Faculty. ?Z a Course . ?X advisor ?Y . ?X takesCourse ?Z . ?Y teacherOf ?Z }
LQ10	SELECT ?X WHERE { ?X a Student . ?X takesCourse <http://Dept0.Uni0.edu/GradCourse0>}
LQ11	SELECT ?X WHERE { ?X a ResearchGroup . ?X subOrganizationOf <http://Uni0.edu/> }
LQ12	SELECT ?X ?Y WHERE { ?X a Chair . ?Y a Department . ?X worksFor ?Y . ?Y subOrganizationOf <http://Uni0.edu/> }
LQ13	SELECT ?X WHERE { ?X a Person . <http://Uni0.edu/> hasAlumnus ?X }
LQ14	SELECT ?X WHERE { ?X a UndergraduateStudent }

Table 7.5: Number of results for LUBM 1

Query	Reference answers	LODR	LODR w/o rules
LQ1	4	4	4
LQ2	0	0	0
LQ3	6	6	6
LQ4	34	34	0
LQ5	719	719	0
LQ6	7790	0	0
LQ7	67	67	0
LQ8	7790	77	0
LQ9	208	0	0
LQ10	4	4	0
LQ11	224	224	0
LQ12	15	15	0
LQ13	1	1	0
LQ14	5916	5916	5916

Table 7.6: Reasoning and query answering time for LUBM queries 1 - 14.
* denotes incomplete results. - denotes timeout.

	LODR			
Query	LUBM1	LUBM5	LUBM10	LUBM20
LQ1	2.38 s	2.38 s	2.38 s	2.38 s
LQ2	264.85 s	-	-	-
LQ3	2.23 s	2.19 s	2.23 s	2.22 s
LQ4	13.37 s	13.46 s	13.08 s	13.35 s
LQ5	25.10 s	24.57 s	25.09 s	24.96 s
LQ6	1.56 s*	1.56 s*	1.58 s*	1.58 s*
LQ7	4.77 s	4.81 s	4.83 s	4.79 s
LQ8	254.15 s	254.40 s	256.92 s	251.81 s
LQ9	2.04 s*	2.02 s*	2.02 s*	2.05 s*
LQ10	2.40 s	2.42 s	2.40 s	2.26 s
LQ11	57.04 s	58.19 s	56.98 s	57.87 s
LQ12	115.65 s	117.81 s	116.05 s	115.23 s
LQ13	2.16 s	4.53 s	5.72 s	10.40 s
LQ14	15.27 s	86.32 s	148.55 s	308.29 s

or subproperty relationships, e.g., stating that a graduate student is also a student. Also included are rules for transitivity (property *is suborganization of*) and existential entailments (e.g., somebody working for an organisation is an employee).

Our first experiment is to compare the number of results found by LODR with the reference answers provided for LUBM 1. In Table 7.5 we list the number of results including the number of results found by LODR without any rules about the domain knowledge. The numbers show that reasoning is necessary to find the correct results for all but four queries (LQ1-LQ3 and LQ14). Furthermore, we see that LODR with rules finds all correct results, except for queries LQ6, LQ8, LQ9. The reason for the missing results is that LODR retrieves the information source for *Student*, which returns no instances, as in the dataset individuals are only specified as one of the subclasses (*undergraduate student* and *graduate students*). The problem could be resolved by rewriting a query according to the domain knowledge to replace queries for instances of a class to queries for instances of all its subclasses. For example, query LQ6 could be transformed to the following union:

```
SELECT ?X WHERE { {?X a Student} UNION
                 {?X a GradStudent} UNION
                 {?X a UndergradStudent} }.
```

We did not implement this rewriting, as classes returning instances when dereferenced are very seldom in real Linked Data [UHPD12]. For queries about concrete instances all relevant inferences can be made from the data obtained when dereferencing the instance IRI. For example, query LQ5 retrieves all members of the specified department which have assigned concrete subclasses of person (e.g., graduate student or assistant professor), which is enough information to infer that the members are all persons.

The limited view of LODR on the dataset which is an disadvantage for some queries, where not all answers are found, is a big advantage in the next experiment, where we evaluate the scalability of the approach. We evaluated the queries on LUBM datasets of different scale factors and measured the time to perform the queries. The results are shown in Table 7.6. We can cluster the queries that are answered correctly (all except LQ6, LQ8, LQ9) into three categories:

- Queries requiring time that grows with increasing dataset size (LQ13, LQ14): the queries return more results when more universities are modelled. The number of undergraduate students grows linearly with the number of universities and the same holds for the query times. For LQ13 the alumni of the university with number zero only grows sublinearly as most of them are already modelled in LUBM 1 under the assumption that the alumni of the university stay at the same university with higher probability than going to another university.

- Queries which time out for scale factors larger than one: LQ2 timed out after more than 1 hour for larger datasets. The reason can be found in the lack of restriction to one single university and the complex query structure including a cycle. The query makes LODR retrieve the complete dataset and evaluating all domain rules leading to a large loaded dataset for which LODR is currently not optimised.

- Queries requiring constant time. Queries LQ1, LQ3, LQ4, LQ5, LQ7, LQ10, LQ11, LQ12 show no significant increase in query time when the size of the dataset is increased. These queries all are about concrete instances of one university and result size does not increase when adding more universities. Thus the queries benefit from the main advantage of LODR that only relevant data is retrieved and thus rules and queries are evaluated only on this subset of the complete data.

7.5.3 Linked Data

For measuring the performance of Linked Data queries we conducted experiments based on the FedBench benchmark [SGH+11]. The FedBench Linked Data benchmark defines eleven queries (FQ1 - FQ11) that can be evaluated over Linked Data on the web. The queries are listed in Table 7.7. Additionally the benchmark provides a dataset of 167,411,991 triples on which the queries can be evaluated to make the results better comparable.

The first experiment is a comparison of LODR to SQUIN in terms of the number of retrieved information sources and the number of found results. In proxy mode we could ensure that Cumulus RDF returns all triples containing the requested IRI in either subject or object position, thus we specified subject-and-object authority for all query patterns. The results are shown in Table 7.8. Both LODR and SQUIN find the same number of results for all queries and for most queries also retrieve the same number of information sources, which means that SQUIN implements a similar completeness notion as our proposed query reachable completeness. For queries FQ2 and FQ4 however we find substantial reductions (72.9 %, respectively 87.7 %) in the number of sources that are retrieved by LODR compared to SQUIN to find the same number of query results. The differences for FQ5 and FQ11 are marginal. No results and no successfully retrieved sources for Q8 are due to Cumulus RDF not returning any triples for the seed IRI in FQ8, probably due to a bug during loading or serving the data.

In the second experiment, we compared the total times for performing queries FQ1 - FQ5 and FQ11 using SQUIN and LODR both in live and proxy mode as well as using Jena TDB. The subset of queries was selected as the others did not deliver results when performed in live mode at the time of experimentation (between 14th May 2012 and 25th May 2012). For the proxy mode and Jena TDB we additionally measured the time to load the FedBench data into Cumulus RDF, respectively a Jena TDB store.

In Table 7.9, we list the times for performing the Linked Data queries and for loading the data if applicable. Both in live and proxy mode SQUIN performs faster on most queries than LODR, supposedly due to its more efficient and more mature implementation. However for FQ4 in live mode, LODR only needs 18 % of the time as SQUIN, which can be attributed to its implementation of query reachable completeness, as we have shown in Table 7.8 that it reduces the required sources for FQ4 by 87.7 %. We have no explanation for the bad performance of FQ3 for SQUIN in proxy mode, but it occurred repeatedly. Query execution of the live systems performed considerable slower than the systems with centralised data, e.g., the total time of LODR live for queries FQ1 - FQ5 and FQ11 is more than 20 times as high as for LODR proxy and more than 145 times as high as for Jena TDB. However, if

Table 7.7: FedBench Linked Data Queries (with abbreviated IRIs)

Query Name	Query Text
FQ1	SELECT * WHERE { ?PAPER swc:isPartOf conf:iswc/2008/posters_demos . ?PAPER swrc:author ?P . ?P rdfs:label ?N . }
FQ2	SELECT * WHERE { ?PROC swc:relatedToEvent conf:eswc/2010 . ?PAPER swc:isPartOf ?PROC . ?PAPER swrc:author ?P . }
FQ3	SELECT * WHERE { ?PAPER swc:isPartOf conf:iswc/2008/posters_demos . ?PAPER swrc:author ?P. ?P owl:sameAs ?X. ?P rdfs:label ?N .}
FQ4	SELECT * WHERE { ?ROLE swc:isRoleAt conf:eswc/2010 . ?ROLE swc:heldBy ?P .?PAPER swrc:author ?P . ?PAPER swc:isPartOf ?PROC . ?PROC swc:relatedTo conf:eswc/2010.}
FQ5	SELECT * WHERE { ?A dbowl:artist dbpedia:Michael_Jackson. ?A rdf:type dbowl:Album . ?A foaf:name ?N . }
FQ6	SELECT * WHERE {?DIR dbowl:nationality dbpedia:Italy. ?FILM dbowl:director ?DIR . ?X owl:sameAs ?FILM . ?X foaf:based_near ?Y . ?Y <http://www.geonames.org/ontology#officialName> ?N .}
FQ7	SELECT * WHERE {?X gn:name ?N . ?X gn:parentFeature <http://sws.geonames.org/2921044/>.}
FQ8	SELECT * WHERE {?DRUG owl:sameAs ?S . ?DRUG drugbank:drugCategory drugbank:micronutrient . ?DRUG drugbank:casRegistryNumber ?ID . ?S foaf:name ?O . ?S skos:subject ?SUB . }
FQ9	SELECT * WHERE { ?P dbowl:managerClub ?X . ?X skos:subject dbp:FIFA_World_Cup-winning_countries . ?P foaf:name "Luiz Felipe Scolari" . }
FQ10	SELECT * WHERE { ?N skos:subject dbp:Chancellors_of_Germany . ?N owl:sameAs ?P2 . ?P2 nytimes:latest_use ?U . }
FQ11	SELECT * WHERE { ?X dbowl:team dbpedia:Eintracht_Frankfurt . ?X rdfs:label ?Y . ?X dbowl:birthDate ?D . ?X dbowl:birthPlace ?P . ?P rdfs:label ?L . }

Table 7.8: Comparison of number of retrieved information sources to find query results (proxy mode)

Query	# results	# sources LODR	# sources SQUIN	Reduction
FQ1	309	315	315	0.0 %
FQ2	185	64	236	72.9 %
FQ3	162	315	315	0.0 %
FQ4	50	87	709	87.7 %
FQ5	28	37	38	2.6 %
FQ6	39	418	418	0.0 %
FQ7	33	34	34	0.0 %
FQ8	0	0	0	0.0 %
FQ9	1	57	57	0.0 %
FQ10	3	41	41	0.0 %
FQ11	376	407	403	-1.0 %

Table 7.9: Performance of FedBench Linked Data queries

System	FQ1	FQ2	FQ3	FQ4	FQ5	FQ11	Load	Sum
LODR live	143 s	31 s	143 s	41 s	10 s	92 s	-	460 s
SQUIN live	88 s	27 s	88 s	248 s	12 s	20 s	-	483 s
LODR proxy	4.2 s	1.9 s	4.0 s	3.4 s	1.7 s	7.7 s	22,957 s	22,980 s
SQUIN proxy	1.7 s	1.1 s	61.0 s	3.4 s	0.6 s	2.8 s	22,957 s	23,028 s
Jena TDB	.61 s	.43 s	.53 s	.60 s	.23 s	.75 s	23,391 s	23,394 s

we consider loading time as part of the centralised systems, the total execution time for the live systems is below 3 % of the centralised systems. Of course the time reduction of the live systems will dramatically decrease for an increasing number of queries, but centralised systems have to be updated with new data.

In Table 7.10, we list the number of results found by the different query engines. As expected, the centralised Jena TDB approach yields the same number of results as LODR with query reachable completeness. Both LODR and SQUIN find more results for some queries when performed live on the actual Linked Data web, which could be expected as the

Table 7.10: Number of results for FedBench Linked Data queries

System	FQ1	FQ2	FQ3	FQ4	FQ5	FQ11
LODR live	334	185	191	50	43	23,301
SQUIN live	334	185	191	50	33	260
LODR proxy	309	185	162	50	28	376
SQUIN proxy	309	185	162	50	28	376
Jena TDB	309	185	162	50	28	376

Table 7.11: Authority of triples in the Billion Triple Challenge 2011 dataset.

Authority type	Relative	Absolute number
no authority	5.6 %	108,628,370
s	90.1 %	1,757,863,321
p	0.1 %	988,489
o	24.7 %	482,222,566
$s \wedge p$	< 0.1 %	653,770
$s \wedge o$	20.4 %	398,177,024
$p \wedge o$	< 0.1 %	279,436
$s \wedge p \wedge o$	< 0.1 %	254,890
$s \vee p$	90.1 %	1,758,198,040
$s \vee o$	94.4 %	1,841,908,863
$p \vee o$	24.8 %	482,931,619
$s \vee p \vee o$	94.4 %	1,842,219,036
Unique triples	100.00 %	1,950,847,406

FedBench dataset is only a partial snapshot of Linked Data and available Linked Data has increased since its creation.

7.6 Completeness

The completeness classes that we proposed in Section 6.2 are based on the notion of authority, i.e., the relation between the identifiers in a triple and the identifiers of the documents in which the triple is stated. One of the assumptions behind Linked Data is that dereferencing the identifier of an entity should provide information about the entity. This assumption alone does however not prohibit that dereferencing returns information about arbitrary other entities nor that arbitrary other documents can contain information about the entity of interest. In order to show that authority is none-the-less a meaningful concept, we analysed a large amount of information, which is representative of the available Linked Data on the web: the Billion Triple Challenge (BTC) 2011 data set. The BTC consists of approximately 2 billion (exactly 2,144,893,389) triples which were obtained in May and June 2011 by crawling Linked Data documents starting from a set of seed IRIs, which were randomly chosen from existing Linked Data crawls. For each triple the documents in which it is stated are recorded. Additionally, HTTP redirects are collected. The whole data set is of size 434 GB. Using IRI normalisation and the recorded redirects, we implemented the co function given us the correspondence between an entity and its authoritive document. For each triple we checked with which atomic authorities it is stated (none, subject authoritive, predicate authoritive, and object authoritive) and computed which complex authorities thus hold for the triple (e.g., a triple stated subject authoritive and object authoritive has the following complex authorities: subject and object authoritive, subject or object authoritive, subject or predicate authoritive, predicate or object authoritive, subject or predicate or object authoritive). The numbers are listed in Table 7.11. For blank nodes, we consider the defining document as authoritive.

One key result is that 94.4 % are stated with some authority, meaning that the vast majority of triples can be found by dereferencing the identifier of one of the entities in the triple. The class of completely answerable queries is defined in a way to ensure that for every relevant triple at least one identifier is known either from the IRIs in the query or from a variable already bound in another triple. The most prevalent authority type is subject authority with a share of 90.1 % of all triples, followed by object authority with 24.7 %, whereas predicate authority is very insignificant with 0.1 %. Exploiting the dominance of subject authority, one can discard the requirement for users to specify authority mappings for answering queries according to the query reachable completeness notion and instead just assume a mapping for all patterns to subject authority.

Umbrich et al. analyse a different Linked Data crawl and come to the similar conclusion that 95 % of the triples having an dereferencable identifier u in subject position can be found by dereferencing u [UHPD12].

7.7 Fulfillment of Requirements

In the following, we go through the requirements identified in Section 2.2 and discuss how our work addresses them including pointers to relevant sections.

R1: *Web Compatibility* The proposed architecture for information systems is based on the Linked Data principles, which embrace the use of web technologies. The LIDS extension for integrating information services into Linked Data is carefully designed to maintain uniform access methods and information models (Section 6.1). While we define the formalism underlying our policy language in an abstract way in terms of first-order logic, we also describe how we can create practical web compatible policy languages based on standardised web languages like OWL and RIF (Section 4.5). We describe the syntaxes and implementations for the practical languages in Section 7.1. The practical web compatibility of our methods is demonstrated in the scenario of Alice, where we integrate existing data sources (DBpedia) with existing information services (Flickr and GeoNames) while considering policies formalising licenses that are in widespread use on the web (Creative Commons) (Section 7.2.1).

R2: *Formal Semantics* We define formal semantics of the policy language using a greatest fixed point model layered on top of standard first-order logic semantics (Section 4.4). The semantics are applicable for clearly defined fragments of first-order logic, which avoid ambiguities that could otherwise occur in practically irrelevant corner cases. We evaluate the appropriateness of the semantics by showing that it corresponds to the intuition behind the Creative Commons licenses (Section 7.2.1).

R3: *Data-centricity of Policies* The defined policy formalism allows to express policies that restrict the actions allowed by other policies, thus enabling the modelling of single actions in isolation. Furthermore, we specified how policies can be linked to information artefacts in a web compliant way, either by exploiting the distinction of information and non-information resources or by using the HTTP link header (Section 4.6). The ability to attach policies to artefacts and the local view enabled by policy restrictions qualifies our policies as data-centric.

R4: *Extendable Vocabulary of Computational Model* As required, we base our vocabulary of artefact usage descriptions on the Open Provenance Model (Section 4.1.1). The vocabulary can be easily extended particularly enabled by using web compliant technologies which assign globally unique identifiers to concepts and properties in the vocabulary.

R5: *Content-based Restrictions on Other Policies* The proposed policy formalism introduces a special containedIn relation that models the containment of policies. Containment is defined in terms of the usages allowed by two policies. The containedIn relation can be used as part of policy conditions, which enables the restriction of admissible policies for generated artefacts based on the actions that they should or should not allow. In contrast to name-based policy restrictions, our formalism leads to increased compatibility.

R6: *Support for Obligations* We introduced an approach for application- and domain-specific distinctions between policy violations and obligations that are not yet fulfilled (Section 5.3). The approach is implemented in a prototype for Datalog-based policies (Section 7.1).

R7: *Expressivity for Common Restrictions* We identified a set of restrictions that are common to many practical policies and showed solutions in our proposed language (Section 4.7). Furthermore, we realised three scenarios in different domains which included the modelling of practical policies (Section 7.2).

R8: *Decidable and Practical Classification* The decidability of the policy language formalism is ensured by introducing restrictions on allowed first-order logic constructs that maintain decidability if the employed first-order logic fragment is decidable (Section 4.4). We implemented prototypes for both Datalog-based and OWL-based policy engines and used them to demonstrate feasibility of the scenarios (Section 7.2) and to conduct performance experiments (Section 7.3). We also showed how scalability restrictions can be overcome for practical problems by partitioning the problem.

R9: *User Interactions with Hidden Formal Logic* We presented a method to construct policies from building blocks described in natural language and backed by formal policies for machine evaluation (Section 5.1). While the method introduces a new layer of formalism, it can be conveniently hidden by easy-to-build graphical user interfaces due to its clear structure. Furthermore, we showed an approach that exploits the structure of such policies to provide natural language explanations for the reasons why an action is classified as non-compliant (Section 5.2). Together the two methods hide the logical formalism underlying policies from the user in the most common interaction tasks: specifying policies and finding reasons for non-compliance.

R10: *Decentralised Architecture for Interlinked Information* As the underlying architecture for decentralised information systems, we chose Linked Data. Linked Data uses RDF as information model, which directly supports links to external data entities via IRIs. Furthermore, Linked Data mandates that the used IRIs are dereferencable via HTTP and return RDF descriptions of the identified data entities. In Section 6.3, we presented a query processor exploiting the links in Linked Data to answer queries over the distributed information space.

R11: *Support for Information Services* The Linked Data Services (LIDS) approach integrates information services in a fully compliant way into Linked Data (Section 6.1).

R12: *Completeness Notions for Queries* We introduced several notions of completeness for querying Linked Data systems in Section 6.2. Besides the theoretical web completeness, and the rather coarse seed completeness, we defined the practical query reachable completeness (QRC). QRC guarantees complete answers if trusted sources for certain kinds of statements are restricted on the notion of authority, which is very common in the existing Linked Data web (Section 7.6).

7.8 Discussion

In this chapter, we described practical systems that implement the technologies that we proposed in this work. Using the implementations, we showed how they can be applied to realise the three scenarios that motivated and framed our work. The scenarios showed the feasibility of building systems that integrate all components developed as part of this thesis. Subsequently, we took an isolated look at different components and conducted performance experiments. We used benchmarks both based on existing, real data (e.g., FedBench) and on data generated explicitly for the benchmark (e.g., policy experiments and LUBM). Finally, we presented how our work addresses the identified requirements.

Chapter 8

Conclusion

In this thesis, we developed methods for decentralised processing of information with usage restrictions. Our methods provide a novel approach that addresses several requirements, which we derived from an analysis of three exemplary scenarios from different domains. Through our contributions, we advanced the state of the art in the areas of knowledge representation, policy-based computing, semantic technologies, and information integration.

We conclude our thesis in this chapter as follows. Section 8.1 summarises our contributions. In Section 8.2, we give an outlook on future directions for which our work can provide the foundation.

8.1 Summary of Contributions

The underlying motivation for our work is that service providers manage and process a large and ever increasing amount of information on behalf of the information owners. Such information is often subject to usage restrictions, which stem from a multitude of sources including copyright laws, privacy laws, social norms, or company guidelines. The providers of services are no longer single entities but in many cases co-operate in dynamically changing networks. The lack of a central view, let alone control, on the processes of such networks requires an information architecture that facilitates interoperability and adherence to usage restrictions. We developed in this thesis a number of solutions in order to verify our overall hypothesis that

> decentralised systems can be built that support end users in the creation of services and applications using information in compliance to applicable usage restrictions.

To further substantiate the goal of our work, we identified a number of requirements by analysing different domains with the help of concrete scenarios. Our approach comprises three components each targeted at a different subhypothesis; together the subhypotheses encompass our overall hypothesis. In the following, we structured the discussion of our contributions along the three components, respectively subhypotheses, of our work.

Language for Data-centric Usage Policies

Formalising usage restrictions in a policy language enables automatically computing whether a specific information usage is compliant or non-compliant. Our approach was thus to develop a suitable language to show the validity of our first hypothesis:

> Information usage restrictions can be formalised in a way such that compliance of an information use can be checked without a complete view on the containing process.

We introduced the concept of data-centric usage policies with content-based policy restrictions. Data-centric policies are attached to information artefacts and take a localised view on isolated information usages. Instead of relying on information about all future usages of an artefact and its derivations, the localised view restricts the policies of the derivations and assumes that they will be used in a compliant way. Compatibility of such policies is increased by restricting admissible policies based on their content, i.e., the usages they allow, and not based on their names. Such content-based restrictions are specified in terms of whether a policy is contained in or contains certain other policies.

We introduced a framework based on first-order logic that specifies the semantics for languages with a special relation that models the containment between policies. The containment relation leads to meta-modelling and self-referentiality in policies, which we support by defining a greatest fixed point semantics for the framework. We instantiated the framework to create concrete policy languages by extending description logics and Datalog with the containment relation. We validated the semantics of the languages by modelling the Creative Commons licenses and ensuring that we infer the correct compatibilities between the individual licenses.

We furthermore identified a number of restrictions that are common in usage policies and gave generic patterns that model the restrictions.

Methods for Interacting with Policies

End users of policy-based systems cannot be expected to be experts in computer science or formal logics. The acceptance of such systems thus depends on the methods with which users interact with policies. We developed a number of methods to substantiate our second hypothesis:

> Policy specifiers and information consumers can interact with the policy-aware system without being exposed to logic formalisms.

We presented a structured model, which enables users to compose policies from existing re-usable building blocks. Behind each building block is a policy that formally defines its meaning. The building blocks can be described with additional meta-data including natural language descriptions of their meaning. Users can select building blocks based on their descriptions without the need to understand their formal definition.

Based on the structured model, we introduced an explanation component that can explain in natural language to a user why an intended usage is non-compliant. The proposed explanation algorithm exploits the natural language labels and the user-given structure of policies.

The generated explanations are complete in the sense, that they present the only way to reach compliance, and adhering to them guarantees compliance.

Furthermore, we developed an approach for automatically handling obligations on behalf of the user. Our approach supports domain-specific definitions that distinguish between unfulfilled obligations and policy violations.

Decentralised Architecture for Information Processing

The policy-aware infrastructure needs to be based on a unifying architecture that gives access to all relevant information sources. Otherwise, much of the processing will take place outside the architecture, which also circumvents the automated methods for ensuring policy compliance. Due to the heterogeneity of the information sources, owners, and processors, we require a decentralised and open architecture. We presented several extensions to the Linked Data architecture in order to validate our third hypothesis:

> Decentralised systems can provide a uniform view with well-defined borders on information and policies distributed over a wide range of data sources.

We extended the Linked Data architecture with support for information services by developing the Linked Data Services (LIDS) approach. We developed a number of LIDS and used them throughout our experiments. We also included support for LIDS in the Linked Data query processor that we developed.

In contrast to previous solutions, our query processor evaluates queries according to formally well-defined completeness notions. We introduced, three formal completeness notions and analysed theoretically their relation to each other. Especially the notion of query-reachable completeness is practical as it requires access only to a manageable set of data sources and provides all results available on the web under certain assumptions. We analysed large amounts of existing Linked Data, to validate the appropriateness of the assumptions.

8.2 Future Work and Outlook

In this section, we discuss a number of open problems that are raised by this thesis and outline possible next steps that can be based on our work.

Combination with Statistical and Heuristic Methods

We consider the methods developed in this thesis as exact in the sense that they clearly and unambiguously specify the expected result. The contact with Linked Data in the real world has shown us limitations of such exact approaches due to the heterogeneity and the lack of quality of the data. In the following, we outline several opportunities to overcome the limitations by combining our work with statistical and heuristic methods.

A core feature of Linked Data Services is identity resolution by defining equivalences between entities in the service response with entities in other information sources. We built the resolution on basic graph patterns, which provide exact descriptions of entities. An interesting idea would be to replace the basic graph patterns by patterns in the SILK language [VBGK09], which supports heuristic conditions such as thresholds on the editing distance of labels.

Furthermore, it would be interesting to experiment with (semi-)automatic schema alignment methods when processing Linked Data and services instead of the static rule-based alignments that we currently use.

We can consider using our completeness notions as a method for quality control by restricting the data sources that can contribute to query results. Combining our completeness with statistical methods that detect outliers or suspicious values in processed information could lead to further increases in quality.

Re-use and Extensions of Language Formalism

We had a clear motivation for the definition of our logic framework with the containedIn predicate for representing formulae containment: we wanted to express data-centric policies with content-based policy restrictions. However, the self-referential and meta-modelling features of our proposed language are interesting in themselves. We see three directions for further developments of the language.

First, it might be worthwhile to experiment with other modelling problems, where the expressivity of our language can bring a benefit. For example, approaches for matching formal service descriptions often check the containment of pre- and postconditions of services. With our language, the semantics of a matching approach could be formally described using the containment predicate.

Second, it would be interesting to study if our closed-fragment-based syntactic restrictions could be further relaxed without giving up the positive properties of the semantics.

A third direction is to investigate further types of content-based policy restrictions, i.e., predicates that model properties of a policy or a relation between policies. One candidate for such a restriction would be a condition that two policies have a non-empty intersection, i.e., there exists a usage that is allowed by both policies.

Completeness

Our work on completeness for Linked Data query processing leaves room for two directions of further developments: (i) extending the notions to consider the effects of reasoning, and (ii) using the completeness notions to support more expressive queries.

We already commented on the effect of equivalences in the form of owl:sameAs statements on the completeness notions. We have not yet considered further modelling features or the additional effort needed for implementing completeness in the light of background knowledge as it is illustrated by the following example. We observed during our experiments with the LUBM benchmark that a lookup for the class student did not return any instances, as they are only specified to be in one of the subclasses of student, such as undergraduate student. A possible implementation strategy could build on query rewriting techniques that query not only for instances of student but also for all known subclasses.

Our completeness notions can enable more expressive queries as they support checking for absence of query results. In future work, we would like to support negation-as-failure in both rules and queries.

Alignment of Efforts for Aligning of Linked Data and Services

Our Linked Data Services approach was developed in parallel to other independent efforts to align Linked Data and services, most notably are Linked Open Services [NK10] and REST-desc [VSD$^+$11]. We are currently in the process of aligning the different efforts under the label of Linked APIs. We already have organised events together, including tutorials at international conferences and the Linked APIs workshop in conjunction with the Extended Semantic Web Conference 2012. For the future, it would be interesting to bring our approaches and experiences into standardisation activities such as the Linked Data Platform Working Group organised by the W3C.

Outlook

We believe that it is an irreversible trend that more and more information is produced, gathered, shared, and used in all contexts of life. This information facilitates the development of new services that provide added value to both individuals and organisations. We expect that the complexity of the provider networks supplying such services will further increase and thus, that there is a growing need for decentralised information processing systems. It is important that such systems respect usage restrictions imposed by information owners in order to avoid misuse.

In this thesis, we developed an approach for decentralised processing of information in compliance with applicable usage restrictions. Our presented work can serve as a solid foundation for both practical applications and future research.

List of Tables

List of Figures

Bibliography

[AALY08]   Hal Abelson, Ben Adida, Mike Linksvayer, and Nathan Yergler. ccREL: The Creative Commons Rights Expression Language. Technical report, Creative Commons, 2008. Available at `http://creativecommons.org/projects/ccREL`.

[ACH⁺07]   Fabian Abel, Juri Luca De Coi, Nicola Henze, Arne Wolf Koesling, Daniel Krause, and Daniel Olmedilla. Enabling Advanced and Context-Dependent Access Control in RDF Stores. In Karl Aberer, Philippe Cudré-Mauroux, Key-Sun Choi, Natasha Noy, Dean Allemang, Kyung-Il Lee, Lyndon Nixon, Jennifer Golbeck, Peter Mika, Diana Maynard, Riichiro Mizoguchi, and Guus Schreiber, editors, *Proceedings of the 6th International Semantic Web Conference and the 2nd Asian Semantic Web Conference (ISWC'07/ASWC'07)*, number 4825 in Lecture Notes in Computer Science, pages 1–14, Busan, Korea, 2007. Springer.

[AD98]   Serge Abiteboul and Oliver M. Duschka. Complexity of Answering Queries using Materialized Views. In *Proceedings of the 17th ACM SIGACT-SIGMOD-SIGART Symposium on Principles of Database Systems (PODS'98)*, pages 254–263, Seattle, WA, USA, 1998. ACM.

[AFRS11]   Darko Anicic, Paul Fodor, Sebastian Rudolph, and Nenad Stojanovic. EP-SPARQL: A Unified Language for Event Processing and Stream Reasoning. In Sadagopan Srinivasan, Krithi Ramamritham, Arun Kumar, M. P. Ravindra, Elisa Bertino, and Ravi Kumar, editors, *Proceedings of the 20th International Conference on World Wide Web (WWW'11)*, pages 635–644, Hyderabad, India, 2011. ACM.

[AGLL05]   Dakshi Agrawal, James Giles, Kang-Won Lee, and Jorge Lobo. Policy Ratification. In *Proceedings of the 6th IEEE Workshop on Policies for Distributed Systems and Networks (POLICY'05)*, pages 223–232, Stockholm, Sweden, 2005. IEEE Computer Society.

[AH10]   Alapan Arnab and Andrew Hutchison. Persistent Access Control: A Formal Model for DRM. In Arne-Jørgen Berre, Asunción Gómez-Pérez, Kurt Tutschku, and Dieter Fensel, editors, *Proceedings of the 3rd Future Internet Symposium (FIS'10)*, volume 6369 of *Lecture Notes in Computer Science*, Berlin, Germany, 2010. Springer.

[AHV94]   Serge Abiteboul, Richard Hull, and Victor Vianu. *Foundations of Databases*. Addison Wesley, 1994.

[AK07]   José Luis Ambite and Dipsy Kapoor. Automatically Composing Data Work-flows with Relational Descriptions and Shim Services. In Karl Aberer, Philippe Cudré-Mauroux, Key-Sun Choi, Natasha Noy, Dean Allemang, Kyung-Il Lee, Lyndon Nixon, Jennifer Golbeck, Peter Mika, Diana Maynard, Riichiro Mizoguchi, and Guus Schreiber, editors, *Proceedings of the 6th International Semantic Web Conference and the 2nd Asian Semantic Web Conference (ISWC'07/ASWC'07)*, number 4825 in Lecture Notes in Computer Science, pages 15–29, Busan, Korea, 2007. Springer.

[API]   OWL API. (Software). http://owlapi.sourceforge.net/, accessed June 15th 2012.

[ARFS12]   Darko Anicic, Sebastian Rudolph, Paul Fodor, and Nenad Stojanovic. Stream Reasoning and Complex Event Processing in ETALIS. *Semantic Web*, 3(4):397–407, 2012.

[AS05]   Sudhir Agarwal and Barbara Sprick. Specification of Access Control and Cer-tification Policies for Semantic Web Services. In Kurt Bauknecht, Birgit Pröll, and Hannes Werthner, editors, *Proceedings of the 6th International Confer-ence on E-Commerce and Web Technologies (EC-Web'05)*, volume 3590 of *Lecture Notes in Computer Science*, pages 348–357, Copenhagen, Denmark, 2005. Springer.

[AV00]   Serge Abiteboul and Victor Vianu. Queries and Computation on the Web. *Theor. Comput. Sci.*, 239:231–255, May 2000.

[AvBN95]   Hajnal Andréka, Johan van Benthem, and István Németi. Back and Forth be-tween Modal Logic and Classical Logic. *Logic Journal of the IGPL*, 3(5):685–720, 1995.

[Baa90]   Franz Baader. Terminological Cycles in KL-ONE-based Knowledge Represen-tation Languages. In *Proceedings of the 8th National Conference on Artificial Intelligence (AAAI'90)*, pages 621–626, Boston, MA, USA, 1990. AAAI Press.

[BBC+09]   Elisa Bertino, Carolyn Brodie, Seraphin B. Calo, Lorrie Faith Cranor, Clare-Marie Karat, John Karat, Ninghui Li, Dan Lin, Jorge Lobo, Qun Ni, Prathima Rao, and Xiping Wang. Analysis of Privacy and Security Policies. *IBM Journal of Research and Development*, 53(2):225–241, 2009.

[BBC+10]   Davide Francesco Barbieri, Daniele Braga, Stefano Ceri, Emanuele Della Valle, and Michael Grossniklaus. Incremental Reasoning on Streams and Rich Background Knowledge. In Lora Aroyo, Grigoris Antoniou, Eero Hyvönen, Annette ten Teije, Heiner Stuckenschmidt, Liliana Cabral, and Tania Tudo-rache, editors, *Proceedings of the 7th Extended Semantic Web Conference*

(ESWC'10) Part I, volume 6088 of *Lecture Notes in Computer Science*, pages 1–15, Heraklion, Crete, Greece, 2010. Springer.

[BBL05]   Ji-Won Byun, Elisa Bertino, and Ninghui Li. Purpose Based Access Control of Complex Data for Privacy Protection. In *Proceedings of the 10th ACM Symposium on Access Control Models and Technologies (SACMAT'05)*, pages 102–110, Stockholm, Sweden, 2005. ACM.

[BCB07]   Mahmoud Barhamgi, Pierre-Antoine Champin, and Djamal Benslimane. A Framework for Web Services-based Query Rewriting and Resolution in Loosely Coupled Information Systems, 2007.

[BCG07]   Christian Bizer, Richard Cyganiak, and Tobias Gauss. The RDF Book Mashup: From Web APIs to a Web of Data. In *Proceedings of the Workshop on Scripting for the Semantic Web (SFSW'07) in conjunction with the 4th European Semantic Web Conference (ESWC'07)*, Innsbruck, Austria, 2007.

[BCGM05]   Christian Bizer, Richard Cyganiak, Tobias Gauss, and Oliver Maresch. The TriQL.P Browser: Filtering Information using Context-, Content- and Rating-based Trust Policies. In *Proceedings of the Semantic Web and Policy Workshop in conjunction with the 4th International Semantic Web Conference (ISWC'05)*, Galway, Ireland, 2005.

[BCM+07]   Franz Baader, Diego Calvanese, Deborah McGuinness, Daniele Nardi, and Peter Patel-Schneider, editors. *The Description Logic Handbook*. Cambridge University Press, second edition, 2007.

[BDOS10]   Piero Bonatti, Juri Luca De Coi, Daniel Olmedilla, and Luigi Sauro. A Rule-based Trust Negotiation System. *IEEE Transactions on Knowledge and Data Engineering*, 22:1507–1520, 2010.

[BDS02]   Piero Bonatti, Sabrina De Capitani Di Vimercati, and Pierangela Samarati. An Algebra for Composing Access Control Policies. *ACM Transactions on Information and System Security*, 5(1):1–35, 2002.

[BEPW03]   Peter Biddle, Paul England, Marcus Peinado, and Bryan Willman. The Darknet and the Future of Content Protection. In Joan Feigenbaum, editor, *Revised Papers of the ACM Workshop on Security and Privacy in Digital Rights Management (DRM'02)*, volume 2696 of *Lecture Notes in Computer Science*, pages 155–176, Washington DC, USA, 2003. Springer.

[BFG10]   Moritz Y. Becker, Cedric Fournet, and Andrew D. Gordon. SecPAL: Design and Semantics of a Decentralized Authorization Language. *Journal of Computer Security (JCS)*, 18:597–643, 2010.

[BH08]   Glenn Bruns and Michael Huth. Access-Control Policies via Belnap Logic: Effective and Efficient Composition and Analysis. In *Proceedings of the 21st*

IEEE Computer Security Foundations Symposium (CSF'08), pages 163–176, Pittsburgh, PA, USA, 2008. IEEE Computer Society.

[BHBL09]   Christian Bizer, Tom Heath, and Tim Berners-Lee. Linked Data – The Story So Far. *International Journal on Semantic Web and Information Systems*, 5(3):1–22, 2009.

[BJC11]   Christian Bizer, Anja Jentzsch, and Richard Cyganiak. State of the LOD Cloud, 2011. Version 0.3, Available at `http://www4.wiwiss.fu-berlin.de/lodcloud/state/`, accessed 7th June 2012.

[BK08]   Greg Barish and Craig A. Knoblock. Speculative Plan Execution for Information Gathering. *Artif. Intell.*, 172(4-5):413–453, 2008.

[BL06]   Tim Berners-Lee. Linked Data – Design Issues, 27th July 2006. Available at `http://www.w3.org/DesignIssues/LinkedData`, accessed July 22nd 2012.

[BL10]   Christian Baumann and Christian Loës. Formalizing Copyright for the Internet of Services. In Gabriele Kotsis, David Taniar, Eric Pardede, Imad Saleh, and Ismail Khalil, editors, *Proceedings of the 12th International Conference on Information Integration and Web-based Applications and Services (iiWAS'10)*, pages 714–721. ACM, 2010.

[BLC11]   Tim Berners-Lee and Dan Connolly. *Notation3 (N3): A Readable RDF Syntax.* W3C Team Submission, 28 March 2011. Available at `http://www.w3.org/TeamSubmission/n3/`.

[BLFM05]   Tim Berners-Lee, Roy T. Fielding, and Larry Masinter. *Uniform Resource Identifier (URI): Generic Syntax.* Number 3986 in Request for Comments (RFC). Internet Engineering Task Force (IETF), January 2005. Available at `http://www.ietf.org/rfc/rfc3986.txt`, accessed July 24th 2012.

[BLK+09]   Christian Bizer, Jens Lehmann, Georgi Kobilarov, Sören Auer, Christian Becker, Richard Cyganiak, and Sebastian Hellmann. DBpedia – A Crystallization Point for the Web of Data. *Journal of Web Semantics: Science, Services and Agents on the World Wide Web*, 7(3):154–165, 2009.

[BM08]   Piero Bonatti and Fabio Mogavero. Comparing Rule-based Policies. In *Proceedings of the 9th IEEE Workshop on Policies for Distributed Systems and Networks (POLICY'08)*, pages 11–18, Palisades, NY, USA, 2008. IEEE Computer Society.

[BM10]   Dan Brickley and Libby Miller. *FOAF Vocabulary Specification 0.98.* 09 August 2010. Available at `http://xmlns.com/foaf/spec/`, accessed July 22nd 2012.

[BMB10]   Moritz Y. Becker, Alexander Malkis, and Laurent Bussard. A Practical Generic
            Privacy Language. In Somesh Jha and Anish Mathuria, editors, *Proceedings of
            the 6th International Conference on Information Systems Security (ICISS'10)*,
            number 6503 in Lecture Notes in Computer Science, pages 125–139, Gandhi-
            nagar, India, 2010. Springer.

[BN08]   Moritz Y. Becker and Sebastian Nanz. The Role of Abduction in Declarative
            Authorization Policies. In Paul Hudak and David Scott Warren, editors, *Pro-
            ceedings of the 10th International Symposium on Practical Aspects of Declar-
            ative Languages (PADL'08)*, volume 4902 of *Lecture Notes in Computer Sci-
            ence*, pages 84–99, San Francisco, CA, USA, 2008. Springer.

[BOP06]   Piero Bonatti, Daniel. Olmedilla, and Joachim Peer. Advanced Policy Expla-
            nations on the Web. In Gerhard Brewka, Silvia Coradeschi, Anna Perini, and
            Paolo Traverso, editors, *Proceedings of the 17th European Conference on Arti-
            ficial Intelligence (ECAI'06)*, volume 141 of *Frontiers in Artificial Intelligence
            and Applications*, pages 200–204, Riva del Garda, Trentino, Italy, 2006. IOS
            Press.

[Bor96]   Alex Borgida. On the Relative Expressiveness of Description Logics and Pred-
            icate Logics. *Artificial Intelligence*, 82(1–2):353–367, 1996.

[BRDM07]   Patricia Beatty, Ian Reay, Scott Dick, and James Miller. P3P Adoption on
            E-Commerce Web Sites: A Survey and Analysis. *IEEE Internet Computing*,
            11:65–71, 2007.

[BS85]   Ronald J. Brachman and James G. Schmolze. An Overview of the KL-ONE
            Knowledge Representation System. *Cognitive Science*, 9(2):171–216, 1985.

[CBHS05]   Jeremy J. Carroll, Christian Bizer, Pat Hayes, and Patrick Stickler. Named
            Graphs, Provenance and Trust. In Allan Ellis and Tatsuya Hagino, editors, *Pro-
            ceedings of the 14th International Conference on World Wide Web (WWW'05)*,
            pages 613–622, Chiba, Japan, 2005. ACM.

[CCG10]   Jean-Paul Calbimonte, Óscar Corcho, and Alasdair J. G. Gray. Enabling
            Ontology-based Access to Streaming Data Sources. In Peter F. Patel-Schneider,
            Yue Pan, Birte Glimm, Pascal Hitzler, Peter Mika, Jeff Pan, and Ian Hor-
            rocks, editors, *Proceedings of the 9th International Semantic Web Conference
            (ISWC'10) Part I*, volume 6496 of *LNCS*, pages 96–111, Shanghai, China,
            2010. Springer.

[COML10]   Madalina Croitoru, Nir Oren, Simon Miles, and Michael Luck. Graph-based
            Norm Explanation. In Max Bramer, Miltos Petridis, and Adrian Hopgood,
            editors, *Proceedings of the 30th SGAI International Conference on Innovative
            Techniques and Applications of Artificial Intelligence (AI'10)*, pages 35–48,
            Cambridge, UK, 2010. Springer.

[CR02]   Hans Chalupsky and Thomas A. Russ. Whynot: Debugging Failed Queries in
            Large Knowledge Bases. In *Proceedings of the 14th Conference on Innovative
            Applications of Artificial Intelligence (IAAI'02)*, pages 870–877, Edmonton,
            Alberta, Canada, 2002. AAAI Press.

[Cre09]   Creative Commons. *Defining "Noncommercial": A Study of How the Online
            Population Understands "Noncommercial Use"*. September 2009. Available
            at http://wiki.creativecommons.org/Defining_Noncommercial.

[CT09]   Michele Chinosi and Alberto Trombetta. Integrating Privacy Policies into Busi-
            ness Processes. *Journal of Research and Practice in Information Technology*,
            41(2):155–170, 2009.

[CVDG12]   Luca Costabello, Serena Villata, Nicolas Delaforge, and Fabien Gandon.
            Linked Data Access goes Mobile: Context-aware Authorization for Graph
            Stores. In *Proceedings of the Linked Data on the Web Workshop (LDOW'12)
            in conjunction with the 21st International World Wide Web Conference
            (WWW'12)*, Lyon, France, 2012.

[DA06]   S. Dietzold and S. Auer. Access Control on RDF Triple Stores from a Se-
            mantic Wiki Perspective. In *Proceedings of the Workshop on Scripting for the
            Semantic Web in conjunction with the 3rd European Semantic Web Conference
            (ESWC'06)*, 2006.

[DDLS01]   Nicodemos Damianou, Naranker Dulay, Emil Lupu, and Morris Sloman. The
            Ponder Policy Specification Language. In Morris Sloman, Jorge Lobo, and
            Emil Lupu, editors, *Proceedings of the 2nd International Workshop on Policies
            for Distributed Systems and Networks (POLICY'01)*, volume 1995 of *Lecture
            Notes in Computer Science*, pages 18–38, Bristol, UK, 2001. Springer.

[DLV]   DLV. (Software). http://www.dlvsystem.com/dlvsystem/index.php/
            DLV, accessed March 14th 2012.

[DM88]   Barry A. Devlin and Paul T. Murphy. An Architecture for a Business and
            Information System. *IBM Systems Journal*, 27(1):60–80, 1988.

[Doc04]   Cory Doctorow. Digital Rights Management (Manifesto), 21st Sep
            2004. ChangeThis Issue 4. Available online at http://changethis.com/
            manifesto/show/4.DRM.

[Dod10]   Leigh Dodds. Rights Statements on the Web of Data. *Nodalities Magazine*,
            pages 13–14, 2010.

[DS05]   Martin Duerst and Michel Suignard. *Internationalized Resource Identifiers
            (IRIs)*. Number 3987 in Request for Comments (RFC). Internet Engineering
            Task Force (IETF), January 2005. Available at http://www.ietf.org/rfc/
            rfc3987.txt, accessed July 24th 2012.

[DSS93]   Randall Davis, Howard E. Shrobe, and Peter Szolovits. What is a Knowledge
             Representation? *AI Magazine*, 14(1):17–33, 1993.

[EMS⁺04]   Ulrich Endriss, Paolo Mancarella, Fariba Sadri, Giacomo Terreni, and
             Francesca Toni. The CIFF Proof Procedure for Abductive Logic Programming
             with Constraints. In José Júlio Alferes and João Alexandre Leite, editors, *Pro-
             ceedings of the 9th European Conference on Logics in Artificial Intelligence
             (JELIA'04)*, volume 3229 of *Lecture Notes in Computer Science*, pages 31–43.
             Springer, Lisbon, Portugal, 2004.

[Erl04]   Thomas Erl. *Service-Oriented Architecture: A Field Guide to Integrating XML
             and Web Services*. Prentice Hall, 2004.

[Eur06]   European Comission Directorate-General for Research and Innovation.
             European Technology Platform – SmartGrids Vision and Strategy For
             Europe's Electricity Networks of the Future, 2006.   EUR 22040.
             Available online at `http://www.ec.europa.eu/research/energy/pdf/`
             `smartgrids_en.pdf`.

[FGM⁺99]   Roy T. Fielding, James Gettys, Jeffrey C. Mogul, Henrik Frystyk, Larry Mas-
             inter, Paul J. Leach, and Tim Berners-Lee. *Hypertext Transfer Protocol –
             HTTP/1.1*. Number 2616 in Request for Comments (RFC). Internet Engineer-
             ing Task Force (IETF), June 1999. Available at `http://www.ietf.org/rfc/`
             `rfc2616.txt`, accessed July 24th 2012.

[FGP12]   Valeria Fionda, Claudio Gutierrez, and Giuseppe Pirró. Semantic Naviga-
             tion on the Web of Data: Specification of Routes, Web Fragments and Ac-
             tions. In *Proceedings of the 21st International Conference on World Wide Web
             (WWW'12)*, pages 281–290, Lyon, France, 2012. ACM.

[FHM05]   Michael Franklin, Alon Halevy, and David Maier. From Databases to Datas-
             paces: A New Abstraction for Information Management. *SIGMOD Record*,
             34:27–33, December 2005.

[Fie00]   Roy T. Fielding. *Architectural Styles and the Design of Network-based Soft-
             ware Architectures*. PhD thesis, University of California, Irvine, 2000.

[FJK⁺08]   Tim Finin, Anupam Joshi, Lalana Kagal, Jianwei Niu, Ravi Sandhu, William
             Winsborough, and Bhavani Thuraisingham. ROWLBAC – Representing Role
             Based Access Control in OWL. In *Proceedings of the 13th ACM symposium
             on Access Control Models and Technologies (SACMAT'08)*, pages 73–82, Estes
             Park, CO, USA, 2008. ACM.

[FK92]   David Ferraiolo and Richard Kuhn. Role-based Access Control. In *In Proceed-
             ings of the 15th NIST-NCSC National Computer Security Conference*, pages
             554–563, 1992.

[FKO⁺12]   André Freitas, Benedikt Kämpgen, Joao Gabriel Oliveira, Sean O'Riain, and
           Edward Curry. Representing Interoperable Provenance Descriptions. In *Pro-
           ceedings of the 3rd International Workshop on Role of Semantic Web in Prove-
           nance Management (SWPM'12) in conjunction with the 9th Extended Semantic
           Web Conference (ESWC'12)*, Heraklion, Crete, Greece, 2012. CEUR-WS.org.

[GD11]   G. R. Gangadharan and Vincenzo D'Andrea. Service Licensing: Conceptu-
           alization, Formalization, and Expression. *Service Oriented Computing and
           Applications*, 5(1):37–59, 2011.

[GF05]   Pedro Gama and Paulo Ferreira. Obligation Policies: An Enforcement Plat-
           form. In *Proceedings of the 6th IEEE Workshop on Policies for Distributed Sys-
           tems and Networks (POLICY'05)*, pages 203–212, Stockholm, Sweden, 2005.
           IEEE Computer Society.

[GK10]   Birte Glimm and Markus Krötzsch. SPARQL Beyond Subgraph Matching. In
           Peter F. Patel-Schneider, Yue Pan, Birte Glimm, Pascal Hitzler, Peter Mika, Jeff
           Pan, and Ian Horrocks, editors, *Proceedings of the 9th International Semantic
           Web Conference (ISWC'10) Part I*, volume 6496 of *LNCS*, pages 241–256,
           Shanghai, China, 2010. Springer.

[GPH04]   Yuanbo Guo, Zhengxiang Pan, and Jeff Heflin. An Evaluation of Knowledge
           Base Systems for Large OWL Datasets. In Sheila McIlraith, Dimitris Plex-
           ousakis, and Frank van Harmelen, editors, *Proceedings of the 3rd International
           Semantic Web Conference (ISWC'04)*, volume 3298 of *Lecture Notes in Com-
           puter Science*, pages 274–288. Springer, Toronto, Canada, 2004.

[GPH05]   Yuanbo Guo, Zhengxiang Pan, and Jeff Heflin. LUBM: A Benchmark for OWL
           Knowledge Base Systems. *Journal of Web Semantics: Science, Services and
           Agents on the World Wide Web*, 3(2-3):158–182, 2005.

[Gro03]   W3C Semantic Web Interest Group. *Basic Geo (WGS84 Lat/Long) Vocabulary*.
           2003. Available at `http://www.w3.org/2003/01/geo/`, accessed July 20th
           2012.

[GRV10]   Birte Glimm, Sebastian Rudolph, and Johanna Völker. Integrated Metamod-
           eling and Diagnosis in OWL 2. In Peter F. Patel-Schneider, Yue Pan, Birte
           Glimm, Pascal Hitzler, Peter Mika, Jeff Pan, and Ian Horrocks, editors, *Pro-
           ceedings of the 9th International Semantic Web Conference (ISWC'10) Part I*,
           volume 6496 of *LNCS*, pages 257–272, Shanghai, China, 2010. Springer.

[Hal01]   Alon Y Halevy. Answering Queries using Views: A Survey. *The VLDB Jour-
           nal*, 10(4):270 – 294, 2001.

[Har11]   Olaf Hartig. Zero-Knowledge Query Planning for an Iterator Implementa-
           tion of Link Traversal Based Query Execution. In Grigoris Antoniou, Marko

Grobelnik, Elena Paslaru Bontas Simperl, Bijan Parsia, Dimitris Plexousakis, Pieter De Leenheer, and Jeff Z. Pan, editors, *Proceedings of the 8th Extended Semantic Web Conference (ESWC'11) Part I*, volume 6643 of *Lecture Notes in Computer Science*, pages 154–169, Heraklion, Crete, Greece, 2011. Springer.

[Har12a]   Olaf Hartig. SPARQL for a Web of Linked Data: Semantics and Computability. In Elena Simperl, Philipp Cimiano, Axel Polleres, Óscar Corcho, and Valentina Presutti, editors, *Proceedings of the 9th Extended Semantic Web Conference (ESWC'12)*, volume 7295 of *Lecture Notes in Computer Science*, pages 8–23, Heraklion, Crete, Greece, 2012. Springer.

[Har12b]   Olaf Hartig. SPARQL for a Web of Linked Data: Semantics and Computability (Extended Version). *CoRR*, abs/1203.1569, 2012.

[HB09]   Matthew Horridge and Sean Bechhofer. The OWL API: A Java API for Working with OWL 2 Ontologies. In Rinke Hoekstra and Peter F. Patel-Schneider, editors, *Proceedings of the 5th International Workshop on OWL: Experiences and Directions (OWLED 09)*, volume 529 of *CEUR Workshop Proceedings*, Washington DC, USA, 2009. CEUR-WS.org.

[HB11]   Tom Heath and Christian Bizer. *Linked Data: Evolving the Web into a Global Data Space (1st Edition)*, volume 1 of *Synthesis Lectures on the Semantic Web: Theory and Technology*. Morgan & Claypool, 2011.

[HBF09]   Olaf Hartig, Christian Bizer, and Johann-Christoph Freytag. Executing SPARQL Queries over the Web of Linked Data. In Abraham Bernstein, David R. Karger, Tom Heath, Lee Feigenbaum, Diana Maynard, Enrico Motta, and Krishnaprasad Thirunarayan, editors, *Proceedings of the 8th International Semantic Web Conference (ISWC'09)*, volume 5823 of *LNCS*, pages 293–309, Washington DC, USA, 2009. Springer.

[HBLK+07]   Chris Hanson, Tim Berners-Lee, Lalana Kagal, Gerald Jay Sussman, and Daniel Weitzner. Data-Purpose Algebra: Modeling Data Usage Policies. In *Proceedings of the 8th IEEE Workshop on Policies for Distributed Systems and Networks (POLICY'07)*, pages 173–177, Bologna, Italy, 2007. IEEE Computer Society.

[Her]   Hermit. (Software). http://hermit-reasoner.com/, accessed June 20th 2012.

[HHK+10]   Andreas Harth, Katja Hose, Marcel Karnstedt, Axel Polleres, Kai-Uwe Sattler, and Jürgen Umbrich. Data Summaries for On-demand Queries over Linked Data. In *Proceedings of the 19th International Conference on World Wide Web (WWW'10)*, pages 411–420, Raleigh, NC, USA, 2010. ACM.

[HHP08]   Aidan Hogan, Andreas Harth, and Axel Polleres. SAOR: Authoritative Rea-
           soning for the Web. In John Domingue and Chutiporn Anutariya, editors, *Pro-
           ceedings of the 3rd Asian Semantic Web Conference (ASWC'08)*, volume 4825
           of *Lecture Notes in Computer Science*, pages 76–90, Bangkok, Thailand, 2008.
           Springer.

[HKR09]   Pascal Hitzler, Markus Krötzsch, and Sebastian Rudolph. *Foundations of Se-
           mantic Web Technologies*. Chapman & Hall/CRC, 2009.

[HKS04]   Markus Holzer, Stefan Katzenbeisser, and Christian Schallhart. Towards a For-
           mal Semantics for ODRL (Extended Abstract). In Renato Iannella and Susanne
           Guth, editors, *Proceedings of the International ODRL Workshop 2004*, 2004.

[HMZ10]   Peter Haase, Tobias Mathäß, and Michael Ziller. An Evaluation of Approaches
           to Federated Query Processing over Linked Data. In Adrian Paschke, Nicola
           Henze, and Tassilo Pellegrini, editors, *Proceedings the 6th International Con-
           ference on Semantic Systems (I-SEMANTICS'10)*, Graz, Austria, 2010. ACM.

[HPB⁺07]   Manuel Hilty, Alexander Pretschner, David Basin, Christian Schaefer, and
           Thomas Walter. A Policy Language for Distributed Usage Control. In Joachim
           Biskup and Javier Lopez, editors, *Proceedings of the 12th European Sympo-
           sium On Research In Computer Security (ESORICS'07)*, volume 4734 of *Lec-
           ture Notes in Computer Science*, pages 531–546, Dresden, Germany, 2007.
           Springer.

[HS04]   Ian Horrocks and Ulrike Sattler. Decidability of $\mathcal{SHIQ}$ with Complex Role
           Inclusion Axioms. *Artificial Intelligence*, 160(1):79–104, 2004.

[HS12]   Andreas Harth and Sebastian Speiser. On Completeness Classes for Query
           Evaluation on Linked Data. In Jörg Hoffmann and Bart Selman, editors, *Pro-
           ceedings of the 26th AAAI Conference on Artificial Intelligence (AAAI'12)*,
           Toronto, Ontario, Canada, 2012. AAAI Press.

[HW08]   Joseph Y. Halpern and Vicky Weissman. A Formal Foundation for XrML.
           Journal of the ACM, 55(1):4:1–4:42, 2008.

[HYP]   HYPROLOG. (Software). `http://akira.ruc.dk/~henning/hyprolog/`,
           accessed March 14th 2012.

[HZB⁺06]   Duncan Hull, Evgeny Zolin, Andrey Bovykin, Ian Horrocks, Ulrike Sattler,
           and Robert Stevens. Deciding Semantic Matching of Stateless Services. In
           Anthony Cohn, editor, *Proceedings of the 21st National Conference on Artifi-
           cial Intelligence (AAAI'06) - Volume 2*, pages 1319–1324, Boston, MA, USA,
           2006. AAAI Press.

[Ian01]   Renato Iannella. Digital Rights Management (DRM) Architectures. *DLib
           Magazine*, 7(6), 2001.

[Ian02]   Renato Iannella. Open Digital Rights Language (ODRL) Version 1.1. W3C Note, 19 September 2002. Available at http://www.w3.org/TR/odrl/, accessed August 8th 2012.

[ISPG08]   Kashif Iqbal, Marco Luca Sbodio, Vassilios Peristeras, and Giovanni Giuliani. Semantic Service Discovery using SAWSDL and SPARQL. In *Proceedings of the 4th International Conference on Semantics, Knowledge and Grid (SKG'08)*, pages 205–212, Beijing, China, 2008.

[IYW06]   Keith Irwin, Ting Yu, and William H. Winsborough. On the Modeling and Analysis of Obligations. In Ferng-Ching Lin, Der-Tsai Lee, Bao-Shuh Paul Lin, Shiuhpyng Shieh, and Sushil Jajodia, editors, *Proceedings of the 2006 ACM Symposium on Information, Computer and Communications Security (ASIACCS'06)*, pages 134–143, Taipei, Taiwan, 2006.

[JCZ07]   Helge Janicke, Antonio Cau, and Hussein Zedan. A Note on the Formalisation of UCON. In Volkmar Lotz and Bhavani M. Thuraisingham, editors, *Proceedings of the 12th ACM Symposium on Access Control Models and Technologies (SACMAT'07)*, pages 163–168, Sophia Antipolis, France, 2007. ACM.

[Jen]   Apache Jena. (Software). http://jena.apache.org/, accessed June 6th 2012.

[JF06]   Amit Jain and Csilla Farkas. Secure Resource Description Framework: An Access Control Model. In David F. Ferraiolo and Indrakshi Ray, editors, *Proceedings of the 11th ACM Symposium on Access Control Models and Technologies (SACMAT'06)*, pages 121–129, Lake Tahoe, CA, USA, 2006. ACM.

[JH08]   Pramod A. Jamkhedkar and Gregory L. Heileman. A Formal Conceptual Model for Rights. In Gregory L. Heileman and Marc Joye, editors, *Proceedings of the 8th ACM Workshop on Digital Rights Management (DRM'08)*, pages 29–38, Alexandria, VA, USA, 2008. ACM.

[JH09]   Pramod A. Jamkhedkar and Gregory L. Heileman. Digital Rights Management Architectures. *Comput. Electr. Eng.*, 35(2):376–394, 2009.

[KA10]   Lalana Kagal and Hal Abelson. Access Control is an Inadequate Framework for Privacy Protection. In *W3C Workshop on Privacy for Advanced Web APIs*, pages 1–6, London, UK, 2010.

[KBK+10]   Ankesh Khandelwal, Jie Bao, Lalana Kagal, Ian Jacobi, Li Ding, and James Hendler. Analyzing the AIR Language: A Semantic Web (Production) Rule Language. In Pascal Hitzler and Thomas Lukasiewicz, editors, *Proceedings of the 4th International Conference on Web Reasoning and Rule Systems (RR'10)*, volume 6333 of *Lecture Notes in Computer Science*, pages 58–72, Bressanone/Brixen, Italy, 2010. Springer.

[KES11]   Szymon Klarman, Ulle Endriss, and Stefan Schlobach. ABox Abduction in the
           Description Logic $\mathcal{ALC}$. *Journal of Automated Reasoning*, 46:43–80, 2011.

[KFJ03]   Lalana Kagal, Tim Finin, and Anupam Joshi. A Policy Language for a Perva-
           sive Computing Environment. In *Proceedings of the 4th IEEE International
           Workshop on Policies for Distributed Systems and Networks (POLICY'03)*,
           pages 63–74, Villa Olmo, Lake Como, Italy, 2003. IEEE Computer Society.

[KHP07]   Vladimir Kolovski, James Hendler, and Bijan Parsia. Analyzing Web Access
           Control Policies. In Carey L. Williamson, Mary Ellen Zurko, Peter F. Patel-
           Schneider, and Prashant J. Shenoy, editors, *Proceedings of the 16th Interna-
           tional Conference on World Wide Web (WWW'07)*, pages 677–686, Banff, Al-
           berta, Canada, 2007. ACM.

[KHW08]   Lalana Kagal, Chris Hanson, and Daniel Weitzner. Using Dependency Track-
           ing to Provide Explanations for Policy Management. In *Proceedings of the
           9th IEEE Workshop on Policies for Distributed Systems and Networks (POL-
           ICY'08)*, pages 54–61, Palisades, NY, USA, 2008. IEEE Computer Society.

[KJK11]   Ankesh Khandelwal, Ian Jacobi, and Lalana Kagal. Linked Rules: Principles
           for Rule Reuse on the Web. In Sebastian Rudolph and Claudio Gutierrez, ed-
           itors, *Proceedings of the 5th International Conference on Web Reasoning and
           Rule Systems (RR'11)*, number 6902 in Lecture Notes in Computer Science,
           pages 108–123, Galway, Ireland, 2011. Springer.

[KOH12]   Benedikt Kämpgen, Sean O'Riain, and Andreas Harth. Interacting with Statis-
           tical Linked Data via OLAP Operations. In *Proceedings of the International
           Workshop on Interacting with Linked Data (ILD'12) in conjunction with the
           9th Extended Semantic Web Conference (ESWC'12)*, Heraklion, Crete, Greece,
           2012. CEUR-WS.org.

[KS11a]   Markus Krötzsch and Sebastian Speiser. Expressing Self-Referential Usage
           Policies for the Semantic Web. Technical Report 3014, Institute AIFB, Karl-
           sruhe Institute of Technology, 2011. Available online at http://www.aifb.
           kit.edu/web/Techreport3014.

[KS11b]   Markus Krötzsch and Sebastian Speiser.   ShareAlike Your Data: Self-
           Referential Usage Policies for the Semantic Web. In Lora Aroyo, Chris Welty,
           Harith Alani, Jamie Taylor, Abraham Bernstein, Lalana Kagal, Natasha Noya,
           and Eva Blomqvist, editors, *Proceedings of the 10th International Semantic
           Web Conference (ISWC'11) Part I*, volume 7031 of *LNCS*, pages 354–369,
           Bonn, Germany, 2011. Springer.

[KSC04]   Apu Kapadia, Geetanjali Sampemane, and Roy H Campbell. KNOW Why
           Your Access Was Denied: Regulating Feedback for Usable Security. In Vijay-
           alakshmi Atluri, Birgit Pfitzmann, and Patrick Drew McDaniel, editors, *Pro-*

ceedings of the 11th ACM Conference on Computer and Communications Security (CCS'04), pages 52–61, Washington, DC, USA, 2004. ACM.

[KSW03] Günter Karjoth, Matthias Schunter, and Michael Waidner. Platform for Enterprise Privacy Practices: Privacy-enabled Management of Customer Data. In Roger Dingledine and Paul F. Syverson, editors, *Revised Papers of the 2nd International Workshop on Privacy Enhancing Technologies (PET'02)*, volume 2482 of *Lecture Notes in Computer Science*, pages 69–84, San Francisco, CA, USA, 2003. Springer.

[KW04] Jeffrey O. Kephart and William E. Walsh. An Artificial Intelligence Perspective on Autonomic Computing Policies. In *Proceedings of the 5th IEEE Workshop on Policies for Distributed Systems and Networks (POLICY'04)*, pages 3–12, Yorktown Heights, NY, USA, 2004. IEEE Computer Society.

[Lam71] Butler W Lampson. Protection. In *Proceedings of the 5th Princeton Symposium on Information Sciences and Systems*, pages 437–443, Princeton University, 1971. reprinted in Operating Systems Review, 8,1, January 1974, pp. 18–24.

[Lam07] Steffen Lamparter. *Policy-based Contracting in Semantic Web Service Markets*. PhD thesis, Universität Karlsruhe (TH), Institut AIFB, 2007.

[Les05] Lawrence Lessig. CC in Review: Lawrence Lessig on Compatibility, 2005. Available at: http://creativecommons.org/weblog/entry/5709.

[LH11] Günter Ladwig and Andreas Harth. CumulusRDF: Linked Data Management on Nested Key-Value Stores. In *Proceedings of the 7th International Workshop on Scalable Semantic Web Knowledge Base Systems (SSWS'11) in conjunction with the 10th International Semantic Web Conference (ISWC'11)*, Bonn, Germany, 2011.

[Lif88] Vladimir Lifshitz. Circumscriptive Theories: A Logic-based Framework for Knowledge Representation. *Journal of Philosophical Logic*, 17:391–441, 1988.

[LK09] Erietta Liarou and Martin L. Kersten. DataCell: Exploiting the Power of Relational Databases for Efficient Stream Processing. *ERCIM News*, 2009(76), 2009.

[LMP07] Vladimir Lifschitz, Leora Morgenstern, and David Plaisted. Knowledge Representation and Classical Logic. In Frank van Harmelen, Vladimir Lifschitz, and Bruce Porter, editors, *Handbook of Knowledge Representation*, chapter 1, pages 3–88. Elsevier Science, 2007.

[LP10]   Ralf Lämmel and Ekaterina Pek. Vivisection of a Non-Executable, Domain-Specific Language - Understanding (the Usage of) the P3P Language. In *Proceedings of the 18th IEEE International Conference on Program Comprehension (ICPC'10)*, pages 104–113, Braga, Minho, Portugal, 2010. IEEE Computer Society.

[LP12]   Ralf Lämmel and Ekaterina Pek. Understanding Privacy Policies (A Study in Empirical Language Usage Analysis). Available at `http://softlang.uni-koblenz.de/p3p/paper.pdf`, accessed November 6th 2012, 2012.

[LPB06]   Yin Hua Li, Hye-Young Paik, and Boualem Benatallah. Formal Consistency Verification between BPEL Process and Privacy Policy. In *Proceedings of the International Conference on Privacy, Security and Trust (PST'06)*, Markham, Ontario, Canada, 2006.

[LRO96]   Alon Y. Levy, Anand Rajaraman, and Joann J. Ordille. Querying Heterogeneous Information Sources using Source Descriptions. In T. M. Vijayaraman, Alejandro P. Buchmann, C. Mohan, and Nandlal L. Sarda, editors, *Proceedings of the 22th International Conference on Very Large Data Bases (VLDB'96)*, pages 251–262, Mumbai (Bombay), India, 1996. Morgan Kaufmann.

[LT10]   Günter Ladwig and Thanh Tran. Linked Data Query Processing Strategies. In Peter F. Patel-Schneider, Yue Pan, Birte Glimm, Pascal Hitzler, Peter Mika, Jeff Pan, and Ian Horrocks, editors, *Proceedings of the 9th International Semantic Web Conference (ISWC'10) Part I*, volume 6496 of *LNCS*, pages 453–469. Springer, Shanghai, China, 2010.

[LT11]   Günter Ladwig and Thanh Tran. SIHJoin: Querying Remote and Local Linked Data. In Grigoris Antoniou, Marko Grobelnik, Elena Paslaru Bontas Simperl, Bijan Parsia, Dimitris Plexousakis, Pieter De Leenheer, and Jeff Z. Pan, editors, *Proceedings of the 8th Extended Semantic Web Conference (ESWC'11) Part I*, volume 6643 of *Lecture Notes in Computer Science*, pages 139–153, Heraklion, Crete, Greece, 2011. Springer.

[LUB]   LUBM. (Project Homepage). `http://swat.cse.lehigh.edu/projects/lubm/`, accessed Jun 6th 2012.

[MCB+11]   James Manyika, Michael Chui, Brad Brown, Jacques Bughin, Richard Dobbs, Charles Roxburgh, and Angela Hung Byers. Big Data: The Next Frontier for Innovation, Competition, and Productivity. Technical report, McKinsey Global Institute, May 2011. Available online at `http://www.mckinsey.com/Insights/MGI/Research/Technology_and_Innovation/Big_data_The_next_frontier_for_innovation`.

[MCF+11]   Luc Moreau, Ben Clifford, Juliana Freire, Joe Futrelle, Yolanda Gil, Paul Groth, Natalia Kwasnikowska, Simon Miles, Paolo Missier, Jim Myers, Beth

Plale, Yogesh Simmhan, Eric Stephan, and Jan Van den Bussche. The Open Provenance Model Core Specification (v1.1). *Future Generation Computer Systems*, 27:743–756, June 2011.

[ME07]   Andrew D. Miller and W. Keith Edwards. Give and Take: A Study of Consumer Photo-sharing Culture and Practice. In *Proceedings of the SIGCHI Conference on Human Factors in Computing Systems (CHI'07)*, pages 347–356. ACM, 2007.

[Mil67]   Stanley Milgram. The Small-world Problem. *Psychology Today*, 2:60–67, 1967.

[Mil99]   Robin Milner. *Communicating and Mobile Systems: π-calculus*. Cambridge University Press, Cambridge, UK, 1999.

[Min74]   Marvin Minsky. A Framework for Representing Knowledge. Technical Report Memo 306, MIT-AI Laboratory, June 1974.

[MKF10]   Hannes Mühleisen, Martin Kost, and Johann-Christoph Freytag. SWRL-based Access Policies for Linked Data. In Philipp Kärger, Daniel Olmedilla, Alexandre Passant, and Axel Polleres, editors, *Proceedings of the 2nd Workshop on Trust and Privacy on the Social and Semantic Web (SPOT'10) in conjunction with the 7th Extended Semantic Web Conference (ESWC'10)*, volume 576. CEUR-WS.org, 2010. Available online at http://CEUR-WS.org/Vol-576/paper1.pdf.

[ML85]   Naftaly H. Minsky and Abe D. Lockman. Ensuring Integrity by Adding Obligations to Privileges. In *Proceedings of the 8th International Conference on Software Engineering (ICSE'85)*, pages 92–102, London, UK, 1985. IEEE Computer Society Press.

[ML05]   Mahdi Mankai and Luigi Logrippo. Access Control Policies: Modeling and Validation. In K. Adi, D. Amyot, and L. Logrippo, editors, *Proceedings of the 5th Colloque International sur les Nouvelles Technologies de la Répartition (NOTERE'05)*, 2005.

[MM97]   Alberto O. Mendelzon and Tova Milo. Formal Models of Web Queries. In *Proceedings of the 16th ACM SIGACT-SIGMOD-SIGART Symposium on Principles of Database Systems (PODS'97)*, pages 134–143, Tucson, AZ, USA, 1997. ACM Press.

[Mot07]   Boris Motik. On the Properties of Metamodeling in OWL. *Journal of Logic and Computation*, 17(4):617–637, 2007.

[NBL09]   Qun Ni, Elisa Bertino, and Jorge Lobo. D-algebra for Composing Access Control Policy Decisions. In *Proceedings of the 4th ACM Symposium on Information, Computer and Communications Security (ASIACCS'09)*, pages 298–309, Sydney, Australia, 2009. ACM.

[Neb91]   Bernhard Nebel. Terminological Cycles: Semantics and Computational Prop-
             erties. In John F. Sowa, editor, *Principles of Semantic Networks: Explorations
             in the Representation of Knowledge*, pages 331–361. Kaufmann, 1991.

[NK10]   Barry Norton and Reto Krummenacher. Consuming Dynamic Linked Data.
             In *Proceedings of the 1st International Workshop on Consuming Linked Data
             (COLD'10) in conjunction with the 9th International Semantic Web Conference
             (ISWC'10)*, Shanghai, China, 2010.

[Not10]   Mark Nottingham. *Web Linking*. Number 5988 (Proposed Standard) in Request
             for Comments (RFC). Internet Engineering Task Force (IETF), October 2010.
             Available at http://www.ietf.org/rfc/rfc5988.txt.

[NTBL07]   Qun Ni, Alberto Trombetta, Elisa Bertino, and Jorge Lobo. Privacy-aware
             Role Based Access Control. In Volkmar Lotz and Bhavani M. Thuraisingham,
             editors, *Proceedings of the 12th ACM Symposium on Access Control Models
             and Technologies (SACMAT'07)*, pages 41–50, Sophia Antipolis, France, 2007.
             ACM.

[OAS05]   OASIS. *eXtensible Access Control Markup Language (XACML) Version 2.0.*
             OASIS Standard, 2005. http://docs.oasis-open.org/xacml/2.0/.

[OAS09]   OASIS Web Services Secure Exchange TC. *WS-SecurityPolicy 1.3.* OASIS
             Standard, 2 February 2009. Available at http://docs.oasis-open.org/
             ws-sx/ws-securitypolicy/v1.3/ws-securitypolicy.pdf.

[PAG09]   Jorge Pérez, Marcelo Arenas, and Claudio Gutierrez. Semantics and Complex-
             ity of SPARQL. *ACM Transactions on Database Systems*, 34:1–45, 2009.

[Pap07]   Mike P. Papazoglou. *Web Services: Principles and Technology*. Pearson –
             Hall, 2007.

[Pei55]   Charles .S. Peirce. Abduction and Induction. In *Philosophical writings of
             Peirce*. Dover Publications, 1955.

[Pfe04]   Götz Pfeiffer. Counting Transitive Relations. *Journal of Integer Sequences*, 7,
             2004.

[PHB⁺08]   Alexander Pretschner, Manuel Hilty, David Basin, Christian Schaefer, and
             Thomas Walter. Mechanisms for Usage Control. In *Proceedings of the 2008
             ACM Symposium on Information, Computer and Communications Security
             (ASIACCS'08)*, pages 240–244, Tokyo, Japan, 2008. ACM.

[PHS⁺08]   Alexander Pretschner, Manuel Hilty, Florian Schütz, Christian Schaefer, and
             Thomas Walter. Usage Control Enforcement: Present and Future. *IEEE Secu-
             rity and Privacy*, 6(4):44–53, 2008.

[PKH05]   Bijan Parsia, Vladimir Kolovski, and Jim Hendler. Expressing WS-Policies in
            OWL. In *Proceedings of the Workshop on Policy Management for the Web
            in conjunction with the 14th International Conference on World Wide Web
            (WWW'05)*, Chiba, Japan, 2005.

[Poo89]   David Poole. Explanation and Prediction: An Architecture for Default and
            Abductive Reasoning. *Computational Intelligence*, 5:97–110, May 1989.

[PS02]   Jaehong Park and Ravi Sandhu. Towards Usage Control Models: Beyond Tra-
            ditional Access Control. In *Proceedings of the 7th ACM Symposium on Access
            Control Models and Technologies (SACMAT'02)*, pages 57–64, Monterey, CA,
            USA, 2002. ACM.

[PS04]   Jaehong Park and Ravi Sandhu. The UCON$_{ABC}$ Usage Control Model. *ACM
            Transactions on Information and System Security*, 7(1):128–174, 2004.

[PSK$^+$09] Nicoleta Preda, Fabian M. Suchanek, Gjergji Kasneci, Thomas Neumann,
            Maya Ramanath, and Gerhard Weikum. ANGIE: Active Knowledge for In-
            teractive Exploration. *PVLDB*, 2(2):1570–1573, 2009.

[PW04]   Riccardo Pucella and Vicky Weissman. A Formal Foundation for ODRL.
            In *Proceedings of the 2004 Workshop on Issues in the Theory of Security
            (WITS'04) in conjunction with the European Joint Conferences on Theory and
            Practice of Software (ETAPS'04)*, 2004.

[Qui67]   M. Ross Quillian. Word Concepts: A Theory and Simulation of Some Basic
            Semantic Capabilities. *Behavioral Science*, 12(5):410–430, 1967.

[RFJ05]   Pavan Reddivari, Tim Finin, and Anupam Joshi. Policy-based Access Con-
            trol for an RDF Store. In Lalana Kagal, Tim Finin, and Jim Hendler, editors,
            *Proceedings of the Workshop on Policy Management for the Web in conjunc-
            tion with the 14th International World Wide Web Conference (WWW'05)*, pages
            78–81, Chiba, Japan, 2005.

[RGM01]   Sriram Raghavan and Hector Garcia-Molina. Crawling the Hidden Web. In
            Peter M. G. Apers, Paolo Atzeni, Stefano Ceri, Stefano Paraboschi, Kotagiri
            Ramamohanarao, and Richard T. Snodgrass, editors, *Proceedings of 27th In-
            ternational Conference on Very Large Data Bases (VLDB'01)*, pages 129–138,
            Roma, Italy, 2001. Morgan Kaufmann.

[RKL$^+$05] Dumitru Roman, Uwe Keller, Holger Lausen, Jos de Bruijn, Rubén Lara,
            Michael Stollberg, Axel Polleres, Cristina Feier, Cristoph Bussler, and Dieter
            Fensel. Web Service Modeling Ontology. *Applied Ontology*, 1(1):77–106,
            2005.

[Ros92]   Kenneth A. Ross. Relations with Relation Names As Arguments: Algebra
            and Calculus. In Michael Stonebraker, editor, *Proceedings of the 11th ACM*

SIGACT-SIGMOD-SIGART Symposium on Principles of Database Systems (PODS'92), pages 346–353, San Diego, CA, USA, 1992. ACM.

[RR07]   Leonard Richardson and Sam Ruby. *RESTful Web Services*. O'Reilly Media, May 2007.

[RS10]   Christoph Ringelstein and Steffen Staab. PAPEL: A Language and Model for Provenance-aware Policy Definition and Execution. In Richard Hull, Jan Mendling, and Stefan Tai, editors, *Proceedings of 8th International Conference on Business Process Management (BPM'10)*, volume 6336 of *LNCS*, pages 195–210, Hoboken, NJ, USA, 2010. Springer.

[San03]   Scott Sanner. Towards Practical Taxonomic Classification for Description Logics on the Semantic Web. Technical Report KSL-03-06, Knowledge Systems Laboratory, Stanford University, 2003. Available online at `http://www.ksl.stanford.edu/KSL_Abstracts/KSL-03-06.html`.

[SGH⁺11]   Michael Schmidt, Olaf Görlitz, Peter Haase, Günter Ladwig, Andreas Schwarte, and Thanh Tran. FedBench: A Benchmark Suite for Federated Semantic Data Query Processing. In Lora Aroyo, Chris Welty, Harith Alani, Jamie Taylor, Abraham Bernstein, Lalana Kagal, Natasha Noya, and Eva Blomqvist, editors, *Proceedings of the 10th International Semantic Web Conference (ISWC'11) Part I*, volume 7031 of *LNCS*, pages 585–600, Bonn, Germany, 2011.

[SH10]   Sebastian Speiser and Andreas Harth. Taking the LIDS off Data Silos. In Adrian Paschke, Nicola Henze, and Tassilo Pellegrini, editors, *Proceedings the 6th International Conference on Semantic Systems (I-SEMANTICS'10)*, Graz, Austria, 2010. ACM.

[SH11]   Sebastian Speiser and Andreas Harth. Integrating Linked Data and Services with Linked Data Services. In Grigoris Antoniou, Marko Grobelnik, Elena Paslaru Bontas Simperl, Bijan Parsia, Dimitris Plexousakis, Pieter De Leenheer, and Jeff Z. Pan, editors, *Proceedings of the 8th Extended Semantic Web Conference (ESWC'11) Part I*, volume 6643 of *Lecture Notes in Computer Science*, pages 170–184, Heraklion, Crete, Greece, 2011. Springer.

[SH12]   Sebastian Speiser and Andreas Harth. Data-centric Privacy Policies for Smart Grids. In *Proceedings of the Workshop on Semantic Cities in conjunction with the 26th Conference on Artificial Intelligence (AAAI'12)*, Toronto, Canada, 2012.

[SKBL09]   Oshani Seneviratne, Lalana Kagal, and Tim Berners-Lee. Policy Aware Content Reuse on the Web. In Abraham Bernstein, David R. Karger, Tom Heath, Lee Feigenbaum, Diana Maynard, Enrico Motta, and Krishnaprasad

Thirunarayan, editors, *Proceedings of the 8th International Semantic Web Conference (ISWC'09)*, volume 5823 of *LNCS*, pages 553–568, Washington DC, USA, 2009. Springer.

[SP] SWI-Prolog. (Software). `http://www.swi-prolog.org/`, accessed March 14th 2012.

[SP11a] Owen Sacco and Alexandre Passant. A Privacy Preference Manager for the Social Semantic Web. In *Proceedings of the 2nd Workshop on Semantic Personalized Information Management: Retrieval and Recommendation (SPIM'11) in conjunction with the 10th International Semantic Web Conference (ISWC'11)*, Bonn, Germany, 2011.

[SP11b] Owen Sacco and Alexandre Passant. A Privacy Preference Ontology (PPO) for Linked Data. In *Proceedings of the Linked Data on the Web Workshop (LDOW'11) in conjunction with the 20th International World Wide Web Conference (WWW'11)*, Hyderabad, India, 2011.

[SPD11] Owen Sacco, Alexandre Passant, and Stefan Decker. An Access Control Framework for the Web of Data. In *Proceedings of the 10th IEEE International Conference on Trust, Security and Privacy in Computing and Communications (TrustCom'11)*, Changsha, China, 2011.

[Spe10] Sebastian Speiser. Semantic Annotations for WS-Policy. In *Proceedings of the 2010 IEEE International Conference on Web Services (ICWS'10)*, pages 449–456, Miami, FL, USA, 2010. IEEE Computer Society.

[Spe11a] Sebastian Speiser. Policy of Composition ≠ Composition of Policies. In *Proceedings of the IEEE Symposium on Policies for Distributed Systems and Networks (POLICY'11)*, pages 121–124, Pisa, Italy, 2011. IEEE Computer Society.

[Spe11b] Sebastian Speiser. Towards Policy-aware Queries over Linked Data (Poster). In *Posters and Demos at the 10th International Semantic Web Conference (ISWC'11)*, Bonn, Germany, 2011.

[Spe12a] Sebastian Speiser. A Data-centric View on Expressing Privacy Policies. Technical Report 3023, Institute AIFB, Karlsruhe Institute of Technology, 2012. Available online at `http://www.aifb.kit.edu/web/Techreport3023`.

[Spe12b] Sebastian Speiser. Distinguishing Obligations and Violations in Goal-based Data Usage Policies. In *Proceedings of the 7th International Conference on Internet and Web Applications and Services (ICIW'12)*, Stuttgart, Germany, 2012.

[SQU] SQUIN. (Software). `http://squin.sourceforge.net/`, accessed June 6th 2012.

[SS89]   Manfred Schmidt-Schauß. Subsumption in KL-ONE is Undecidable. In *Proceedings of the 1st International Conference on Principles of Knowledge Representation and Reasoning*, pages 421–431, 1989.

[SS10a]   Sebastian Speiser and Rudi Studer. A Self-Policing Policy Language. In Peter F. Patel-Schneider, Yue Pan, Birte Glimm, Pascal Hitzler, Peter Mika, Jeff Pan, and Ian Horrocks, editors, *Proceedings of the 9th International Semantic Web Conference (ISWC'10) Part I*, volume 6496 of *LNCS*, pages 730–746, Shanghai, China, 2010. Springer.

[SS10b]   Sebastian Speiser and Rudi Studer. Usage Policies for Document Compositions. In Lora Aroyo, Grigoris Antoniou, Eero Hyvönen, Annette ten Teije, Heiner Stuckenschmidt, Liliana Cabral, and Tania Tudorache, editors, *Proceedings of the 7th Extended Semantic Web Conference (ESWC'10) Part II*, volume 6089 of *Lecture Notes in Computer Science*, Heraklion, Crete, Greece, 2010. Springer.

[SSD10]   Sebastian Speiser, Rudi Studer, and Thomas Dreier. Requirements for Formalizing Usage Policies of Web Services. In Thomas Dreier, Jan Krämer, Rudi Studer, and Christof Weinhardt, editors, *Information Management and Market Engineering, Vol. II*, number 11 in Studies on eOrganisation and Market Engineering. KIT Scientific Publishing, Karlsruhe, 2010.

[SSS91]   Manfred Schmidt-Schauß and Gert Smolka. Attributive Concept Descriptions with Complements. *Artificial Intelligence*, 48:1–26, 1991.

[TAK04]   Snehal Thakkar, José Luis Ambite, and Craig A Knoblock. A Data Integration Approach to Automatically Composing and Optimizing Web Services. In *Proceedings of Workshop on Planning and Scheduling for Web and Grid Services at International Conference on Automated Planning and Scheduling (ICAPS'04)*, Whistler, British Columbia, Canada, 2004.

[TFHS10]   Raphael Troncy, Andre Fialho, Lynda Hardman, and Carsten Saathoff. Experiencing Events through User-Generated Media. In *Proceedings of the 1st International Workshop on Consuming Linked Data (COLD'10) in conjunction with the 9th International Semantic Web Conference (ISWC'10)*, Shanghai, China, 2010.

[The10]   The Economist. Data, Data Everywhere. *The Economist - Special report: Managing Information*, 2010. Available online at http://www.economist.com/node/15557443.

[TM69]   Jeffrey Travers and Stanley Milgram. An Experimental Study of the Small World Problem. *Sociometry*, 32(4):425–443, 1969.

[UBJ+03]   Andrzej Uszok, Jeffrey M. Bradshaw, Renia Jeffers, Niranjan Suri, Patrick Hayes, Maggie Breedy, Larry Bunch, Matt Johnson, Shriniwas Kulkarni, and

James Lott. KAoS Policy and Domain Services: Toward a Description-Logic Approach to Policy Representation, Deconfliction, and Enforcement. In *Proceedings of the 4th IEEE International Workshop on Policies for Distributed Systems and Networks (POLICY'03)*, pages 93–96, Villa Olmo, Lake Como, Italy, 2003. IEEE Computer Society.

[UHPD12]   Jürgen Umbrich, Aidan Hogan, Axel Polleres, and Stefan Decker. Improving the Recall of Live Linked Data Querying through Reasoning. In Markus Krötzsch and Umberto Straccia, editors, *Proceedings of the 6th International Conference on Web Reasoning and Rule Systems (RR'12), Vienna, Austria*, volume 7497 of *Lecture Notes in Computer Science*, pages 188–204, Vienna, Austria, 2012. Springer.

[VBGK09]   Julius Volz, Christian Bizer, Martin Gaedke, and Georgi Kobilarov. Discovering and Maintaining Links on the Web of Data. In Abraham Bernstein, David R. Karger, Tom Heath, Lee Feigenbaum, Diana Maynard, Enrico Motta, and Krishnaprasad Thirunarayan, editors, *Proceedings of the 8th International Semantic Web Conference (ISWC'09)*, volume 5823 of *LNCS*, pages 650–665, Washington DC, USA, 2009. Springer.

[VDGG11]   Serena Villata, Nicolas Delaforge, Fabien Gandon, and Amelie Gyrard. An Access Control Model for Linked Data. In Robert Meersman, Tharam S. Dillon, and Pilar Herrero, editors, *Proceedings of the Confederated International Workshops and Posters On the Move to Meaningful Internet Systems (OTM'11)*, volume 7046 of *Lecture Notes in Computer Science*, pages 454–463. Springer, 2011.

[VSD⁺11]   Ruben Verborgh, Thomas Steiner, Davy Van Deursen, Rik Van de Walle, and Joaquim Gabarr Valls. Efficient Runtime Service Discovery and Consumption with Hyperlinked RESTdesc. In *Proceedings of the 7th International Conference on Next Generation Web Services Practices (NWeSP'11)*, Salamanca, Spain, 2011.

[W3C99]   W3C. *HTML 4.01 Specification*. W3C Recommendation, 24 December 1999. Available at http://www.w3.org/TR/html4/.

[W3C02]   W3C. *The Platform for Privacy Preferences 1.0 (P3P1.0) Specification*. W3C Recommendation, 2002. http://www.w3.org/TR/P3P/.

[W3C04a]   W3C. *OWL-S: Semantic Markup for Web Services*. W3C Member Submission, 2004. Available at http://www.w3.org/Submission/OWL-S/.

[W3C04b]   W3C. *RDF Vocabulary Description Language 1.0: RDF Schema*. W3C Recommendation, 2004. http://www.w3.org/TR/rdf-schema/.

[W3C04c]   W3C.   *Resource Description Framework (RDF): Concepts and Abstract Syntax*.   W3C Recommendation, 2004.   `http://www.w3.org/TR/rdf-concepts/`.

[W3C07]   W3C. *Web Services Policy 1.5 – Framework*. W3C Recommendation, 2007. `http://www.w3.org/TR/ws-policy/`.

[W3C08]   W3C. *SPARQL Query Language for RDF*. W3C Recommendation, 2008. `http://www.w3.org/TR/rdf-sparql-query/`.

[W3C09a]   W3C. *OWL 2 Web Ontology Language: Document Overview*. W3C Recommendation, 27 October 2009.   Available at `http://www.w3.org/TR/owl2-overview/`.

[W3C09b]   W3C. *OWL 2 Web Ontology Language Mapping to RDF Graphs*.   W3C Recommendation, 27 October 2009. Available at `http://www.w3.org/TR/owl2-mapping-to-rdf/`.

[W3C09c]   W3C. *OWL 2 Web Ontology Language: New Features and Rationale*. W3C Recommendation, 27 October 2009. Available at `http://www.w3.org/TR/owl2-new-features/`.

[W3C09d]   W3C.   *OWL 2 Web Ontology Language XML Serialization*.   W3C Recommendation, 27 October 2009.   Available at `http://www.w3.org/TR/owl2-xml-serialization/`.

[W3C10a]   W3C. *RIF Basic Logic Dialect*. W3C Recommendation, 22 June 2010. Available at `http://www.w3.org/TR/rif-bld/`.

[W3C10b]   W3C. *RIF Core Dialect*. W3C Recommendation, 22 June 2010. Available at `http://www.w3.org/TR/rif-core/`.

[W3C11]   W3C. *RIF in RDF*. W3C Working Group Note, 12 May 2011. Available at `http://www.w3.org/TR/rif-in-rdf/`.

[W3C12a]   W3C. *The RDF Data Cube Vocabulary*. W3C Working Draft, 05 April 2012. Available at `http://www.w3.org/TR/vocab-data-cube/`.

[W3C12b]   W3C. *RIF Overview*. W3C Working Group Note, 22 June 2012. Available at `http://www.w3.org/TR/rif-overview/`.

[WA91]   Annita N. Wilschut and Peter M. G. Apers. Dataflow Query Execution in a Parallel Main-memory Environment. In *Proceedings of the 1st International Conference on Parallel and Distributed Information Systems (PDIS'91)*, pages 68–77, Miami Beach, FL, USA, 1991. IEEE Computer Society Press.

[WABL⁺08] Daniel J. Weitzner, Harold Abelson, Tim Berners-Lee, Joan Feigenbaum, James Hendler, and Gerald Jay Sussman. Information Accountability. *Communications of the ACM*, 51(6):82–87, 2008.

[Wei07]   Daniel J. Weitzner. Beyond Secrecy: New Privacy Protection Strategies for Open Information Spaces. *IEEE Internet Computing*, 11:96, 94–95, 2007.

[Wes67]   A. Westin. *Privacy and Freedom*. Atheneum Press, New York, 1967.

[WHBLC05] Daniel J Weitzner, Jim Hendler, Tim Berners-Lee, and Dan Connolly. Creating a Policy-aware Web: Discretionary, Rule-based Access for the World Wide Web. In Elena Ferrari and Bhavani Thuraisingham, editors, *Web and Information Security*. IRM Press, 2005.

[WJSH11]   Andreas Wagner, Martin Junghans, Sebastian Speiser, and Andreas Harth. Privacy-aware Semantic Service Discovery for the Smart Energy Grid (Poster). In *Posters Track at the 8th Extended Semantic Web Conference (ESWC'11)*, Heraklion, Crete, Greece, 2011.

[WLD⁺02]   Xin Wang, Guillermo Lao, Thomas Demartini, Hari Reddy, Mai Nguyen, and Edgar Valenzuela. XrML – eXtensible Rights Markup Language. In Michiharu Kudo, editor, *Proceedings of the 2002 ACM Workshop on XML Security (XMLSEC'02)*. ACM, 2002.

[WSRH10]   Andreas Wagner, Sebastian Speiser, Oliver Raabe, and Andreas Harth. Linked Data for a Privacy-aware Smart Grid. In Klaus-Peter Fähnrich and Bogdan Franczyk, editors, *Informatik 2010: Service Science - Neue Perspektiven für die Informatik, Beiträge der 40. Jahrestagung der Gesellschaft für Informatik e.V. (GI), Band 1*, volume 175 of *LNI*, pages 449–454, Dresden, Germany, 2010. Springer.

[XF11]   Cheng Xu and Philip W. L. Fong. The Specification and Compilation of Obligation Policies for Program Monitoring. Technical Report 2011-996-08, Department of Computer Science, University of Calgary, Canada, April 2011. Available at http://pages.cpsc.ucalgary.ca/~pwlfong/Pub/UC-CPSC-TR-2011-996-08.pdf.

[YLA04]   Ting Yu, Ninghui Li, and Annie I. Antón. A Formal Semantics for P3P. In *Proceedings of the 2004 Workshop on Secure Web Services (SWS'04)*, pages 1–8, 2004.

[ZC06]   Wen-Feng Zhao and Jun-Liang Chen. Toward Automatic Discovery and Invocation of Information-providing Web Services. In Riichiro Mizoguchi, Zhongzhi Shi, and Fausto Giunchiglia, editors, *Proceedings of the 1st Asian Semantic Web Conference (ASWC'06)*, number 4185 in Lecture Notes in Computer Science, pages 474–480, Beijing, China, 2006. Springer.

[Zha10]   Jun Zhao. *Open Provenance Model Vocabulary Specification*. 06 October
            2010. Available at `http://purl.org/net/opmv/ns`, accessed July 20th
            2012.

[ZPPPS04]   Xinwen Zhang, Jaehong Park, Francesco Parisi-Presicce, and Ravi Sandhu. A
            Logical Specification for Usage Control. In Trent Jaeger and Elena Ferrari,
            editors, *Proceedings of the 9th ACM Symposium on Access Control Models
            and Technologies (SACMAT'04)*, pages 1–10, Yorktown Heights, USA, 2004.
            ACM.